BIHAR AND ORISSA DISTRICT GAZETTEER
HAZARIBAGH

BIHAR AND ORISSA DISTRICT GAZETTEER

HAZARIBAGH

BY

E. LISTER, C I. E.,
INDIAN CIVIL SERVICE.

GYAN

ISBN: 978-81-212-1402-5(HB)

First Published in 1917
Indian Reprint in 2017

Published by

Gyan Publishing House
5, Ansari Road
Daryaganj, New Delhi-110002
Phone: 9811692060
E-mail: books@gyanbooks.com

Cataloging in Publication Data—DK
Courtesy: D.K. Agencies (P) Ltd. <docinfo@dkagencies.com>

Lister, Edward, 1871- **author.**
Hazaribagh / by E. Lister.
pages cm. — (Bihar and Orissa district gazetteers)
Reprint. Originally published: Patna : Superintendent, Government Printing, Bihar and Orissa, 1917.
Includes index.
ISBN 9788121214025 (HB)

1. Haza˜ri˜ba˜g (India : District)—Gazetteers. 2. Haza˜ri˜ba˜g (India : District)—Economic conditions. I. Title. II. Series: Bihar and Orissa district gazetteers.

DS485.H36L57 2017 DDC 915.4127003 23

PREFACE.

THIS Gazetteer has been compiled on the basis of the Statistical Account of Hazāribāgh, which was prepared about 1875 under the supervision of Sir William Hunter. It follows closely the form of the corresponding volume on Mānbhum which was written by Mr. H. Coupland, I.C.S., and much of its matter has been suggested by the gazetteers of Mānbhum and Gaya. In addition to published books, which have been indicated in the appropriate places, valuable original contributions have been received on special subjects from the Rev. S. L. Thompson (Botany), Mr. L. L. Fermor (General Geology), Mr. Thomas H. Ward (Giridih Coal-field), Mr. G. C. Lathbury (Bokāro Colliery), Dr. A. Jowett (Karanpura Valley), Mr. E. Lane (Mica), Mr. C. J. B. Wight Boycott (Emigration), the Rev. J. C. Forrester (Anglican Mission), the Rev. J. A. Dyer (U. F. Church of Scotland Mission), and Babu Bisheshvar Mukharji (Agriculture). The statistics of the recent years have been compiled by Babu J. C. Datta, Deputy Magistrate and Collector of Hazāribāgh.

Extracts from or references to the Settlement Report of Hazāribāgh appear throughout the book, and I take this opportunity of acknowledging my great indebtedness to its author, Mr. J. D. Sifton, I.C.S., late Settlement Officer of Chotā Nāgpur.

E. LISTER.

The 15*th July* 1917.

PLAN OF CONTENTS.

TABLE OF CONTENTS.

CHAPTER I.

PHYSICAL ASPECTS.

CHAPTER II.

GEOLOGY AND MINERALS.

CHAPTER III.

HISTORY.

CHAPTER IV.

THE PEOPLE.

CHAPTER V.

PUBLIC HEALTH.

CHAPTER VI.

AGRICULTURE.

CHAPTER VII.

NATURAL CALAMITIES.

CHAPTER VIII.

RENTS, WAGES AND PRICES.

CHAPTER IX.

OCCUPATIONS, MANUFACTURES AND TRADE.

CHAPTER X.

MEANS OF COMMUNICATION.

CHAPTER XI.

LAND REVENUE ADMINISTRATION.

CHAPTER XII.

GENERAL ADMINISTRATION.

CHAPTER XIII.

LOCAL SELF-GOVERNMENT.

CHAPTER XIV.

EDUCATION.

CHAPTER XV.

GAZETTEER.

GAZETTEER
OF THE
HAZARIBAGH DISTRICT.

CHAPTER I.

PHYSICAL ASPECTS.

The district of Hazāribāgh forms the north-eastern portion of the Chota Nāgpur Division and lies between 23° 25′ and 24° 48′ north latitude, and 84° 29′ and 86° 38′ east longitude. Its area has not been determined with precision: in the recent traverse survey it has been estimated at 7,000 square miles; but the summation of fields in the cadastral survey shows a total of 6,987 square miles. The population in 1911 was 1,288,609. The principal town and administrative headquarters is Hazāribāgh, which is situated towards the west of the higher plateau at an elevation of about 2,000 feet. GENERAL DESCRIPTION.

The town and district take their name from the mango grove at Hazāri, one of the villages which make up the town of Hazāribāgh. The local vernacular spelling, omitting the final 'h', follows the Hindi form of the word which means grove. This village of Hazāri was on the military road from Calcutta to Benares, which was made about 1782 and coincided at this stage with an earlier road between Kendi and Makundganj. It still possesses the remains of a fine mango grove and it is a reasonable conjecture that it was the usual halting place for travellers, and so obtained a pre-eminence over the neighbouring Origin of name.

villages. The selection of the locality about 1780 as the head-quarters of the Rāmgarh Battalion and its adoption in 1834 as the centre of a new civil administrative unit which included both Rāmgarh and Kharagdiha, and could not with propriety bear the name of either, appear to be the sole reasons for the application of its name to the entire district.

Boundaries.

The adjoining districts are, on the north Gayā and Monghyr, on the east the Santāl Parganas and Mānbhum, on the south Rānchi, and on the west Palāmau and Gayā. On the east there are no natural divisions for the greater part of the boundary. On the north the face of the lower Hazāribāgh plateau coincides roughly with the border. On the west the boundary is physically capricious, except where the Morhar river is followed. To the south the crest of the Rānchi plateau is utilized irregularly, and in places the Dāmodar and Subarnarekha rivers. Two villages which are included in the criminal and revenue jurisdiction of Gayā are entirely isolated in Hazāribāgh, and similarly Harni and Pathra lie wholly in Gayā but are administratively a part of Hazāribāgh.

NATURAL DIVISIONS AND SCENERY.

The following description of the general aspect is borrowed largely from a report by Major Sconce who was Deputy Superintendent of Revenue Survey about fifty years ago.

The district forms part of the chain of high land, sometimes a range of hills, sometimes a high cultivated plateau, which extends across the continent of India south of the Narbada river on the west, and south of the Son river on the east. This chain has nearly reached its eastern extremity in Hazāribāgh, the rivers begin to take an easterly course, and the general level of the country begins to lower. The district cannot therefore be considered entirely an elevated plateau, nor does it contain any extensive range of high hills: but both features are met with; and viewing the elevated face of the district from the plains of Bihar on the north it may well be considered to form a part of the extensive highland chain. This elevated northern face, not scarped, but most clearly defined, has the appearance of a range of hills uniform in height; but in reality it is the edge of a plateau elevated about 800 feet from the level of the Gayā plain. Eastward this northern edge

The lower plateau.

forms a well-defined water-shed between the heads of the tributaries of the rivers of Gayā and those of the Barākar river, which traverses Hazāribāgh district in an easterly direction. The slope of this plateau to the east is uniform and gentle, and is continued past the river, which bears to the south-east, into the Santāl Parganas, and finally disappears in the lower plains of Bengal. The western boundary of the plateau is formed by the deep bed of the Lilājān river. The southern boundary consists of the face of the higher plateau as far as its eastern extremity, where for some distance a low and undistinguished water-shed runs eastward to the western spurs of Pārasnāth. The drainage to the south of this low line passes by the Jamunia river to the Dāmodar. The plateau so contained has a general elevation of about 1,300 feet.

The higher plateau, on which the station of Hazāribāgh is built, is about forty miles east by west and fifteen miles north by south, with an average height of 2,000 feet. Its north-eastern and southern faces are mostly abrupt; but to the west it narrows and descends slowly in the neighbourhood of Simaria and Jabra, where it curves to the south and connects with the Rānchi plateau through Tori pargana. The higher plateau.

The third great subdivision is the Dāmodar basin, which commences from the ridge just described. The essential constituent of this basin is a trough between the Rānchi and Hazāribāgh plateaus, resulting from enormous fractures at their present edges, which caused the land between to sink to a great depth and incidentally preserved from complete denudation the measures of the Karanpura, Rāmgarh, and Bokāro coalfields. This trough is not continuous, for it is interrupted where the Karanpura Valley to the west is separated from Māndu to the east by a lofty spur from the higher plateau which terminates by the bank of the Dāmodar in Aswa Pāhār. The northern boundary of the Dāmodar valley is steep as far as the south-eastern corner of the higher plateau, where the Konār river carries away most of its drainage and has modified its abruptness. The lower basin of the Konār river falls somewhat steeply from the water-shed which separates it from the Jamunia, and in consequence this part of the district is rough and largely uncultivated. To the east the latter river descends from its The Dāmodar basin.

higher level in a wide eastward curve; and so its journey to the Dāmodar is easy and gentle, and its basin forms a gradual slope to the south-east. On the south of the trough the Dāmodar river keeps close to the edge of the Rānchi plateau till it has passed Rāmgarh, after which a turn to the north-east leaves on the right hand a wide and level valley, on which the Subarnarekha river begins to intrude south of Gola, till the Singhpur hills divert it abruptly to the south. Further to the east the Dāmodar basin passes tamely into Mānbhum.

Scenery of the higher plateau.

The scenery varies in each of the three main divisions. On the higher plateau the country is open and cultivation fairly extensive. The surface is never level, but the undulations are usually gentle. Near the headquarters station a few rocky hills break the skyline, and in the distance appear the summits of the cliffs which skirt the edges of the plateau. It is at the end of the rains, in late October and November, that the landscape is most attractive. The rice in the terraced valleys is turning into yellow, and the grazed uplands are still tinged with green. Interspersed are great blotches of pale gold where fields of surguja fringe the rice lands or penetrate the glades of the sāl woods; and the distant horizon is broken by the misty violet hills. The days are lazily warm and the nights cool. By December the rice crops are harvested, and the grass is withered; only the sāl trees and gardens of primrose-coloured rape break the drab monotony from which there is no relief till the rains in June bring back the herbage.

Scenery of the lower plateau.

On the lower plateau, the scenery is tame when one has passed beyond the dominance of the steep cliffs of the descent. The surface is still undulating, but the jungle is rarely better than scrub, and the grazing lands are barren; and scattered rocky ridges disclose the severity of the denudation to which this ancient land surface has been exposed. From one of these at Simrādhāb on the Dhanwār road an extensive prospect of the Barākar basin clearly reveals its character. The land is seen inclining gently eastward with the river's course; but north and south and west it rises slowly as though to a shallow saucer's rim. On the south-east and south the horizon is shut in by the masses of Pārasnāth and the buttresses of the higher plateau, but in other directions a few isolated peaks alone interrupt the sky line. In the middle distance village sites are indicated by their scanty screen of jack and mango trees: and near at hand the terraces of the rice fields are seen in sharp relief. The absence of water is the most striking feature in the scene.

Scenery of the Dāmodar Valley.

The most interesting portion of the Dāmodar basin is the Karanpura valley, of which a description is given in Chapter II. The northern side of the valley, after leaving Karanpura, is broken forest country, with a scanty population of aboriginals until the level basin of the Jamunia is reached. The south is much more fertile, containing some of the best rice land in the district; and is still decently clad with jungle, while the proximity of the Rānchi plateau breaks the monotony of the landscape.

HILLS. The higher plateau.

The higher plateau may be regarded as the most important hill in the system of the district. The western portion constitutes a broad water-shed between the Dāmodar drainage on the south and the Lilājān and Mohani rivers on the north. The highest hills on this side are called after the villages of Kāsiātu, Hesātu and Hudua, and rise fronting the south 600 feet above the general level of the plateau. Further east along the southern face a long spur projects right up to the Dāmodar river, where it ends in Aswa Pāhār (2,465). This spur as stated above serves to isolate Karanpura pargana from the rest of the Dāmodar Valley. From the south-eastern corner of the plateau Jilinga ("long") Hill runs down to the Bokāro river. It is 3,057 feet high and has a very extensive base and rounded face, on which there used to be a tea garden. Mahābar Jārimo (2,185) and Barsot (2,120) stand in isolation to the east; and on the north-west edge of the plateau Sendraili (2,216) and Māhuda (2,409) are the most prominent features. Isolated on the plateau in the neighbourhood of Hazāribāgh station are four hills, of which the highest (Chendwār) rises to 2,816 feet.

Sātpahri.

In Karanpura there are two conspicuous masses of sandstone hills. South of Tandwa and near the Palāmau border Sātpahri (2,241) is roughly triangular in shape. Eastward stretches

Māhudi. Māhudi Hill, rising to 2,437 feet, of which the last 800 are a bold scarp of sheer sandstone, and from the north side a detached crescent forms a striking outwork. An abandoned garden on its undulating summit recalls the early experiments in the cultivation of tea. Further down the Dāmodar valley, Lugu Hill. away to the east of Māndu the great sandstone mass of Lugu compels attention by the boldness of its outline. On all sides it has an exceedingly abrupt scarp, modified only on the south-east, where the stream which drains its summit has made a less impracticable path. On the north it falls almost sheer in a swoop of 2,200 feet to the bed of the Bokāro river, which separates it from the opposing cliff of Jilinga. Its greatest height is 3,203 feet. Inaccessible and covered with thick forests of sāl trees, it is the appropriate scene of sombre legends of the neighbouring tribes. A demon has his dwelling in great caves in its summit, and girls, venturing alone on the hill, re-appear after the lapse of many years crazy and unable to reveal the secrets of their imprisonment. If however they are seen from the west modified by the distance Lugu and Jilinga with the steep wooded cliffs of the plateau suggest the curve of a beautiful sea-coast indented by deep and tranquil bays. On the south of the Dāmodar river the ground rises sharply to the level of the Rānchi plateau, of which the highest station on the border is Barāgai or Marang Buru (3,445). Seen from the north the edge of this plateau has the appearance of a range of hills, in whose shadow are many secluded valleys of peaceful beauty. Further to the east, where the river has turned northwards and left a wide plain on the right hand, a triangle of hills rises east of Gola to 2,083 feet. Thence to the east the valley extends without interruption to Mānbhum. As one proceeds north wards to the conspicuous block of Pārasnāth immediately north of the Dāmodar a stretch of wooded country is crossed which rises up to the water-shed of the Jamunia. Though of no great height the hills (for they appear to be hills when seen from the south) are a formidable obstacle to communications all the way from the junction of the Konār and Dāmodar rivers to the border of Mānbhum.

Pārasnāth Hill. In the east of the district, on the border of Mānbhum, the great mass of Pārasnāth (4,481) overhangs the Grand Trunk Road for many miles. The physical character of this hill, of which a description has been given by Sir William Hooker in his Journal, is a central narrow ridge, with many rocky peaks, irregular in shape but taking the general configuration of a crescent, with its ends pointing to the north-east and north-north-west. In these directions the principal spurs of the hill extend, and they are of the same rocky character as the central ridge. On the south-west there are no spurs, and the greatest continuous rise occurs. To the north and west the spurs are very extensive and of a part with the Pārasnāth upheaval; and high country of a broken rocky character stretches to the Barākar river. To the south-east there is one spur of importance which forms the boundary with Mānbhum.

Across the Barākar river no hills of magnitude are met with till one reaches the northern edge of the lower plateau. Thence is seen to the north a confused tract of rocky hills and steep ravines, through which the Sakri and its tributaries have worn out their gradually widening valleys. To the east and on the borders of Monghyr Ghoranji hill (1,984) is prominent, and northward the Sātpahri hill (1,806) lies on the border, rising 1,200 feet above the plain of Monghyr. North of the Sakri basin the most prominent hills are Rheowa (1,673) on the Gayā border and Bhandeswar (1,759) a rocky peak about three miles north-east of Gāwān. South of the river is Mabābar (2,210), a very prominent landmark, lying south of Satgāwān, and the highest point of a ridge stretching far into Gayā. From Mahābar south-westward the edge of the lower plateau continues to form the district border with Gayā, marked by the heights of Mārāmoko (2,050), Durbasha (2,209) in the Kodarma forest, Lohābar (1,788) overlooking Danua Ghāt on the Grand Trunk Road, and Kuluha (1,575) near Hunterganj, now a resort of Hindu pilgrims. Throughout its length it is a mass of broken ravines, unfit for cultivation, and important mainly by reason of its deposits of mica. At Kuluha the valley of the Lilājān is reached, westward of which is the confused mass of spurs and ranges that make up the Kunda country and attach themselves to the western extremity of the higher plateau. In the neighbourhood of Kodarma Nero (1,737) and Banda (1,853) bear witness to the denudation of the lower plateau.

Mahābar Hill.

RIVERS. The outstanding feature of the drainage of the district is the water-shed which separates the basin of the Dāmodar from that of the streams which flow north to join the Ganges. Within that basin the distribution between the Dāmodar and its tributary the Barākar is of great importance. The main water-shed starts on the western boundary south-west of Simaria on the northern side of Kāsiātu hill, whence it runs north and east along the higher plateau, passing about seven miles north-west of the town of Hazāribāgh. Thence it curves beyond Itkhori and meets the edge of the lower plateau, with which it coincides till the eastern boundary of the district is reached. The drainage north and west of this line finds its way into the Ganges, through the districts of Gayā and Monghyr. After the Ganges water-shed leaves the district the Barākar has a common water-shed on the east with the Ajay and its tributaries. The term basin is peculiarly applicable to the country drained by the northern feeders of the Barākar. The elevated lip follows a crescent-like line of great regularity for nearly 100 miles, and the windings of the river are markedly regular, so few are the disturbing features which break the uniformity of the gradient. The Dāmodar and its tributaries drain about 4,510 out of the 7,000 square miles in the district.

(The Damodar water-shed.)

The Dāmodar River. The source of the Dāmodar or Deonad is in Palamau, twenty-five miles from the boundary of Hazāribāgh. After a course of ninety miles in the district it traverses Mānbhum. Bānkura Burdwān and Hooghly till it joins the river Hooghly below Calcutta. Near its entrance into the district, where it is joined by the Garhi, its bed is 1,326 feet above sea level. At Rāmgarh in thirty-eight miles it has fallen to 1,030 feet, and at the junction with the Konār after a further course of thirty-five miles the elevation is 713 feet. So far the fall averages about 8·9 feet per mile; but for the remaining twenty miles to its junction with the Jamunia, when it is 582 feet above sea level, the fall is 6·5 feet only. For the greater part of its course it passes through a sparsely-peopled forest country, and the quiet solitudes of its long sandy reaches are very pleasant. Near Rājābera, where it prepares to leave the district, it has worn for itself a rocky bed, where save in times of heavy rain it sleeps in a chain of deep and placid pools. Everywhere fordable in the dry season it is liable to severe floods in the rains, which frequently cause great damage in the lower districts.

Tributaries.

The first tributary from Hazāribāgh is the Garhi or Tandwa river, which rises near Kāsiātu hill and drains the area included in Tandwa police-station. Next comes the Haharo, on the east of the Māhudi hill, bearing the drainage of the eastern Karanpura valley. Then follows Naikāri from the south, the Mārāmarha from the north and Bhera from the south. At Jaridih comes the Konār from the north which, with its tributary the Siwāni, drains the greater portion of the higher plateau, and then descending through desolate and barren wastes of scrub and jungle passes Gumia to receive the waters of the Bokāro shortly before its union with the Dāmodar. The Bokāro also rises on the plateau south of Hazāribāgh town but quickly escapes to skirt the southern face and to pass in a narrow and beautiful valley between Jilinga and Lugu hills. Below the junction with the Konār the Khanjo comes from the south: and the last important affluent is the Jamunia, which rises near Bishungarh, and after running near the Grand Trunk Road from Bagodar past Dumri turns south to form the boundary with Mānbhum.

Konār river.

Bokāro river.

Barākar.

Descending from its source in the higher plateau the Barākar flows northward till it reaches the neighbourhood of the Grand Trunk Road, which crosses it by a new iron bridge (1914) two miles west of Barhi. Thence it flows east by south with a moderate fall in a succession of regular windings, passing north of the Pārasnāth range until it leaves the district thirty-two miles before its junction with the Dāmodar. From the north its main tributaries are the Leruja, Gokhāna, Akta, Kisko, Bareto, Arga and Usri, of which the two last are of considerable size. From the south the Barahkatha river is the only large stream. Its basin of 2,050 square miles is comparatively level; and after heavy rain the river remains in flood for a long time. As it is unbridged below Barhi (save for a railway bridge at Parsabād) it is a serious obstacle to communications.

Sakri.

The Sakri river drains an area of 810 square miles, which it has carved out of the northern face of the lower plateau. Seen from above on the Jamdār road in the cold weather the nearer view is of steep ridges clothed by forest, narrowing till they sink below in a wide level plain which bears thick crops of *rakar*, sugarcane and oil-seeds. Through the middle runs a wide river of sand, and on the far side the valleys narrow rapidly, and climb steeply till they merge in the dark hills. To the west is seen the mouth of a similar plain from Pihra, and beyond is the great mass of Mahābar hill overhanging Sātgāwān. As it passes to the north-west the river of sand widens, and on its level surface trickles of water wander in apparent aimlessness. In reality they are jealously enticed to one or other bank, to be lifted for the watering of the crops. In times of flood the absence of a definite channel brings disaster; for the waters spread over the nearer fields and ruin them by the deposit of their enormous burden of sand.

Mohani. The Mohani rises about twelve miles from Hazārībāgh and drains the west of the upper plateau. Thence, running north past Itkhori, it descends to the Gayā plain and crosses the Grand Trunk Road about two miles from the foot of the Danua pass. Near Itkhori it intersects the Chatra-Chauparan road with its wide and sandy channel, which still remains unbridged.

Lilajān. The Lilajān begins its journey north of Simaria in broken country and flows through a deep and rocky channel until it reaches the neighbourhood of Jori. There the hills begin to recede and the stream flows sluggishly over a wide sandy bed. From this point to the Gayā border beyond Hunterganj the valley resembles on a minor scale that of the Sakri described above. Six miles south of Gayā town it unites with the Mohani to form the Phalgu and ultimately discharges into the Ganges.

General characteristics. The rivers of Hazārībāgh are alike in that they are fed by the surface precipitation of rain water. This is for the most part promptly discharged by the water-courses, and very little sinks below the surface; and though springs are numerous there is no single one which yields a copious supply of water. The river basins are for the most part steep, and frequently rocky; and rainfall is succeeded by sudden floods of brief duration. At other times a scanty stream trickles over the river's rocky channel or is lost beneath a deep bed of gravel and sand. Navigation is impossible, fisheries valueless and irrigation impracticable except on the lower courses of the Sakri and Lilajān, whose level valleys have been formed from the débris of the ravines above.

The following is a statement of the areas drained by the rivers and river systems of Hazāribāgh :— Area of drainage basins.

System.	River.	River drainage, square miles.	System drainage square miles.
1	2	3	4
1. Dāmodar ...	Dāmodar ...	2,440	4,510
	Barākar ...	2,040	
2. Ganges	Mohani ...	490	2,170
	Lilajān	380	
	Morhar	170	
	Dhadhār, Tilaya, Dhanarji ...	200	
	Sakri	810	
	Kiul	70	
	Barnar	50	
3. Son	Jhikia Chako ...	170	170
4. Ajay... ...	Patro, Jainti ...	100	100
5. Subarnarekha ...	Subarnarekha ...	50	50
	Total area ...	...	7,000

There are no lakes or marshes in the district. Artificial lakes are made by means of dams across the heads of valleys for irrigating crops, but they are neither numerous nor of great size. Lakes and Marshes.

The following description of the flora of the district has been contributed by the Reverend S. L. Thompson, formerly Principal of St Columba's College, Hazāribāgh, whose studies were directed largely to verifying the local occurrence of the forms of vegetation reported in Mr. Haines's book on the province of Chota Nāgpur. Flora.

"The indigenous vegetation of Hazāribāgh is mainly a combination of two distinct types corresponding to the dry and damp conditions of the district. The first type is semi-xerophytic, consisting of trees and shrubs very often stunted, and now mostly coppiced, and the other is the damp tropical flora confined to the damper tracts and to the rainy season.

"The thorny scrub jungle covering large areas of uplands and rapidly taking the place of the true forest is an example of the first type, as is also the number of dry rock-loving plants.

Khair and five other Acacias, Bair and four other Zizyphus, Carissa, Capparis horrida, Mimosa rubicaulis, Flacourtia, Limonia acidissima, Vangueria spinosa and three Randias, all thorny plants, compose this scrub jungle. Odina Wodier, Anogeissus, latifolia, Nyctanthes arbortristis, the dwarf palm Phoenix acaulis, Alangium Lamarckii and Cleistanthus, the last two curiously local, are other common plants of the scrub jungle of this semi-xerophytic type.

" Common plants growing in cracks of the driest rocks are Gardenia latifolia and G. turgida, Ficus Arnottiana, and F. tomentosa, Hamiltonia suaveolens, Euphorbia nivulia, and Anisochilus carnosus, the last often adapting itself to the dry habitat by developing little more than a fleshy pyramidal cactus-like stem.

, " A considerable number of larger trees occupying a dry habitat on the hills and scarps of the plateau are deciduous during at least a part of the long dry season, and are a characteristic feature of the district. Some have very thick corky twigs or coriaceous or tomentose leaves and thus resist the desiccating influence of the climate. Sterculia urens, Cochlospermum gossypium, Odina Wodier are leafless for nearly half the year, and others of this kind are Boswellia serrata, Garuga pinnata, Ailanthus excelsa, Erythrina suberosa, Butea superba and frondosa, Ougeinia dalbergioides (stunted), Indigofera arborea and Phyllanthus emblica, Casearia tomentosa and graveolens are very common in dry scrub jungle, the latter rather conspicuous in the cold weather because of its leaves turning copper-coloured before their fall.

" The damp tropical type is represented by a considerable number of Cucurbitaceae, Apocynaceae, Asclepiads and six vines. A large number of Acanthaceae, Labiatae, Scrophulariaceae, Liliaceae, and Commelinaceae compose the short-lived vegetation which grows under the jungle trees. Rubiaceae, Compositae and Leguminosae are very abundant during the rains. Along rivers and streams with constant water-supply the following plants are more or less common :—

" Salix tetrasperma, Diospyros, Eugenia Heyneana, the beautiful Reinwardtia, Homonoia riparia, Phyllanthus Lawii, Crinum defixum,

Tamarix ericoides, Dalbergia volubilis, Breynia rhamnoides, Kirganelia reticulata. On the northern and damper sides of hills and along ravines is the usual habitat of Kydia calycina, Helicteres Isora, three Glochidions, four Flemingias. Pterocarpus Marsupium, Dalbergia latifolia and lanceolaria, Combretum decandrum and two Bridelias. Generally distributed throughout the district are Bombax malabaricum (in the deeper jungle usually almost strangled by Zizyphus, Œnoplia, Ichnocarpus, etc.), six Grewias, Aegle marmelos, Soymida febrifuga (usually only a mutiliated stump). Semecarpus Anacardium, Buchanania latifolia, the Kusum, Elaeodendron glaucum, the Mahua, Oroxylum, indicum, Hollarrhena antidysenterica and Wrightia tomentosa.

"Although almost all the plants above mentioned are trees or shrubs it must not be imagined that Hazāribāgh has not an abundant and interesting herbaceous flora. The grasses and Leguminosae are of course the most numerous; but in paddy fields and damp places in the rains there is the greatest variety of beautiful and interesting plants. There are no less than eleven bladderworts, two of which have not yet been reported from this province and are very minute, growing among moss where water trickles over rocks on Pārasnāth and other hills. Two sundews, Begonia picta, Didymocarpus pygmaea, and Rhynchoglossum obliquum are very interesting little flowers in damp and shady places.

"There is a considerable number of climbing and scandent herbs and shrubs and in the rains in some damp ravines the jungle has all the appearance of a tropical forest. Bauhinia Vahlii, Ventilago, Celastrus, Butea superba, Atylosia crassa, Olax scandens, Smilax macrophylla, Gloriosa superba, Erycibe, Porana, Ichnocarpus, Hemidesmus, Cryptolepis and several yams are among the commonest climbers. Cissampelos, Cocculus, Tinospora, about fourteen gourds, Helinus, Holostemma, Marsdenia, Pergularia, Dregea, Ceropegia and many Leguminosae and Convolvulaceae are more or less common in the rains climbing over bushes and trees. The annual screen of cultivated creepers which every villager plants round his little garden or courtyard is composed of Basella rubra, Dolichos Lablab, two or three edible Ipomeas and two or three bright Cucurbitaceae, and hardly a single garden is without the useful and beautiful Munga.

"The parasitic and epiphytic plants in Hazāribāgh form an interesting part of the vegetation. A very conspicuous object in the jungle is Loranthus scurrula, which becomes a very noticeable object on deciduous trees in the cold season. It is often like a large inverted bush hanging from trees and is especially found on Butea frondosa, Woodfordia and Wendlandia. Loranthus longiflorus and globosus are not so common, and chiefly live on the sāl and mango respectively. The three mistletoes are not nearly so common. There are several root parasites including the sandalwood. Alectra Thomsoni, Aeginetia indica and Orobanche indica are also parasitic on roots, while two or three figs are epiphytic when young. Cassytha filiformis and Cuscuta reflexa are slender leafless parasites enveloping bushes in a net of yellowish threadlike branches. More than half the orchids are epiphytic; the commonest and most showy are Saccolabium papillosum, Vanda Roxburghii and Aerides multiflorum.

Economic uses.

a. Timber trees.

"It would be quite impossible to enumerate the various useful, fantastic, and superstitious purposes for which plants are employed in Hazāribāgh. The principal trees used for timber are the sakua or sal (Shorea robusta), paisar (Pterocarpus marsupium), tun (Cedrela toona), the karam (Adina cordifolia) and gamhar (Gmelina arborea). The kend (Diospyros tomentosa), ām (Mangifera indica), sali (Boswellia serrata), āsan (Terminalia tomentosa), Artocarpus integrifolia, and several other trees are used but yield bad timber.

"The jamun (Eugenia jambolana) and simal (Bombax malabaricum) do not rot in water and are therefore much used for '*jamots*' of wells and such purposes. Dhaunta (Anogeissus latifolia), pandan (Ougeinia dalbergioides), sidha (Lagerstroemia parviflora) and dhelha (Alangium Lamarckii), though only small trees, yield very hard wood and are much prized for agricultural implements. For this reason they are rapidly disappearing.

b. Oils.

"Oil is locally manufactured from the seeds of following trees and cultivated plants:—Three or four kinds of mustard, linseed (Linum usitatissimum), gingili (Sesamum indicum), sarguja (Guizotia abyssinica), karanj (Pongamia glabra), bherenda (Jatropha curcas) and the castor oil plant Ricinus communis, as well as from the following wild plants :—bhelwa (Semecarpus anacardium), Celastrus paniculata, the nim (Azadirachta indica), the kusum (Schleichera trijuga) and the mahua (Bassia latifolia).

"Several varieties of Gossypium herbaceum are cultivated for their cotton, but for ordinary domestic purposes the cotton of simal (Bombax malabaricum) and Cochlospermum gossypium is used. *c.* Cotton.

For tanning the bark of Zizphus xylopyra and of the sāl is used, but Terminalia tomentosa and Arjuna are considered better. *d.* Tanning. The principal trees used for the cultivation of lac are Butea frondosa and the kusum. Different kinds of gum or resin are obtained for incense and other purposes from Boswellia serrata, Bursera serrata, the sāl, Buchanania latifolia, paisār and other trees. *e.* Lac. *f.* Gums. Dyes are obtained from Mallotus philippinensis, Woodfordia floribunda, Oroxylum indicum, Symplocos racemosa and Lawsonia alba. *g.* Dyes.

"There are so many plants yielding strong fibres that the traveller through the jungle and the villagers can always obtain a strong cord with little trouble. *h* Fibres. '*Chop*' the commonest fibre used for all sorts of rough purposes, and sold in the bazar, is obtained from Bauhinia vahlü, an extensive creeper which is as useful to the villager as it is injurious to the forest. Great numbers of Malvaceae, Tiliaceae, Sterculiaceae and Asclepiads yield strong fibre. The san hemp (Crotolaria juncea) and Hibiscus cannabinus are sometimes cultivated for their fibre, and the two jute plants, Corchorus olitorius and capsularis, are apparently wild but are never used for their fibre. Marsdenia tenacissima, Pergularia pallida and Dregea volubilis are remarkable for the strength of their fibre but are not very common.

"A considerable number of plants are used to intoxicate fish, e.g., *i.* Fish poisons. Randia dumetorum, Cleistanthus collinus, Milletia auriculata and Polygonum glabrum. A large number of plants are of great use in times of famine and are continually used by the very *j.* Famine foods. poor. The commonest are several Bauhinias, Antidesma diandrum and many wild and cultivated Amarantaceae and Chenopodiaceae. The plants used for medicinal and superstitious purposes are too many to mention. The bel, nim, Tinospora cordifolia, akon,

k. Medicines and magic.

Holarrhena antidysenterica, anant-mul and a great number of others are of the greatest utility, while some have only an imaginary value. Helicteres Isora is, for example, considered a cure for colic because its twisted carpels are supposed to resemble the intestines, and Vallaris Heynei when suspended from the roof of a certain day in June is believed to keep away snakes throughout the rains, probably because of its snaky stems. The nim is used in exorcising those who are supposed to be possessed of devils, and the extraordinary herb called agni khair (Lepidagathis Hamiltoniana) is used in the capture of evil spirits.

Foreign trees.

" A very large number of trees and shrubs have been introduced and grow well in Hazāribāgh and many are half wild. The following trees are planted commonly along roads and in compounds :—pipal, banian, tun, nim, ām, amra, karanj, teak, sissu, gold mohar, tamarind babul, siris, Eucalyptus, Millingtonia hortensis, Casuarina equisitefolia, Grevillea robusta and Pterospermum acrifolium. Very occasionally planted may be found Polyalthia longifolia and Saraca indica, both called asoka, Erythrina suberosa and indica, kadam, nagesar, Guazuma tomentosa, Eleocarpus serratus, Sapindus trifoliatus, Acacia suma, Caesalpinia coriaria, Cassia fistula and siamea and Adenanthera pavonina.

Garden fruits.

" Fruit trees cultivated in gardens and sometimes running wild are the ām, guava, lichi and ashphal, pear and peach, loquat, pomegranate, gulabjamun, saripha and bullock's heart, papita, plantain, three or four Citrus, bel, phalsa, mulberry, Mimusops elengi and hexandra.

Garden flowering trees.

"The following flowering shrubs are found commonly in gardens :— Michelia Champaca and Artabotrys odoratissima, both called champa, oleander, Plumeria acutifolia and various varieties of Jasminum sambac, Lagerstroemia flos-reginae, myrtles, Ixora coccinea, Caesalpinia pulcherrima, Euphorbia pulcherrima and several showy Hibiscus, Tecoma Stans, Adhatoda, Vasica, Bougainvillea glabra, Vinca rosea and Jatropha multifida. The following very fine creepers have established themselves near houses :—Thunbergia grandiflora, Clitoria ternatea, Beaumontia grandiflora, Antigonum leptopus, Hiptage Madablota and Porana paniculata. The opium poppy is no longer cultivated, but is still found occasionally; Argemone mexicana has become abundant in waste places and the pretty little Evolvulus nummularius is curiously creeping into the district along the Grand Trunk Road.

"Parasnāth hill deserves special mention because of its great botanical interest. Being the highest peak in the province, and till recently well covered with virgin forest, it possesses a large number of plants not found elsewhere in Hazāribāgh. Sir J. D. Hooker who visited the hill in 1848 noted that the mountain top 'presents a mixture of the plants of a damp hot, a dry hot and of a temperate climate in fairly balanced proportions'. Clematis nutans, and C. goureana, Thalictrum javanicum, Berberis asiatica, Hoya pendula, Cynanchum callialata, Osbeckia truncata, Dumasia villosa, Pygeum lucidum, Kalanchoe heterophylla, Rubia cordifolia and the beautiful Geranium ocellatum are very interesting plants confined to the summit of the mountain and forming a little Himalayan flora in the middle of the plains. Other plants found only on Pārasnāth in this district are Naravelia zeylanica, Sterculia colorata, Eriolaena quinque locularis, Bridelia montana, Antidesma Bunius, Bischofia javanica, Glycosmis pentaphylla, Murraya exotica, Cipadessa fruticosa, Mucuna imbricata, Erythrina resupinata, Boerhaavia scabrella, Linociera intermedia, Stereospermum chelonoides, Plectranthus ternifolius, Smilax Roxburghiana, Disporum pullum, Phoenix robusta, Drymaria cordata, Santalum album, Vitis lanceolaria, Coleus barbatus, Gymnema tingens, Polygonum alatum, Sophora Bakeri, Smithia ciliata and Desmodium polycarpum Var. trichocaulon. Botany of Pārasnāth hill.

"A considerable number of grasses and Cyperaceae are confined to Pārasnāth in this district, e.g., Carex stramentitia, Kyllinga cylindrica, Panicum plicatum, Pollinia ciliata, Pennisetum pedicellatum, Arthraxon lanceolatus, Garnotia stricta, Eragrostis nardoides, Tripogon capillatus and Dendrocalamus sericeus.

Several Ferns and other Cryptogams are peculiar to Pārasnāth such as Davallia pulchra, Asplenium parasnathensis, A. drepanophyllum, Neprodium crenatum and Ophioglossum reticulatum. For orchids both terrestrial and epiphytic Pārasnāth is unparalleled in Hazāribāgh. Microstylis congesta, Dendrobium bicameratum, and Habenaria Lawii are examples of many orchids which have not been found elsewhere in the district.

Destruction of forests.

" Unfortunately no report on the Hazāribāgh flora can omit the most striking fact about it, i.e., its rapid disappearance. The forest is being most wastefully destroyed, and with it a great number of plants of great botanical and economical interest are becoming extinct. Mutilated stumps are all that remains of many valuable trees like Dillenia aurea, Sterculia villosa, kusum, paisar, Dalbergia latifolia, Soymida febrifuga and Ailanthus excelsa, where even ten years ago there was considerable jungle. Whether one considers the disastrous effect on the cultivated fields lying below the ruined jungle, or the loss to the villagers of their invaluable forest produce, or merely the botanical loss, this is by far the most important fact about the vegetation of Hazāribāgh."

Early history.

This destruction of forests has been in progress for a very long time. In the report of the Geological Survey of 1848-9 there is a note on the more important timber trees, of which the sāl (Shorea robusta) was then, as now, by far the most valuable. Young trees were in such general demand for house-building and agriculture that they were rarely allowed to grow beyond the size required for such purposes, especially as the only carpenter's tool then in use was the axe. The practice was to encourage only the growth of saplings, and the absence of big trees was very marked. In 1873 Dr. Schlich, the Conservator of Forests, came to the same conclusions as a result of a professional inspection of the south-west of the district, and at the present day it is very rare to find a sāl tree of large size except in sacred groves.

Present condition.

Elsewhere the repeated cutting to which the saplings have been subjected has exhausted the vitality of the tree, and sāl is now extinct over large areas. In the north of Barākar basin there are extensive tracts where all jungle has entirely disappeared, and elsewhere, as in the plains of the Sakri and Lilājān, wide stretches are found which contain nothing but thorny shrubs. These results have been brought about not only by the actual cutting of the trees, but also by unrestricted grazing, and by the pernicious practice of setting fire to the jungle in March, with the object of improving the growth of grass.

Destructive agencies.

In these fires the weaker saplings and practically all the seedlings perish. There is also a mischievous practice of cutting the sāl saplings for the purpose of fencing the homesteads, an object which would be served equally well, with little more trouble, by the use of thorny shrubs. Still, in spite of all the destructive forces at work, there remain extensive areas covered with forest. The sides of the plateaus are naturally unfit for cultivation, and are comparatively inaccessible; and the hills which are scattered about the district for the most part retain a covering of jungle. Recently there has been extensive felling by the proprietor of Sirāmpur in the Giridih subdivision, where the entire contents of whole jungles have been completely removed, by the proprietor of Dhanwār round Bharkatta, and again by tenure-holders in the neighbourhood of Bishungarh. When the clearance of jungle is not accompanied by the introduction of cultivation an immediate result is the cutting up of the country by deep ravines, and the affected tract is rendered permanently unfit for agriculture. Rain water which would have gradually percolated through wooded soil is carried off on the surface with great rapidity and floods in the rivers are aggravated. The problem of conserving the forests with due consideration for existing customary rights and for the normal agricultural development of the country has been under consideration for some years; but up till now no adequate solution has been found.

Forest Scenery.

In the appearance of the typical forest there is little trace of tropical luxuriance, and the general effect is dull and uninteresting. In March the hill sides of the lower plateau are yellow with the great flowers of the golgol (Cochlospermum Gossypium). More rare are the Butea superba, with its orange-red flowers, and the yellow clusters of the Indian laburnum, or amaltās (Cassia fistula). On the outskirts of the jungle the gregarious parās trees (Butea frondosa) make a striking show with their red flowers in March and April, and serve as pasturage for the lac insects. The asan (Terminalia tomentosa) which is sometimes pollarded to feed silkworms, is less common. The kusum (Schleichera trijuga) is beautiful in April when its new leaves and twigs emerge a deep claret colour. Its seeds yield oil, and the lac which it produces is of the best quality. The kend too (Diospyros melanoxylon) is often found on the waste lands: its hard black heart is a valuable wood. The main function of the karam (Adina cordifolia)

Trees outside the jungle.

is to provide a karam branch at the festival which bears its name in the month of October. The bar (Ficus bengalensis) spreads by means of aerial roots and sometimes attains a great size : when its round red fig is ripe flocks of crows, pigeons and mainas crowd to its branches, and foxes and jackals at night eat what has fallen to the ground. The pipal (Ficus religiosa) is a favourite with green pigeons and other birds, who carry its fruit away to their perches ; and the seeds, falling into the crevices of masonry buildings or the bark of trees speedily bring them to decay. Another fig, the dumar (Ficus glomerata) is conspicuous by its fruit, which ripens at all times of the year and grows out of the trunk and larger limbs. It is not used much for human food, but is an important part of the diet of birds and beasts.

Whatever other trees may be destroyed with the forest, the mahua (Bassia latifolia) is jealously preserved. Its dried flowers are valuable not only as a food, but also for making mahua spirit, the chief intoxicating drink of the district ; and the seeds when dried are pressed for oil. On the success of the mahua crop depends the comfort, during some months of the year, of a large part of the people. The simal (Bombax malabaricum) is also usually spared. Its large fleshy flowers of dark red announce the end of the cold season ; and from its large green pods a fine silky cotton is obtained, which is exported under the name of kapok. Its light white wood is suitable for packing cases, and the tree is becoming scarce. Like mahua it is for some unknown scruple never grown from seed. The mango (Mangifera indica) apparently grows wild in the jungles, where its fruit has a scanty stringy envelope tasting of turpentine, and a comparatively large stone. Outside the jungles it is planted largely along the roads, and more rarely in groves. Garden mangoes, carefully cultivated, and bearing really good fruit, are quite uncommon. Near the village sites are found the jamun (Eugenia jambolana) whose purple fruits ripen in the early rains ; the bair (Zizyphus Jujuba) which yields a poor plum, but often grows a crop of lac; the bel (Aegle marmelos) and imli (Tamarindus indica) of which the fruits are medicinally, but not otherwise, attractive ; and the much-prized kathal or jack fruit (Artocarpus integrifolia) whose dark-green glossy foliage shows black from the distance. Round the borders of the courtyards, which are fenced with bean poles, is planted the munga (Moringa pterygosperma) whose leaves, flowers and fruit are all eaten. The nim (Azadirachta indica) yields a medicinal oil from its seeds, and the bean of the karanj (Pongamia glabra) an edible oil. Timber trees growing in the open are the tun (Cedrelă toona), siris (Dalbergia lanceolaria) and sisu (Dalbergia Sissoo). The tār (Borassus flabelliformis) and khajur (Phoenix sylvestris) are tapped for their sugary sap, which is fermented to produce tāri, a beverage with slightly intoxicating powers. The former is rare except in the valleys of the Sakri and Lilājān. The tapping is usually in the cold weather and the round pot into which the sap falls from the incision are very attractive to bears. Bamboos grow wild in the hills, especially round the Lilājān, down whose stream they are floated in large quantities to the plains: they are however too small and heavy for ordinary scaffolding. Bamboos are also cultivated, but somewhat sparingly. Of the other grasses sabai is found in the jungles, but the quantity is comparatively small. There are also other fruits, flowers, leaves and roots, edible or medicinal, which in the aggregate contribute largely to the comfort of the poorer classes, more especially in the jungle areas, when ordinary foods are scarce; and the use of various herbs and grasses as *sāg* is universal. The virtues of many of the medical remedies are, as has been indicated in Mr. Thompson's note, frequently assumed merely on the basis of some supposed physical resemblance.

RESERVED AND PROTECTED FORESTS.

Direct protection of the forests by Government agency has so far been confined to two areas, of which the Kodarma Forest is the larger.

Kodarma.

An area of 19,720 acres was originally demarcated in 1879, and gazetted as reserved forest in 1880, and three years later a contiguous area of 10,047 acres was added lying to the west. In the survey of 1901 the total area was calculated afresh as 28,969 acres. In addition there is a fringe of protected forest of 7,300 acres. When the reserved forest was taken up it consisted of little more than scrub jungle, with large blocks of bare waste interspersed; and it has required careful preservation and improvement for over 30 years to bring it to the workable stage. It is expected in time to become a valuable source of supply of pit props and small building timber. The forest contains valuable mines of mica, which yield a good income to Government. The financial results in 1911-12 were an income of Rs. 29,154 from mica and Rs. 5,825 from other sources; and a total expenditure of Rs. 6,765. In 1915-16 the corresponding figures were Rs. 29,362, Rs. 5,166 and Rs. 5,936. These figures reveal the necessity of patience, and the inevitableness of temporary financial loss, in restoring a typical area of reserved sāl jungle.

Khurchuta. The Khurchuta block, which consists of 6,625 acres of reserved forest and 13,580 acres of protected forest, is situated in the north of Bengābād police-station, and was brought under control in 1893. The revenues of 1911-12 and 1915-16 were Rs. 1,609 and Rs. 657 and expenditure Rs. 1,627 and Rs. 1,569, respectively; but in the last 12 years as a whole there has been a surplus of income over expenditure amounting to about Rs. 5,000. These figures, like those of Kodarma, indicate that the regeneration of forests in Chota Nāgpur is, at least in its earlier stages, far from lucrative.

ZOOLOGY. There has been no zoological survey of this district, and very little has been recorded with special reference to Hazāribāgh. It is however probable that the wild animals to be found there are practically the same as those in the rest of Chota Nāgpur. There is no reason to believe that tigers are specially numerous, in spite of the large number of victims with which they have recently been credited. In a year not more than five or six tiger skins are brought to the Courts for the customary reward of Rs. 25, and the number killed by European sportsmen is quite small. It is probable that owing to accidental circumstances tigers take to man-killing more freely in this district than elsewhere, and some have been credited with an extraordinary number of victims. They still haunt the Kodarma forest, and are permanent residents of the hills near Dānto, north of the headquarters station. In Khesmi and Doranda, Sātgāwān and Partāppur there appear to be families ordinarily in residence. The great difficulty in meeting with them is the enormous extent of continuous cover over which they may wander free from observation, and the absence of favourite resorts. It is not safe after a kill in any particular place to assume that the animal will be anywhere in the same locality immediately afterwards. Leopards are much more common, and frequently visit the town of Hazāribāgh. Each year they kill large numbers of cattle, but they rarely attack human beings unless provoked. Bears are not numerous except in the south and east, whence skins are often brought in. They belong to the ordinary sloth variety. Hyaenas are fairly numerous in the neighbourhood of the headquarters station, whither they are attracted by the bodies of the dead cattle at the Jain pinjrapole near Seotāgarha Hill. Wolves for about four years from 1910 to 1914 killed a large number of human beings near Chaupāran ; but a special reward of Rs. 50 led to the hunting out of the cubs, and the evil has now ceased. They are found over the whole of the district and take considerable toll of goats. Jackals and foxes are common, as there is abundant food over the greater part of the district in the form of feathered game and wild fruits. Pigs are numerous in the west and south, and the great damage which they cause to the crops is usually put forward as the reason for applications for gun licenses received from that part of the district. Hares are common, except in tracts occupied by the Santāls, whose methods of hunting quickly exterminate all game save snipe. Of deer sāmbar are still found, more especially in Gāwān and Partābpur. Spotted deer, hog deer, four-horned deer and ravine deer are met with, but are not plentiful. Nilgai are found in Partābpur.

The statistics relating to deaths caused by wild animals are as follows :— Deaths caused by wild animals.

NUMBER OF HUMAN BEINGS KILLED.

Year.	Tigers.	Leopards.	Bears.	Wolves.	Hyaenas.	Others.	Snakes.	Reward paid.
1	2	3	4	5	6	7	8	9
								Rs.
1910 ...	31	8	11	3	2	3	92	471
1911 ...	10	4	0	44	1	0	125	2,052
1912 ...	16	2	6	86	2	2	128	3,349
1913 ...	28	9	8	21	1	2	97	4,140
1914 ...	21	2	5	6	0	0	117	10,200
1915 ...	57	7	4	3	1	5	144	3,338

The larger number of the deaths caused by tigers in 1915 was due to a single animal near Katkamsānri, for whom a special reward has been offered. The great increase in the rewards distributed was due to the special rate of Rs. 50 paid for wolves until the end of March 1915.

BIRDS.
Game-birds.

Precise information about the birds of this district is almost completely wanting, and the following paragraph is necessarily restricted to a mere impression of its sporting resources. Peafowl are fairly numerous in suitable localities, and jungle fowl are wide-spread. The grey partridge is common all over the district, but the black species is confined to the more wooded parts, as also is the much less numerous spur-fowl. Field quail may be found in spring in the *rabi* crops of the west, and bush quail are common. Snipe, though not present in large numbers, are wide-spread in the cold weather. Green pigeons are common, and golden-plover are sometimes found. A small species of sand-grouse is occasionally met with in the north. The great drawback to shooting in the district is the fact that the game is rarely to be found concentrated, and very large bags are seldom obtained. Geese and duck are comparatively very rare, as the rivers are too small to be safe resorts, and there are few artificial sheets of water of any size.

Fish.

This same want of large permanent bodies of water necessarily results in the absence of fisheries of serious value. Most of the larger tanks contain fish, which are however liable to total destruction in the not unusual event of complete de-watering, after which the tanks are re-stocked with fry. There has so far been no detailed scientific examination of the rivers and *bāndhs*, but it is scarcely likely that when made it will reveal anything of commercial importance.

Reptiles.

Regarding reptiles it is at present safe to say little more than the fact that the reported human deaths from snake-bite were 92 in 1901, 125 in 1911, and in the four following years an average of 120.

CLIMATE.

The climate of the Hazāribāgh plateau is much the same as that of Rānchi, differing from the other neighbouring districts not only in its lower average temperature, but also in the comparative dryness of the air in the rainy season. After the break of the rains in June the first three months are usually quite pleasant, and by the middle of September the mornings already promise the cold weather. In contrast with Bihar October is a delightful month. From November to the middle of February the only drawback is the occasional excessive cold which follows on rain. If there is a good fall of rain in February it remains cool till the middle of March. From April to the rains the day temperature, though high, is always below that of the neighbouring districts, and it is rare for the nights to be oppressive. The prevailing winds, are, in the rains from the south-west, in the cold weather from the west, and in the hot weather from the north-west.

Since the last three years the registration of temperature has been discontinued by the Meteorological Department. Roughly it may be said that the day temperature in most years does not rise beyond 107° Fah., and that it does not fall below 40° Fah. The average day temperature for the whole year is about 75° Fah. The mean humidity is about 51, compared with 76 in Calcutta. Temperature.

The average monthly rainfall of the district was computed as follows up to and including 1914 :— Rainfall.

	Inches.
January	0·73
February	1·32
March	0·86
April	0·54
May	1·70
June	8·04
July	12·77
August	12·80
September	8·75
October	2·63
November	0·20
December	0·18
	50·52

There are thirteen measuring stations, but owing to defects in the records the figures for eight only are of value. Whilst these do not disclose any great inequality in the distribution, it is commonly understood that Gola with eastern Rāmgarh has the steadiest rainfall, and Chaupāran, northern Dhanwār and Kharagdiha the least regular. The distribution of the rains in the year is a much more important factor than the total amount precipitated. Continuous rainfall in the end of June and July coupled with absence of sunshine is injurious to the maize and other autumn (*bhadai*) crops, though it does not prejudice the far more important rice crop. Heavy rain in July is needed for the transplantation of rice and *marua*, though it can be postponed as regards the former crop till the middle of August without serious loss; but none of the crops already in the ground in July can bear a long drought in that month. The rains should continue at short intervals and in fairly heavy quantities till the middle of September, when slightly longer breaks are desirable for the harvesting of the earlier *bhadui* crops. But it is most important that there should be a good fall in the first week of October, to fill the ears of the early rice, and to give a final supply of water to the lower terraces in which are planted the late maturing varieties. It is on this rain that the fortunes of the raiyat's year depend; for without it even the lowest lands will disappoint, and higher terraces will yield little or nothing. Owing to the great importance of the *mahua* crop it is very necessary that there should be no rain whilst the buds are maturing from about the middle of March, or earlier, to the middle of April, during which period untimely showers may arrest or prevent the formation of the flowers.

The heaviest recorded rainfall in any one year was in 1911, when the Hazāribāgh station recorded 75·24 inches, of which 30·49 inches fell between the 5th and 25th June, including 9·81 inches on the 24th. The lowest rainfall recorded was 40·58 inches in 1915.

CHAPTER II.

GEOLOGY AND MINERALS.

The following brief account of the geology of the district has been contributed by Dr. L. L. Fermor, Superintendent of the Geological Survey of India :— General account.

" Broadly speaking the geological formations found in the Hazāribāgh district may be grouped into two chief divisions;

(1) Archaean, comprising a great variety of gneisses, schists, and granites, and occupying by far the greater portion of the district, and (2) the Gondwāna System, in the form of seven coalfields, four of which—namely, Bokāro, Rāmgarh, and North and South Karanpura—occupy a portion of the Dāmodar river valley lying to the south of the Hazāribāgh plateau, whilst one—the small Chope field—lies on the plateau itself, the two remaining fields—Giridih and Itkhori—being situated on the lower plateau. These coalfields or patches of Gondwāna rocks are surrounded on all sides by crystalline rocks of Archaean age and owe their preservation in the main to a series of boundary faults by which they have been let down into the Archaean foundations. There is no doubt that formerly these Gondwāna rocks occupied a much larger area, and it seems probable that the four southern coalfields were once united.

The Archaean formations of this district have not yet been surveyed or studied in detail. But such information as we have shows that in general the Archaean rocks of this district are similar to those of any ordinary Archaean area. The old felspathic gneisses, with the composition of typical igneous rocks, are associated with schistose forms, and may be the results of intermingling of ancient sediments with igneous matter. Among these are intrusive masses of granite, which under pressure have assumed a gneissose structure, and on account of the way in which they stand up as small hills of Archaean.

rounded hummocks have sometimes been referred to as the 'dome gneiss'. They rise up in the midst of bands of schists, which are cut in all directions by veins of acid pegmatite. These pegmatites in the northern portion of the district often carry valuable supplies of mica, and the belt of mica mines stretching from southern Gayā through northern Hazāribāgh as far as Jhājhā (Nawādih) in the Monghyr district is one of the most valuable mica fields in the world.* In addition to the muscovite mica obtained from these mines several other minerals of interest have been found: namely, apatite, especially near Kodarma; leucopyrite, near Dabaur, south of Gāwān, and near Dhāb; and transparent green tourmaline, sometimes suitable for optical uses, near Manimundar, where it is associated with the blue variety, indicolite, and with lepidolite. If there were any market for a porcelain industry an abundance of felspar now rejected would be available in any part of the mica belt.

Amongst the schistose rocks crystalline, dolomitic limestones occur near Gāwān and at Dhelua, where also small fragments of noble serpentine were found associated with the dolomite. Garnets are common throughout the district and some of those in the coarse, flaky biotite schist have the correct colour, but are rarely clear enough, for the manufacture of cheap jewellery.

Some of the gneissic rocks are more correctly designated granulites, and amongst these granulites must be mentioned an intrusive cassiterite-granulite† containing a large proportion of cassiterate or tinstone, and found hitherto at two localities, namely, Chappatānd and Naranga, at the latter of which localities an attempt has been made to mine the tin-bearing rock.

Gondwāna.

In the seven patches of Lower Gondwāna rocks comprising the coalfields already enumerated the following subdivisions of this system have been recognized :—

Tālcher Series	Tālcher. Karharbāri.
Dāmodar Series	Barākar. Ironstone shale. Rāniganj.
Pānchet	Lower Pānchet. Upper Pānchet.

* T. H. Holland, "The Mica Deposits of India", Memoirs, Geol. Surv. Ind., XXXIV., pages 44—53 (1902).

† L. L. Fermor, Records, Geol. Surv. Ind., XXXIII, page 235 (1906), XLII. page 79 (1912).

It is not certain, however, that some of the rocks regarded as Upper Pānchet may not be the equivalent of rocks regarded as Upper Gondwāna in other parts of India, for example the Upper Pānchet of Lugu Hill in the Bokāro coalfield.

A general account of the characters of the Gondwāna system will be found in the Manual of the Geology of India, and we may proceed at once to give an account of the separate coalfields, which will be treated in the following order* :—

(1) Bokāro. (3) & (4) North and South Karanpura.
(2) Rāmgarh. (5) Chope.
(6) Itkhori.

[An account of the Giridih field is omitted here.]

Bokāro.—The Bokāro coalfield lies some two or three miles west of the termination of the Jharia field. Its greatest length is in an east and west direction and is about 40 miles; its maximum breadth from north to south does not exceed 6½ miles. The total area is 220 square miles.

The rocks represented range from Tālchers to Upper Pānchet and are much disturbed by faulting, high dips being the rule rather than the exception. Although coal-seams are found in the Rāniganj beds, yet the whole of the workable coal occurs in the Barākars. In the opinion of Mr. Hughes† who mapped the area in 1866 the coal cannot be compared in its general quality with that obtained from the Jharia coalfield. The number of coal-seams is very large and some of them are enormously thick. In many places they have been much damaged by intrusions of trap. The most productive portion of the field lies between the Konār river and the eastern boundary. Among several thick seams in this latter area, one measuring 88 feet in thickness (the Kargāli seam) stands pre-eminent. In the same locality the dips vary from 5° to 10° and the ground is, therefore, much more favourable for working than in other parts of the field.

Mr. Hughes mentions that 1,500 million tons is the probable amount of available fuel which the field can yield. During the past few years considerable attention has been given to the prospecting of this coalfield. The rights to work this coalfield have been secured by a company known as the Bokāro and Rāmgarh,

* These accounts have been taken from "The Coalfields of India" by V. Ball and R. R. Simpson; Memoirs, Geol. Surv. Ind., XLI., Part I.

† Memoirs, Geol. Surv. Ind., VI., page 58 (1867).

Limited, which has come to an arrangement with the Bengal-Nagpur and the East Indian Railway Companies by which an extension has been constructed as far as Bermo. In return for their enterprise in constructing this extension these two railway companies are to receive a certain proportion of the blocks demarcated in this coalfield. Up to the present two blocks have been marked out, of which the above railway companies have obtained one, which is now producing coal, whilst the other block has been sold by the coal company to the Great Indian Peninsula Railway Company, who are laying out a second colliery. In each case the Kargāli seam is the object of exploitation, and hitherto no other seams approximating to first-class quality have been located. Prospecting operations are now being prosecuted to the west of the Konār river, and future extensions of the railway depend upon the results of these operations.

Rāmgarh.*—This coalfield lies along the valley of the Dāmodar river, some 5 miles to the south of the Bokāro coalfield. Its area is about 40 square miles. The rocks exposed have a total thickness of more than 5,600 feet and consist of Dāmodars and Tālchers. The rocks of the Barākar stage contain a large number of thick coal-seams, of which some are of fair quality, but much disturbed; on the east where low dips prevail the coal is very inferior.

Ball† estimated that about five million tons of coal are available, but did not think it probable that the coalfield would ever be worked to any great extent. Small quantities of coal have been worked by local residents and carried to Rānchi and Hazāribāgh for sale.

North and South Karanpura.—These extensive coalfields occupy the head of the Dāmodar valley and lie at the base of the southern scarp of the Hazāribāgh table-land, from one to four miles west of the Bokāro and Rāmgarh coalfields. Their respective areas are 472 and 72 sq. miles. Although separated from one another by a strip of their common gneissic floor, from one and half to three miles in width, for all intents and purposes they form one field.

The rock groups represented within the area are the same as those which occupy the easterly fields of the Dāmodar valley, i.e.,

* Ball: Memoirs, Geol. Surv. Ind., VI, page 109 (1867).
† Manual, Vol. III, page 84 (1881).

Pānchets, Dāmodars and Tālchers. The structure of the field is that of a comparatively shallow and somewhat oval basin, or broad synclinal trough, with a general dip inwards of the strata from all parts of the periphery towards the centre ; but it is not exempt from local undulations. Except for the well-defined fault on the south of the fields, dislocations of the strata are few and unimportant. There is an extraordinary absence of trappean intrusion and with the exception of two in the southern field the dykes which are seen are not traceable for any distance. There is a number of thick coal seams but they are much less numerous than in the eastern fields. Mr. Hughes,* who mapped the area in detail in 1867-8, estimated that in the northern field, presuming an average thickness of 35 feet of coal to occur over an area of only 250 sq. miles, there is a total quantity of 8,750 million tons of coal. In the southern field he assumed an average thickness of 50 feet of coal over an area of only 15 sq. miles, and a total quantity of 75 million tons of coal. Mr. Hughes points out that these estimates are extremely conservative ones. Much of the coal is of excellent quality ; the following assay is a fair measure of the quality of the better seams :—

Volatile matter	27·00
Fixed carbon	64·50
Ash	8·50

The position of the coalfields between the elevated table-lands of Hazāribāgh and Rānchi renders them somewhat difficult of access. In time to come, however, the continuation of the Bermo-Mahuda branch to Daltonganj, via the Dāmodar valley, will afford them communication with both up and down-country markets. From the latter the heavy freight charges would probably keep out the coal until such time as the better coals of the lower coalfields become exhausted ; in the former market, however, Karanpura coal would probably be in considerable demand at highly remunerative prices.

Chope.—This small coalfield is situated on the Hazāribāgh plateau at an elevation of 2,000 feet above sea-level, and lies about 8 miles a little north of west from the civil station of Hazāribāgh. It consists of Tālcher and Barākar rocks and has an area of about three-fourths of a square mile. There is only one coal-seam, with a thickness of about 4 feet, and it is found

---

* Memoirs, Geol. Surv. Ind., VII, page 285 (1878).

over a very small portion of the area and is of poor quality. Ball* considered that some of the coal might be made use of locally for brick and lime-burning.

Itkhori.—At a very much lower elevation and nearly 20 miles north of the Chope field another small area of Tālcher-Barākar rocks is found on the Mohani, a tributary of the Phalgu river. The Barākars occupy only about half a square mile or $\frac{1}{46}$th of the area. They contain three seams of coal of from four to eight feet in thickness, but the quality is inferior, the average coal containing more than 30 per cent of ash. Hughes † estimated that from one and a half to two million tons of coal were available, but did not predict its use for more than lime and brick-burning purposes in the locality.

Bokaro Colliery.

The recent history of the colliery which has been opened in the Rāmgarh-Bokāro area is contained in the following note contributed by Mr. G. C. Lathbury, Superintendent of the East Indian Railway Company :—

"In the year 1908 Mr. Thos. H. Ward, who was at that time the Superintendent of East Indian Railway Collieries, made a detailed survey and report on that portion of the field which lies to the east of the Konār river. As a result of this report, and in accordance with an agreement between the East Indian and Bengal-Nagpur Railway Companies and the Bokāro-Ramgarh Company, Limited (who had obtained the prospecting and mining rights in this coalfield), the two railways obtained the mining rights for an area measuring 3,750 standard bighas situated in Baidkāro, Bermo and Jaridih villages. The surface rights were acquired under the Land Acquisition Act. A railway was built from Mahuda on the Bengal-Nagpur Railway to the colliery, a distance of 22 miles, and was completed in 1914. The area surveyed by Mr. Ward was found to contain three thick seams of coal, of which one seam (called the Kargāli) contains a large proportion of first-class coal. The total thickness of this seam is about 90 feet of which about 65 or 70 feet are first-class. The other two seams do not contain good coal.

"The railways commenced operations in August 1914, and in April 1916 the development of the colliery had proceeded fast, about 12,000 to 15,000 tons being despatched monthly.

* Memoirs, Geol. Surv. Ind., VIII, page 321 (1872).

† Memoirs, Geol. Surv. Ind., VIII, page 347 (1872).

A certain area of coal is at such a shallow depth that it can be quarried; but two shafts are being sunk to the deeper portions and the production will be increased later.

"A weekly market (held on Sundays) has been opened on the colliery which has proved very popular, and should help to settle labour, which is not plentiful in the district. Water for drinking purposes is carried by pipes all over the colliery and to the market."

Regarding the Rāmgarh coalfield, Mr. Lathbury is satisfied about its entire separation from that of Bokāro and does not consider that it holds coal of commercial value.

It may be added that the colliery maintains an adequate medical staff and has provided suitable houses for the miners. In view of the inaccessibility of the field from the established courts arrangements are being made for a local court of justice and a special staff of police.

The following account of the small but very important Giridih coalfield has been prepared by Mr. Thos H. Ward, late Superintendent of the East Indian Railway Company's Collieries:— Giridih coalfield.

"The Giridih coalfield is perhaps the smallest of the Indian coalfields, the coal-bearing rocks extending over an area of only seven square miles.

"The coalfield used to be known as the Karhārbāri coalfield and is so called in the Records of the Geological Survey of India down to 1894.* Karhārbāri is the name of the village in which the Tikāit lived who had the proprietary rights over the western and major part of the field. The proprietary rights of the eastern portion belong to the Sirāmpur estate. The town of Giridih is situated just off the coal-bearing area to the northeast. It is the terminal station of the Madhupur-Giridih branch line.

The town of Giridih has a population of about 11,000, and lies at an elevation of 1,000 feet above sea-level. This brings the Karharbāri Lower Seam, where it is deepest, to about sea-level. The name (from 'Giri' a hill and 'dih' a village) means "the village in the hills". There are many hills around, picturesque peaks of diorite-trap, in the crystalline area surrounding the coalfield: Bankunju hill is about one mile to the north,

* Saise. Rec. Geol. Surv. Ind. XXVII 86-100.

and Gajhandi and Chope hills, on the west, are close to the coalfield; and in the coalfield itself the bold sandstone escarpment of Lanki hill, Keri hill and Bhaddoah hill, across the centre of the field, and the Jatkoti hills on the west, all caused by deep erosion of the coal-bearing rocks, form striking topographic features of the country. All these, except Keri hill and one of the Bhaddoah hills, are covered with sāl forest. Keri hill was in the land owned by the Bengal Coal Company (now East Indian Railway property) and the forest disappeared 25 years ago. In Bhaddoah a fire occurred in 1909 in a worked-out area of the lower Bhaddoah coal-seam (*vide infra*), and the rock cover being only 30 to 50 feet, the heat generated and the hot gases, escaping from fissures caused by the collapse of the strata over the coal-seam when it was worked out, have entirely destroyed the forest over a considerable area. The extensive bald patch resulting is very conspicuous and disfiguring.

The official history of the coalfield begins in 1848, when Dr. McClelland visited it. He reported in 1850 that the coal in almost every section was superior.

In 1851 coal, mined at Rāmnadih in the west of the coalfield by Mr. Inman, was carted to the Ganges, and up to 1862 coal was mined and carted more than 70 miles to Lakhisarai to burn bricks for the construction of the bridges on the Loop Line of the East Indian Railway. Mr. Inman's properties, Kuldiha (in the centre of the field) and Rāmnadih, appear to have passed into the hands of the Bengal Coal Company about 1886-7.

In 1852 a small quantity of the coal from the field was sent to the Agent, East Indian Railway, but was not very favourably reported on at home.

In 1857 the Government of India employed Mr. David Smith, iron and coal viewer, to report on the coalfield. He reported :—

"The quality of this coal is different to any I have seen in India: It is bituminous, will coke well by the ordinary mode, and is, therefore, applicable for a great variety of purposes. It likewise ignited readily, leaving a comparatively small amount of ash of a light fawn colour.

"Although the field cannot be, by a great deal, so extensive as that of the Dāmuda (Rāniganj), the superior quality of the coal, the highly favourable condition in which it lies, with the important circumstance that the labour of 400 to 500 miners now resident in the neighbourhood may be commanded, constitute it well deserving the attention of mining speculators. All that is required is to remove the only disadvantage I could discover by providing proper communication to transfer the barren (and almost poverty-stricken) locality to a state of prosperity."

In 1859 Mr. Wilson was deputed by the Director of Geological Survey "to examine this coalfield in detail" but no report appears to have resulted.

In 1868 Mr. T. H. Hughes* who opened his report on the coalfield by pointing out that it had "attracted the attention of Government and private individuals owing to the admitted superiority of its coals to those from any of the fields of the Dāmuda valley, and of its position", proceeds: "Those, however, who have so strongly upheld the advantages possessed by the Karharbari field, seem to me to have failed when desirous of making a true valuation of its resources, in giving sufficient weight to the drawback of its limited area, the character of its seams, and its geological structure" and criticized Dr. McClelland's opinion, quoted above, remarking. "This term, superior, however, seems to have been indiscriminately applied to shaly coals, slaty coals, and bituminous coals."

In commenting on Mr. Hughes' report, the Director of Geological Survey, Mr. T. Oldham, remarked :—

"The only workings at present in actual operation (that is in 1868) are those of the Bengal Coal Company, who have been very vigorously raising coal for sometime past, in anticipation of the demand for the railway on the opening of the 'Chord Line', and have further been wisely proving the extension of the beds of coal within their property, and with much success. Nothing has yet been done towards reopening the works which had been carried on by the East Indian Railway." (This refers to the exploration by pits and borings carried out by Mr. T. F. Cockburn, Resident Engineer, East Indian Railway, from 1862) "so that there has unfortunately been very little opportunity of obtaining information as to the nature and continuity of the coal beds. The report is, therefore, unavoidably less full and satisfactory on these points than it was hoped we should have been able to render it".

* Memoirs, Geol. Surv. Ind., VII.

Notwithstanding this somewhat lukewarm attitude the potentialities of this coalfield formed a powerful incentive to the early construction of the Chord Line, East Indian Railway, which passes, in going north, some 20 miles to the east of Giridih. The branch from Madhupur was put in hand at the same time as the Chord Line works, and was opened for traffic in 1871, when the East Indian Railway at once recommenced operations which had been suspended in 1867 for that event.

In 1876 the Rāniganj Coal Association leased the east end of the coalfield from the Sirāmpur Estate. They had a very extensive and valuable property where the Lower Karharbāri seam was very thick and regular. This property was completely worked out in 1905. The Bengal Coal Company had in 1914 finished the working out of Kuldiha, having sold the remainder of their central property to the East Indian Railway Company in 1907. Their interest in the coalfield is now confined to the properties they had in the west. These they have consolidated and are now exploiting by means of the Bengal-Giridih Coal Company, Limited. Practically the rest of the coalfield belongs to the East Indian Railway.

It is an unusual task for an engineer to attempt to describe the physical features of a coalfield without the aid of plan, a but the task must be essayed. The coalfield is a tiny fragment preserved from the planing down process which has gone on over thousands of square miles of the surrounding country, by the accident that it was dropped a little lower than the contiguous portions by the faults which bound it on the north and south. These faults have a west-north-west and east-south-east direction.* The fault on the south has the greater throw, taking the coal-bearing rocks down more than 1,000 feet below the present surface of the earth. The fault on the north has about one-half this throw. About half way between these faults is another parallel fault running right down the centre of the field. This fault brings the northern area up, and the combined effect of this fault, and the smaller throw of the fault on the north, was to bring the northern section under the influence of the planing and eroding action referred to, and has resulted in this northern area having only about half the extent, in an easterly and westerly direction, that the southern area has. The latter is about six miles in

* T. H. Holland & T. H. Ward. Trans. Min. Geol. Inst. Ind., 1906.

length, the former has an extreme limit of three miles; again the latter has an average width of about one mile, while the former has such irregular boundaries as to make it difficult to fix an average width.

It was not until 1880* that the physical structure of the coalfield was finally elucidated. It was then established that the whole of the seven square miles occupied by the coal-bearing rocks was underlain by the seam of coal then named the "Karhārbāri lower seam". This seam or stratum of coal, is no less than 24 feet in thickness at the east of the coalfield but gradually thins out, towards the west, until it is about 8 feet in thickness only. This thinning out is contributed to by the top portion of the seam being gradually separated by a thickening stratum of sandstone. On the east the coal seam is complete. A couple of miles to the west one of the shale bands gradually thickens and changes into very hard sandstone 8 or 10 feet in thickness about 5 or 6 feet below the top of the coal-seam. Further west this band of sandstone has varying thicknesses but eventually thickens while the separated section of the coal seam gets thinner and unworkable.

In the northern part of the field the Karhārbāri lower seam is separated in one area into three sections, by intercalated sandstone bands. All this part has been entirely worked out, as has the eastern portion of the coalfield.

Over a portion of the northern area, as just described, there was a seam 5 to 6 feet in thickness known as the "Karhārbāri upper seam". This seam was of excellent quality. It is represented in the southern area by a thin unworkable seam of poor quality. It lay, in the northern area, about 300 feet above the "Karhārbāri lower seam". Three hundred feet higher still in the section brings in what is known as the "Bhaddoah main seam". This is 8 feet of the inferior coal which was extensively worked in the eighties, and down to 1905, in the East Indian Railway Collieries. The Bhaddoah seams were known as the hill seams because they outcropped on the northern escarpments of Lanki, Keri and Bhaddoah hills. The southern dips prevailing carry them below the surface of the ground in the southern area of the coalfield. Above this horizon—the Bhaddoah main seam—there are several hundred feet of strata, consisting of coarse

* W. Saise. N. of E. Inst. M. & M. Eng., Vol. XXX., 1880.

sandstones, with several seams of poor coal, one at least very thick, as seen in the Jatkoti hill, where these upper sandstones seem to have their greatest thickness.

The thickness, or vertical depth of the strata constituting the coal-bearing rocks, does not greatly exceed 1,000 feet, perhaps 1,200 feet. Of this 964 feet were cut in sinking the "Deep pit" (finished in 1908) in the East Indian Railway Collieries where the Lower Karhārbāri seam was found to be dipping at an angle of 1 in 5·8 a little (14°) to the south of west. In this direction the cover must be greater.

The coal-bearing rocks appear to rest conformably on the Tālchers (in other coalfields there is unconformity) and are known as Barākars.

The relations of the beds are best illustrated thus :—

Lower Gondwān	Dāmodar	Rāniganj.
		Ironstone shales.
		Barakar.
	Tālcher.	

To the Dāmodar stage of the Gondwāna system, belong all the great Dāmodar valley coalfields—Rāniganj, Jharia, Bokāro, Karanpura and other smaller ones including Giridih. Indeed all the coalfields of the Indian Peninsula belong to the Dāmodar stage. In the Giridih coalfield the only representatives of the Gondwānas are the Barākar substage and the Tālcher stage.

The Tālchers, in which no coal seams or carbonaceous shales occur, have been found to exist all over the coalfield. There is an extensive and very interesting spread of these rocks, having an area of about 4 square miles, on the north-west of the field, which includes two in-liers of the crystalline rocks on which the Tālchers directly lie, one of these being 1½ miles in length by a mile wide. Very sparse vegetation always marks the areas occupied by the Tālchers, as the rocks do not weather so as to form soil. The fine-grained arenaceous grey-green shales weather into acicular fragments, and on that account are called "needle shales". Some of the shales are much jointed, one set of joints being crossed by another set. In some cases the included fragment weathers by exfoliating approximately parallel to the jointing, leaving a central mass of irregular shape. This gives the appearance of a tessellated pavement where a bedding plane has been laid bare.

Towards the top of the section thick-bedded sandstones of coarser materials predominate, and at the base of the stage the well-known "Boulder bed" occurs. These boulders, some 6 feet in length and of considerable dimensions on the other axes—are embedded in fine mud shales and must have been ice-borne, as most of them consist of rocks which do not occur in the neighbourhood of the Tālcher exposures in which they are found. The fact that this period was glacial, and that the glaciation extended over an enormous area, has been proved by observations in distant countries. It has been surmised that this glaciation was co-extensive with the supposed Permian ice-age of Europe. The Gondwāna system, of which the Tālchers form the base, or lowest stage, homotaxically corresponds to the Permian=Triassic horizon of Europe.

This sketch of the coalfield would be incomplete if no reference were made to the dykes, or trap intrusions, which are so conspicuous at several places, and which have wrought such terrible destruction in the coal-seam. There are two * distinct classes of igneous rock intrusive into, and younger than, the Tālcher and Barākar stages. To one of these belong the large basaltic dykes, which probably represent the Rājmahāl trap flows of the Upper Gondwāna system. To the other belong the phosphatic mica, † peridotites. These rocks contain large quantities of olivine and are distinguished from all previously known peridotites, in fact from all previously known igneous rocks, by the large quantity of apatite (phosphate of lime) contained. This in some specimens amounted to over 11 per cent of the total rock.

A very remarkable and deeply interesting fact in connection with the peridotites is that, though they occur in the Giridih coalfield, in all the coalfields of the Dāmodar valley, and in the Darjeeling coalfield more than 200 miles away, no instance has been discovered of this rock cutting the metamorphic, or crystalline,

* Holland & Saise, Rec. Geol. Surv. Ind., XXVIII., 121—138, 1895.

† Holland, Rec. Geol. Surv. Ind., XXVII., 129—146, 1894.

areas lying between. Why it should be so common in the coalfields and not in the older rocks around remains a mystery.*

The fact that by far the larger portion of the coalfield belongs to the East Indian Railway makes its history practically the history of the East Indian Railway Collieries. The management of these collieries can claim that it has taken a leading part in the development of coal mining in India; has developed a method of working thick coal seams; has improved the mechanical arrangements for sinking, making deeper shafts practicable; has trained labour for coal-cutting, sinking, and workshops, which has found its way to the Rāniganj and Jharia coalfields in large numbers; and has given the lead in erecting by-product coke-ovens, an example which has already been followed, and will result in an enormous conservation of the natural resources of the coalfields. But perhaps the most interesting development in the East Indian Railway Collieries, to those who are not engineers, is the organization of the labour force. Thirty-four years ago there were no direct relations between the management and the labourer. The mines were let to contractors. This system has been replaced by the direct employment of the labour, with the happiest results to the employés and satisfactory and economical advantages to the employer. The miners and labourers have, without any agitation on their part and without any help from labour combination attained an unique position. Every man subscribes a farthing and every woman half-a-farthing each week to a miner's benefit fund. This is the mainstay of an institution which pays fourteen annas and eight annas weekly to a man or woman who is sick; Rs. 5 and Rs. 2 when an adult (of either sex), or a child dies; a bonus of Rs. 4-8-0 for a birth; and a marriage allowance of Rs. 7-8-0. The other sources of income are insignificant, but it may be mentioned that all fines inflicted for disciplinary reasons are paid into the fund. This institution has been self-supporting since its initiation in 1892. When a workman is accidently killed the Railway Company pays 12 months' earnings to the family of the victim, and for serious injury often as much, besides making itself responsible for the future of any person crippled. As a result, when a serious accident happens, those concerned do not run away.

Holland & Ward. Trans. Min. Geol. Inst. of I (1906).

An old-age pension is earned by every one, male or female, who can prove that he, or she, has worked continuously for the Railway Company. The conditions are that, in the opinion of a committee of Indian subordinate officials, the applicant is not less than 50 years of age and is unable to earn his living. Practically all miners over 50 are eligible for this pension, which is paid by the Railway Company.

There were nearly 14,000 people living on the Railway Company's estates at the last census. A very large contingent of miners, some thousands, is drawn from the surrounding villages to make up the labour force required. In the Chief Inspector's report for 1914 the daily average attendance in the coalfield is returned as being underground 5,221, aboveground 3,358. No one under 12 is employed except those in the Industrial School who are undergoing their training in the workshop, and work under restrictions. A condition of residence on the Railway Company's estate is that all male children under 12 must attend school. Several hundred girls also attend. The daily attendance at the elementary schools is between 1,500 and 1,600, which is about 70 per cent of the number on the rolls. The schools are managed by a committee and receive liberal support from the Railway Company and the District Board. Any boy who passes the upper primary examination has a chance to enter the industrial school which is an appanage of the colliery workshops. There is very keen competition to enter here, as a boy gets a daily wage at once, which gradually increases, if he proves useful, until he is getting 4 or 5 annas a day by the time he has completed his training, at 12 or 13. In a few years he may be earning Rs. 2 a day. The labour employed in the coalfield is entirely indigenous; there is not a single imported worker. For many miles around the coalfield many of the villagers follow a dual occupation, working in their fields in the seasons of planting and harvesting, and cutting coal for the rest of the time. The male population of many villages around the fields migrates in a body to the Jharia or the Rāniganj coalfields for the working months and returns together. All these men have learned their trade in the Giridih coalfield.

All castes are represented amongst the underground workers from Bābhan to Dom; Muhammadans constitute a large fraction. Good wages can be earned, "main gallery" drivers earning sometimes as much as Re. 1 a day. Ordinarily a miner can earn from 6 annas to 8 annas. He does not put in more than eight hours underground (oftener six), and very few work more than five days a week, unless the price of rice is very high. The Indian collier is not a strong or a heavy man, but he has great staying power. As a rule he does not like regular work, and the "out-putting" factor is about 100 tons per person employed per annum. Taking underground workers alone the figure is 160 tons (nearly), as compared with over 400 tons in the "thick-coal" of the South Staffordshire coalfield.

The output of coal from this, the smallest of the coalfields, in 1915 was 872,647 tons, compared with 825,026 in 1914. This is the largest output on record. The East Indian Railway Collieries contributed about 812,000 tons, and the balance was almost entirely from the Bengal-Giridih Colliery Co.'s collieries in the west of the coalfield.

Up to December 1915 the total output from this coalfield has been 25,339,227 tons. Taking into account the Lower Karhārbāri seam only, an annual output of nearly 900,000 tons will exhaust the available coal in about 35 years. In other words there is probably not much more than 30,000,000 tons of this coal available. This does not mean that the coal-mining activities of Giridih will suddenly cease in the year 1950. There will be a prolonged period during which the output will dwindle, the poorer hill seams probably being exploited to some extent.

It may be added that the medical and sanitary arrangements of the East Indian Railway Company's collieries are distinguished by their completeness and efficiency.

Karanpura valley. Physical description.

The account of the geology of the district may be completed by the following popular description of the Karanpura Valley by Dr. Albert Jowett, who is engaged on the geological survey of the coal-bearing rocks in the Karanpura field. Unfortunately the examination of the coal measures is at present so incomplete that a description of them cannot be given.

"The greatest diversity of surface configuration in the Hazāribāgh district is to be found towards its southern boundary. This region not only includes examples of every important type of scenery in the whole district, but they are so well displayed as readily to reveal the more obvious principles by which they may be interpreted.

"The road from Hazāribāgh to Barkāgāon crosses a gently undulating plateau for about ten miles and then descends a very steep slope into a broad east and west valley, some 600 feet below. On the south side of this valley rises the precipitous northern face of the Māhudi Hill mass, which reaches approximately the same general altitude as the Hazāribāgh plateau. The landscape that opens out as one approaches the edge of the plateau is one of striking interest and of great beauty. The wooded rocky slope passes generally abruptly, although sometimes by a number of foot-hills, into a broad valley which looks like a plain. Strips of jungle of varying width, continuous with that on the hill-slopes, occur on both sides of the valley, and here and there approach each other closely and actually unite. A large part of the valley however is cultivated and treeless, except for the clumps of palms and in the neighbourhood of the villages, which are generally almost hidden amongst trees of a larger growth than those of the jungle. Patches of yellow sand mark the *nalas*, which, during the rains, become the courses of broad winding rivers. The well-wooded hills beyond are isolated by an almost continuous precipice of bare rock, at the foot of which there is a steep talus-slope covered by jungle that is continuous with the uncultivated strip on the southern margin of the main valley.

"An attempt will now be made to indicate in broad outline how the distinct types of scenery thus briefly described are related to differences in the nature and structure of the rocks beneath.

"The Hazāribāgh plateau is an excellent example of what even geologists speak of as an ancient land surface. It is composed of very old rocks which have been so intensely crushed and crumpled and injected with molten material from below as to be entirely changed in their mineral structure and are hence termed metamorphic. The "strike" of the rocks is roughly east and west, indicating that the rocks have yielded to forces mainly applied in a north and south direction. Under the long-continued action of the complicated forces which are generally alluded to by the term "weathering", the surface of these rocks has been levelled, only the bands of the most resistant rocks forming the sharp ridges of variable length that emerge at intervals above the general surface of the plateau. The rocks beneath the latter are covered by an irregular thickness of débris that is perhaps mostly derived from the rotting of the rocks immediately beneath it, but is in part derived from the material washed down from the projecting ridges. The best sections of the solid rocks are exposed in the stream courses, which are generally shallow and broad on the plateau, but more deeply incised towards its edges where the scenery becomes wilder and more picturesque.

"The broad valley trending east and west of Barkāgāon is underlain by the consolidated sediments—sandstones, shales and coal seams of the Dāmodar series. These rocks, although still ancient, are not nearly so old as the floor of metamorphic rocks upon which they rest. Comparatively small isolated patches of the Dāmodar rocks occur here and there on the plateau to the north. A careful examination shows that the southern edge of the Hazāribāgh plateau coincides in general direction with a zone of shattering and earth movement, in consequence of which the rocks in the valley to the south have been tilted and thrown down relatively to the rocks on the plateau, to which process they owe their preservation. The almost vertical fissures produced along with this earth movement have generally been filled with chalcedonic silica, in places so wide as to have given rise, after subsequent denudation, owing to its hardness, to hill ridges. The silica appears to have been deposited by the welling up of hot water with silica in solution along the fissures, for hot springs still occur in this district and in districts further west, along such lines of fracture. The silica has not merely been deposited in the fissures, but also in broad strips of porous rock on each side of them, rendering the rock intensely hard and compact. It is probably chiefly owing to the induration of the rocks along this zone of fracture that the southern edge of the Hazāribāgh plateau retains its steepness and is being cut back so slowly by the many streams which fall over it in cascades during the rains.

"The precipices of Māhudi Hill are composed of massive sandstone—not very hard throughout—but strengthened by the deposition amongst it of films of ironstone. It occurs in more or less horizontal beds with well-developed joints (planes of weakness) which cause it to break away readily into great cuboidal masses. It is the falling away of these blocks when their foundation is disturbed by the action of the weather that leads to the preservation of the vertical precipices, the fallen blocks forming a characteristic talus-slope beneath. The only perennial streams in the neighbourhood are fed from springs that emerge from the lowest beds of these massive sandstones. The top of the hill is a gently-stepped plateau, the harder beds of rock producing an increase in slope where they crop out, above which the surface becomes more level again. The streams that flow away from this hill mass, owing to their very steep gradient, have excavated wild and deep ravines. The Dāmodar rocks dip underneath the rocks of which Māhudi Hill is composed, re-appearing on the south of it, where they are thrown down along another line of fracture against the metamorphic rocks to the southward, thus repeating the conditions which exist to the north of Māhudi Hill."

It has been stated in the section relating to geology that muscovite mica is found embedded in reefs of pegmatite, and that these are found in the north of the district in such quantities as to make it one of the most valuable fields at present known. The area in which mica mines are now being worked commences in the west near Gajhandi station on the East Indian Grand Chord line, and passes eastwards through Kodarma, Khesmi, Doranda and the north of Kharagdiha, extending northwards to Gāwān and Sātgāwān with the adjoining parts of Monghyr and Gaya. In this area the proprietary rights in the land are in numerous hands, a fact which has a considerable bearing on the conduct of the industry; but perhaps the best deposits are found in the Government estate of Kodarma. Mica.

The reefs of pegmatite are usually extremely irregular in their development, and the occurrence of mica within the reefs is very capricious. A complete scientific account of the mineral in India is contained in Volume XXXIV, part 2, pages 11 to 121 of the Memoirs of the Geological Survey of India, to which it was contributed by Sir Thomas Holland.

Mica was used for ornaments, and in medicine in ancient India, and it is reasonable to suppose that surface deposits have been worked for many ages. In modern times it appears that there were as many as nine mines in existence in the Government estate alone as early as 1843, each of which was allowed to employ a maximum of 10 labourers, and paid Rs. 12-10 as annual rent. In 1849 it appears from Dr. McClelland's report that there was a very extensive mine at Dhanwi, but it is difficult to credit the statement that it exported 100,000 maunds of mica to Calcutta in a single year. The mining which he saw there was mere burrowing along the reefs of pegmatite, and for the product the mahajans apparently paid an all-round rate of Rs. 4 a maund, selling it in Calcutta at Rs. 7-8.

Twenty-five years later, in 1874, Mr. R. F. Mallet visited the mines of Dhāb and Jāmtara near Doranda. He found that the ordinary method of working was to dig a trench along the course of the reef, in which a depth of 50 feet was never exceeded. In a few cases horizontal galleries were driven into the hill sides. Sometimes, where thick layers of decomposed mica covered the uninjured mineral, shafts were driven to the required depth, and the burrowing commenced from this new level. Roof supports were not in use and accidents were frequent. Some of these old mines have recently been reopened, but the task is both difficult and dangerous owing to the nature of the old methods of working. After rough dressing with a sickle and sorting according to colour, freedom from stain and absence of minor cleavages the mica was separated into six sizes, and sold by the load of 46 lbs. at rates ranging from three annas to nine rupees. A maund of really first-quality mica 18 inches in diameter would however sell for as much as Rs. 60.

From notes contributed by Mr. E. Lane of Kodarma it appears that Mr. F. F. Chrestien of Tisri was the first European to deal with the mineral. It chanced about 1870 that he collected a small quantity and sent it to London, where it was sold at a price which justified him in taking up the business in earnest. At that time electricians were searching for an insulator, and an American experimenting with mica found it greatly superior to the asbestos previously employed. The demand thus created was timely for Mr. Chrestien's new enterprise ; and he improved the methods of extraction by using European explosives and exercising greater care in attacking the matrix. After a few years some Indians took up small areas on short leases, from which they extracted the outcrops, and afterwards two or three Europeans established themselves and the industry developed rapidly. The progress made will appear from the rents paid by

Government lessees, which amounted to Rs. 285 in 1887, to Rs. 8,029 in 1892 and Rs. 30,736 in 1914. Up to 1890 Mr. Chrestien was the sole lessee under Government, but the number had increased to 22 in 1914. Formerly the term of a lease was five years only, with no guarantee of renewal; and this was sufficient in itself to prevent the working of mines to the best advantage. Now the term is practically 30 years; and partly in consequence of this increase, and partly as a result of the exhaustion of the outcrops, improved methods are being employed by the principal European firms. Vertical shafts are sunk to a depth of from 50 to 100 feet along the strikes of the most promising reefs, and these are connected underground by galleries at different levels. In other cases when a hill is known to contain mica in paying quantities adits or tunnels are driven in the hill side. In this way the dangers of burrowing along the reef are avoided. These methods are of recent introduction and involve considerable expense, and their commercial success has not yet been established.

In the Government estate the system of royalties was introduced in 1903, prior to which it was the practice to pay a dead rent. The rules of 1903 prescribed at the option of Government a dead rent of Re. 1 per acre or a 5 per cent *ad. valorem* royalty on all mica at the pits mouth. Somewhat complicated forms of accounts had to be prepared, which were quickly found to be unsuited to the industry, nor were the returns submitted to Government by lessees in all cases of a reliable character. It was accordingly agreed that the system of accounts complained of should be abandoned and a dead rent of Re. 1-8 per acre substituted: but Government reserved to itself the right to introduce the royalty system on giving two years' notice. This dead rent system has satisfied the lessees and brought in a large income without friction or trouble. The wages paid to workmen before the outbreak of the European war in 1914 were from 3½ to 5 annas a day for a man and 2 annas a day for women and children; and in the case of more inaccessible mines the full 5 annas were paid to men and up to 3 annas to others. The workers are by caste mainly Ghātwārs, Goālas, Bhuiyas, Turis, Musahars and Jolahas; and the chief centres of the industry are at Tisri, Kodarma, Dabaur, Dhāb, Domchānch, Gāwān, Bendi and Charki.

Mica is classed as ruby (clear or stained), white, and black spotted. It is sorted into 8 grades as follows :—

Extra specials, 48 square inches and upwards.

Special	... ...	36	to 48	square inches.
1	... ...	24	to 36	Do.
2	... ...	15	to 24	Do.
3	... ...	10	to 15	Do.
4	... ...	6	to 10	Do.
5	... ...	3	to 6	Do.
6	... ...	1	to 3	Do.

The local value of mica fluctuates within wide limits. White mica is valued at 15 per cent below ruby. In 1914 the respective prices of clear ruby and black spotted mica were as follows :—

Class of Mica.	Price per maund.	
	Clear ruby mica.	Black spotted mica.
	Rs.	Rs.
Extra specials	500	200
Specials	400	140
1	300	120
2	225	100
3	170	75
... ...	105	40
5	55	10
6	8	22

The most serious difficulty which now confronts the industry is the prevalence of mica thieving. In the earliest days the disposal of mica was not the business of the miners, but was entirely in the hands of the mahajans or dealers. At the present time some of the miners export direct to Europe and America, and others sell their outturn to these exporters or to large Calcutta dealers. But there is still a not inconsiderable number of miners who dispose of it locally; and it is this local dealing which affords opportunities, and, it is to be feared, furnishes an active incitement to the thieves who pilfer in the mines or steal from the godowns. In some cases an attempt is made to cloak the real business of receiving under the guise of mining; and owing to the subdivision of proprietary rights it is not difficult to acquire the ownership of a mine of some sort. The workings are usually situated in the depths of the jungle and individually are too small to bear the cost of an expensive preventive staff; and mica itself is scarcely capable of certain identification. Consequently detection is infrequent and conviction extremely difficult. The Kodarma Mica Mining Association, which was formed with the objects of safeguarding the interests of mica miners, and advising Government and the local authorities in all matters connected with the industry, has been trying for some years past to devise an acceptable Bill for the prevention of theft; but so far the attempt has not been successful.

Iron.

At the time when the Statistical Account of the district was written in 1875 the smelting of iron was still an important local industry, and hopes were being entertained that convict labour could be employed in the production of iron at such a cost as would make it cheaper in Bengal than iron imported from England: but at the present time it is doubtful whether there is any place in the district where a furnace can be found. Enormous mounds of slag at Tandwa in the Karanpura valley still testify to the old importance of the industry, and round the skirts of Lugu Hill there are abundant traces of former furnaces; and in Kharagdiha also smelting used to flourish. Iron ores occur in Karanpura in comparative abundance, mainly as clay ironstone. It is understood that they are not so rich as to excite commercial curiosity; but with the completion of the geological survey of Karanpura which is now in progress speculation will be laid at rest regarding both coal and iron.

Tin.

Tin ore is found at Narangā, a village of the Pālganj estate near the south bank of the Barākar river, about 4 miles south-west of Leda. The present lessee has so far done little in the shape of mining.

Copper.

At Bāraganda in the same locality the mining of copper was formerly of great importance but work has long since ceased.

Other minerals.

In the mica country are found numerous other minerals, among which are included apatite, leucopyrite, green tourmaline and excellent felspar, with garnets and noble serpentine; but their commercial development has not yet been undertaken.

Lime and road metal.

Kankar or *ghuting* used in lime burning is widely scattered, and stone suitable for metalling is usually obtainable within a reasonable distance of the roads of the district.

Mineral springs.

Five groups of springs are known of a temperature above the normal. They are all sulphurous and are resorted to by persons suffering from skin diseases. Three of them are situated at the base of the central plateau, and a fourth at the base of the spur which projects from the central plateau southwards to the Dāmodar. This last is near the village of Kanki at the southern end of the track which leads from Bādam in the Karanpura valley to Rāmgarh. Its temperature is 92° Fah. The fifth is at Beko in police-station Birni, near the left bank of the Barākar, where the north-western spurs from Pārasnāth finally subside into the lower plateau. It has a temperature of 182° Fah. The spring at Duāri (110°) is on the left bank of the Mohani river where it crosses the Katkamsānri road, and that of Indra Jarba (102°) near the 12th mile of the provincial road from Rānchi to Hāzāribagh.

Surnj Kund springs.

The springs at Suruj Kund, about a mile from the police-station of Barahkatha on the Grand Trunk Road are of much more importance, and are the scene of a large annual *mela* held in January. The place was visited by Sir William Hooker in 1848, and a careful description is found in his Himalayan Journals (Vol. 1, Chapter II). The temperature of the hottest spring is 190° Fah.

CHAPTER III.

HISTORY.

THE materials for a history of Hazāribāgh prior to the late Muhammadan period are extremely meagre and may be classified as follows :— EARLY HISTORY.

(a) Natural routes.
(b) Tribal legends.
(c) Family traditions.
(d) Survivals in the land tenures.
(e) Place names.
(f) Archæological remains.
(g) Present geographical distribution of tribes and castes.

NATURAL ROUTES. It has been stated in the first chapter that the lower plateau is guarded on its western and northern borders by a steep face confronting the Gayā plains. On the south stretches the corresponding face of the higher plateau, until the latter is replaced by a low water-shed between the basins of the Barākar and the Dāmodar rivers, after which the lower plateau and the Dāmodar valley alike merge gently into the eastern plains of the Santāl Parganas and Mānbhum. To the east therefore the lower plateau has no natural physical defence ; but from the eastern terminus of its northern face right round to Kunda the whole north and west is guarded by an escarpment which though nowhere so formidable either by its steepness or its height as to oppose an absolute barrier to an invader, would present considerable difficulties to the movement of large bodies of enemies and would afford great help to the defence. Peaceful intruders would use one or other of the passes, of which the best known are as follows :—

(1) The Sakri valley route leads up through Gāwān thana to the water-shed of Kharagdiha Pargana which is reached near Tisri. The valley is wide and open till it reaches Gumgi, where it narrows and the road commences to climb one of the spurs

which lead up to the plateau. These are so numerous that an enemy would have a wide choice of fairly easy slopes.

(2) South-westward along the Gayā border is the pass which leads from Rajauli to Kodarma, through the Government Reserved Forest. It is even now little better than a track which scrambles up the side of the plateau.

(3) In Rennell's map what is now called Danua Ghāt is named the Champa Pass, and a second route starting from the same base but emerging towards Itkhori is called by him the Donoh Pass. The former gives the easiest access to the plateau and is now utilized for the Grand Trunk Road. It emerges near Chauparan, in the west of Chhai Pargana. The latter road is now abandoned.

(4) Further to the west is the Dhangāin Pass which at the end of the eighteenth century was selected for the Benares military road then under construction.

(5) Next to the west is the mouth of the Lilājān river, which in Hunterganj and Simaria has eroded much the same sort of valley as the Sakri has carved for itself in Gāwān. There is however no spur which affords a reasonably gentle gradient, and the Jori Ghāt, as it is called, leads to Chatra by a road which is too steep for carts. From the south-west a gentle valley comes down from Partābpur; but the spurs round Kunda and the deep valley of the Lilājān prevent the possibility of outflanking the plateau from that side.

It was probably by one or other of these five passes that the people who are found now in north Hazāribāgh must have come, if their approach was from the Ganges valley. Along the district boundary south of Kunda, there is no steep face, but an elevated water-shed, eastward of which the northern tributaries of the Dāmodar give easy access to Karanpura from Palāmau. On this side the physical obstacles to invasion are slight.

Passing to the south the Dāmodar valley lies under the face of the Rānchi plateau much as Gayā lies under the Hazāribāgh lower plateau. From this side there is no tradition that aggression was either expected or suffered; and racial movements appear to have been solely from the north towards the south.

TRIBAL LEGENDS.

In estimating the value of tribal legends for purposes of history it is desirable to inquire whether the legends are uniform or multiform, whether any trace of modification is discernible since they were first reported, and whether they are generally accepted as true by the tribe. It is also necessary to scrutinize carefully the qualifications of those who reported them, to inquire how far they were competent to understand with precision the language of their informants, to avoid the danger of involuntary suggestion and to receive the impression like a photographic plate without preconception and bias. If the records or the traditions of a tribe can stand these tests they obviously possess great value; if they fail, their value is diminished or entirely disappears.

SANTAL MIGRATION LEGEND.

(1) According to Campbell.

The latest form of the Santāl migration legend was published in the Journal of the Bihar and Orissa Research Society for March 1916, by Dr. Campbell of Tundi in the north-west of Mānbhum. According to this account the race originated in Hihiri Pipri, and moved successively to the Sui forest, Haradata, Khojkāman, Chāe and Chāmpa where a long halt was made, forts were built, and the present social divisions were created. Thence they fled out of fear of the half Santāl, half Birhor Mādho Singh, leaving behind a remnant who now form the Bedia tribe, and came to Aire Kāinde, where they remained for many years. Next they crossed the Sang and Aser rivers, and came to the Singh door and Bahi door, which they managed to pass through at the price of adopting the worship of the local *bongas* or spirits. Then they came to Bhelwa Ghāt and the plain of Chitri Hatup, where they halted for many years. Water failing they went to Murup Goda and thence to Amber, the jungle of Kaker, the forest of Bare Bārāngaon, Kadmabeda, Belāonga, Sir and Sikhar. From Sikhar they spread over the parganas of Pālganjo (in Dumri of Hazāribāgh) Tundi, and Pandra (both in North Mānbhum) and the adjoining parts. A portion went south to Midnapore and the others spread over the Barākar to the Santāl Parganas.

(2) According to Dalton.

In Dalton's Ethnology at page 209 is given the narrative of Bāgh Rai Parganāit, a resident of Sonabādi in thana Rāmgarh of Hazāribāgh, according to whom the race originated in Ahiri Pipri and migrated to Hara Duttee, where they were called Kharwārs. Thence they moved to Khairagarh and Hurradgarhi and eventually settled in Chhāi Chāmpa in Hazāribāgh district, where they remained for several generations. Thence they fled from fear of a Birhor, Madho Singh, towards Chota Nāgpur, where the hill god, Marang Buru, in response to their prayer, interposed the mountain in the path of the pursuers, and so won for himself a place in their worship. Thence they proceeded to Jhalda, Pātkum, Sāont (where their name of Kharwār was changed to Santāl) and Sikhar, whence they spread westward.

A tradition not less discrepant is reported in Appendix VIII of Risley's 'Peoples of India'.

It may be noted that Bāgh Rāi's overlord was the proprietor of Rāmgarh, a Kharwār by race, and that Bāgh Rai's district magistrate held his court in pargana Chāmpa, adjoining pargana Chhāi. These two confident identifications made by Bāgh Rai may perhaps be ascribed to the influence of local associations; and it is sufficient for the present purpose to note that so far as regards the early history of Hazāribāgh there are various Santāl legends which are seriously discrepant. The Bedia caste is now living in thana Rāmgarh of this district and numbers about 12,000.

MUNDARI MIGRATION LEGEND.

(1) According to Babu S. C. Ray.

In his book on the Mundās, Babu S. C. Ray does not discuss the sources from which his legendary account was derived. Briefly, the race originated at Azabgarh, and migrated thence to Kalangjar, Garh Chitra, Garh Pali, Garh Pipra, Mandar Pahar, Bijnagarh, Hardinagar, Laknourgarh, Nandangarh, Rijgarh, and Ruidāsgarh, and thence across Burmu Ghāt to Omedanda.

Ruidāsgarh is identified with Rohtās, and Babu S. C. Ray states that up to this stage the Mundās and Santāls had kept company. They were attacked there by a Kharwār chief called Madho Dās, who drove them eastward. They arrived at what is now the trijunction of Gaya, Palāmau and Hazāribāgh and finally parted company at that point, the Santāls proceeding down the Dāmodar valley to Mānbhum.

(2) According to Dalton.

Dalton emphasizes the difficulty of obtaining any clear tradition of the origin and wanderings of the Mundās, and contents himself with an abstract obtained from papers of the Chota Nāgpur Raj family, that they came successively from Pipra, Paligarh, Jaipur, Chitor, Simaliya and Ruidās.

It is not obvious how Colonel Dalton could have failed to come across a tradition of the detailed character reported by Babu S. C. Ray, had it been wide-spread among the race. It may also be noted that the versions of the Santāl traditions given above are silent regarding any close association with the Mundās, that their Mādho Singh is emphatically not a Khārwār, and that the Dāmodar valley is not their route. Bāgh Rāi's ancestors had come to Rāmgarh and the Dāmodar valley from the east.

FAMILY TRADITIONS. Dhanwar.

Family traditions.—The Zāmindār of Dhanwār is the present representative of the Rajas of Kharagdiha. He claims to be descended (through 52 generations) from one Hansrāj Bhut Deo, from Southern India, who is said to have expelled a raja of the Bandāwat caste, and conquered for himself a kingdom in Gayā and Hazāribāgh 600 miles long. The family intermarries with the Bābhan zamindars of North Bihar. It appears that in the adjoining district of Gayā certain Rājput and Bābhan zāmindārs gained considerable influence and power in the fifteenth century, and it is possible that this was the period in which the Dhanwār family succeeded in impressing itself on the Kharagdiha Ghātwāls.

Kunda.

The Kunda estate lies in the south of Hunterganj and west of Simaria, where the hills and valleys are specially confused and difficult. The family claims to be descended from a Garhwāl Rājput of Bundelkhand, a personal servant of the Emperor Aurangzeb, named Rām Singh. In the Fasli year 1076 (1669 A. D.) he was granted a *thānādāri jāgir* by Dāud Khān and Mangal Khān, subordinates of a subordinate of that emperor, "for the care and guarding of the roads". The analogy of the Ghātwāls would suggest that he was a chieftain of the locally predominant race; and so probably a Kharwār. The mother of the present heir is a member of a minor branch of the Rāmgarh family.

Rāmgarh.

The Rāmgarh family claims descent from one Singdeo, who took service, along with his brother, Bāgdeo Singh, under the Maharaja of Chota Nāgpur. These brothers were, it is said, Rājputs from Bundelkhand. "Bāgdeo, the younger and more astute, observing that the portion of the Chota Nāgpur territory now called Rāmgarh was composed of petty estates governed by rājās, who were the vassals of the Nāgpur Rāj, and at enmity with each other, determined to carve out a kingdom for himself. Assisted by Singdeo, he quarrelled with the Chota Nāgpur Rājā, and led a body of adventurers into pargana Karanpura (i e. thana Barkāgāon) then governed by one Kapper Deo, defeated him, and made himself master of that pargana, and then gradually extended his conquests over twenty-one other parganas. Bagdeo in time became the rājā of the following twenty-two parganas :—

1. Karanpura.
2. Goria.
3. Jagesar.
4. Chaingara.
5. Palāni.
6. Gola.
7. Kaliānpur.
8. Basantpur.
9. Champa.
10. Bamhanbai.
11. Barsot.
12. Gumo.
13. Markacho.
14. Katkamsānri.
15. Ahuri
16. Dantār.
17. Sardam.
18. Sāram.
19. Singpur
20. Tisri.
21. Holang.
22. Rāmpur.

" He made his elder brother *fauzdar* with the title of Thākur.

" I give below the generations of Bāgdeo and Singdeo in parallel lines till the year A. D. 1771.

Bāgdeo line	Years	Seat	Singdeo line
1. Bāgdeo	... 1368-1402	at Urda	Singdeo.
2. Kerat Singh	... 1402-1459	at Urda	Mān Singh.
3. Ram Singh	... 1459-1537	at Urda	Newal Singh.
4. Mādho Singh	... 1537-1554	at Urda	Rām Singh.
5. Jagat Singh	... 1554-1604	at Urda	Darjhudan Singh.
6. Hemat Singh	... 1604-1661	at Bādam	Rajbal Singh.
7. Rām Singh	... 1661-1667	at Bādam	Ajit Singh *fauzdar*,
8. Dalel Singh	... 1667-1724	at Rāmgarh.	Golal Singh.
Maharudar Singh			Manir Singh and five others.

Sons of Maharudar Singh: 9. Bishan Singh, 1724-1763. Puratan Singh. 10. Makund Singh 1763-1772.

Sons of Manir Singh: 11. Tej Singh, 1772. Sibnāth Singh.

" Maharúdar Singh died in his father's lifetime and Bishun Singh succeeded his grand-father and died childless. Puratan Singh died childless, and Makund Singh succeeded his brother. All three resided at Rāmgarh.

" Rajbal Singh's elder son was called Kerat Singh. He was set aside in favour of his younger brother Makund Singh. Added to his rāj parganā Chhāi, driving therefrom Raja Lāl Khān, and giving him a precarious *nānkār* allowance of Rs. 1,200 a year. This pargana was owned by five petty rājās, (1) Rāmpur, (2) Jāgodih, (3) Parwaria, (4) Itkhori and (5) Pitij. A former rājā, name now unknown, also added pargana Khāspur, in zila Purulia, to his rāj, but when the English settlement was made, this pargana reverted to the Pānchet Rājā, why or wherefore it is now impossible to say. Tej Singh, the *fauzdar* , quarrelled with Makund Singh ; and assisted by Fateh Singh of Markacho, and Bechu Singh of Bagro, he put himself into communication with the English, and offered his assistance to conquer the country for the English. His offer was accepted, and a force being led into Rāmgarh, Makund Singh was defeated and fled for his life. Tej Singh was placed by the English in possession of Rāmgarh, but only styled *fauzdar*." (Report of Mr. Robinson, Commissioner of Chota Nāgpur in 1876, quoted in the Hazāribāgh Settlement Report.)

It may be observed that apparently the first of these rājās of whom there is independent evidence is Hemat Singh, whose fortified house still stands in partial ruin at Bādam. The doorway has an inscription that it was built for him in 1699 Sambat (i.e. 1642 A. D.) by a Patna builder. In the neighbourhood is Māhudi Hill, which contains some sandstone caves which were originally excavated for religious recluses, and one of them is dated shortly after the building of the Bādam residence. We may conclude from these facts that Hemat Singh was in close touch with the civilization of Bihar.

His five predecessors cover no less than 223 years : and if, as Mr. Robinson's narrative suggests, they were all in direct lineal descent, it is an impossibly long period. Probably it is the creation of that spirit which according to the settlement report has since 1876 given three new ancestors to Bāgdeo Singh.

The family residence was first at Sisia, then Urda, and finally Bādam, moving from west to east of the Karanpura valley (thana

Barkāgāon). The removal from the valley to Rāmgarh, considerably to the east, was probably due to the inconvenient proximity of Bādam to the route by which the Muhammadans reached Chota Nāgpur, which went from Sherghāti, through Chatra and Jābra and brought them close to the head of the Karanpura valley.

SURVIVALS IN THE LAND SYSTEM.

The earliest view afforded of the district discloses Kunda and Bādam ruled by Kharwār chiefs, of whom the latter was gradually reducing to his authority the chieftains of the east and north, whose estates probably corresponded with the parganas enumerated above, wholly or in part. The Settlement Officer notes that ruins of forts are to be found in parganas Chaingara, Palāni, Jagesar and Karanpura; and that there are traditions of rājās at Gola, Durgāpur, Pirgul and Choti. It is possible that these chieftains were Kharwars, for the rājā of Gola in Bāgh Rāi's narrative given above was a Kharwār. In the north and north-east were the five rājās of Chhai, owning allegiance to Raja Lāl Khān, and then came a line of Ghātwār chieftains extending from Kodarma to the borders of Monghyr and the Santāl Parganas, more or less under the authority of the Bābhan Raja of Kharagdiha. Kharwār *khuntkattidars* held subordinate tenures near Chatra, and a Mundāri Manki held a *patti* south of Tandwa at Laranga. Another Mundāri family held a *khuntkatti* tenure at Korāmbe in Rāmgarh. Practically all the jagirdars of the Rāmgarh estates are aliens who received their tenures on service conditions; and from this the Settlement Officer concludes that it was by the help of these foreigners that the Kharwār Chief of Karanpura was able to reduce his neighbours to subjection, and to retain his hold over the conquered territory.

PLACE NAMES

A mere glance at the map will disclose large numbers of place names obviously belonging to one or other of the Mundā languages:* but they have not, it is believed, been subjected to a systematic and detailed examination. To what particular tribes they are severally to be assigned might receive some illumination from the results of such a scrutiny. There are at present several Mundā-speaking tribes in the district, and

* Mundā is the name given by Max Müller and Sir George Grierson to the linguistic family which includes the languages spoken by the Mundā, Santāl, Ho and allied tribes.

there may have been others in the past : and still others, e. g., the Kharwārs, may have adopted Hindi after, and not before, their advent to the district.

ARCHÆOLOGICAL REMAINS.

There has been very little systematic survey of those archæological remains which survive above ground, in the shape of ruined forts, and erect or flat stones. These last are found in various places in the south-west, and closely resemble Mundāri *bid-diris* and *sasan-diris*. The amount of work done under ground is so far very small indeed. The Archæological Survey of India has found little in this district to throw light on its secular history, the remains on Kuluha and Pārasnāth hills being of recent and purely religious origin. The temple ruins near Itkhori have not been scientifically examined, and the ascertainment of their probable age might throw some light on the date of the Hindu immigration into Chhāi.

PRESENT RACIAL DISTRIBUTION.

The present distribution of the more populous castes and tribes is described in detail in Chapter IV. While there is no part of the country in which caste concentration is so marked as it is in parts of Rānchi the predominance of aboriginal tribes is clearly seen in an area which starts from the north-east corner and runs a few miles inside the district down to the Barākar river, where it meets the Pārasnāth hill system. To the west of this line are mixed Hindu races, and to the east Ghātwārs and Santāls. The boundary line continues up the Barākar to the east of Bagodar thana, then south as far as the Jamunia river, and then due west to the face of the upper plateau, the south of which is followed to the Māndu, Hazāribāgh and Simaria thana trijunction. The line crosses the Simaria plateau ridge to its north face and then runs westward, north of Partābpur to the trijunction of Gayā, Palāmau and Hazāribāgh districts. North and west of this rough demarcation the people are predominantly Hindu, south and east they are predominantly aboriginal. The distribution of the Santāls and Kurmis is almost identical (leaving out the Santāl fringe along Monghyr and the Santāl Parganas). They share the Pārasnāth block in Dumri thana, and then, after an interval in Nawādih police-station, they run right across the Dāmodar valley from the border of Mānbhum on the east to the western face of the high ridge which forms the eastern boundary of Barkāgāon. In Chatra, Hunterganj, Chaupāran and Simaria the three castes of

Santāls, Kurmis and Mundās are alike in being practically without representation. Elsewhere in the district the Santāls are found sporadically, and in somewhat larger numbers than the Kurmis. The similarity of the distribution of these two castes is a most striking fact which cannot be left out of count. The Mundās have representatives in Barkāgāon, Māndu and Gumia; but are concentrated in Rāmgarh, with a slight extension eastward into Petarbār. The Bhogta Kharwārs are numerous in Hunterganj, Chatra, Simaria and Barkāgāon, rare elsewhere, and notably scarce in Chaupāran.

Throughout the entire district the Bhuiyas form a numerous underlying element, in a very humble position as landless labourers or petty cultivators, except in Kharagdiha pargana, i.e., thanas Kodarma, Dhanwār, Kharagdiha, Gāwān and Giridih where many of them have contrived to retain their tenures, the so-called Kharagdiha *gādis*, up to the present time.

CONCLUSION. From these materials it is not possible to form more than a mere conjecture of the early history of the country; and it would appear that any serious addition to the existing stock of knowledge can be expected only from an extensive and systematic collection and examination of those ancient remains which are from time to time disinterred from the ground. This is one of the main tasks proposed by the newly-founded Bihar and Orissa Research Society; and in view of the striking results of the methodic work of western scholars in the valleys of the Euphrates and the Nile, and in the isle of Crete, it is permissible to hope that in spite of obvious difficulties the secrets of the past will be partially laid bare here also. Meantime, as a vague surmise, it may be conjectured that the Bhuiyas once occupied the land under a large number of tribal chiefs, that through its western margin passed the Mundās pressed onward by the Kharwārs to the borders of Rānchi; that the western chiefs of the Bhuiyas were conquered and degraded by the Kharwārs; while to the north and east a wedge of Hinduism was driven between the Bhuiya chieftains and their fellow tribesmen, and Santāls and Kurmis pressed up from the south-east into the empty lands of Gola and Jagesar—the area now known as Petarbār, Gumia and Māndu.

MUHAMMADAN CONNEXION. Apparently the first interference of the Muhammadans with the affairs of 'Jhārkhand', by which term they meant the whole of the jungle land between Bihar and Orissa, was in 1585 A.D., when the Emperor Akbār sent an expedition commanded by Shāhabāz Khān which reduced the Rājā of Chota Nāgpur to the position of a tributary. In 1591 this Rājā took part in the Muhammadan expedition to Orissa. There was a second invasion of Chota Nāgpur in 1616 when Ibrāhim Khān, general of the Emperor Jahangir, captured the rājā and sent him as a prisoner to Gwalior. In 1632 the Emperor Shāh Jahān included Chota Nāgpur in the *jāgir* of Palāmau, which he gave to the Subadar of Patna on an annual rental of Rs. 1,36,000; and about 1686 this rental was raised to Rs. 1,61,000, ".Koira Orissa, or Nagpur, with Karanpura, or Badaun, being rated at Rs. 40,505." Between these two dates the following facts are known to have intervened :—

(*a*) In 1642 a Patna mason had built for the Karanpura Raja Hemat Singh the fortified residence at Bādam (probably the "Badaun" referred to above).

(*b*) In 1659 Aurangzeb had defeated Shāh Shuja at Kudwa near Allahabad, and the latter retired on Monghyr, prepared to resist an attack from the west. Prince Muhammad, son of Aurangzeb, and Mir Jumla obtained information after that defeat of a new road into Bengal different from the ordinary Ganges route, "by the route of Sherghāti which is situated in the mountains of Jhārkhand; it was circuitous, narrow and steep, and little used on account of the difficulties it presented, and the savage manners of the mountaineers". Mir Jumla took a force of 12,000 cavalry by this route and so arrived behind (east of) Monghyr, whereupon Shāh Shuja abandoned Monghyr and fled to Rājmahāl.

(*c*) In 1660 Hindu ascetics were making caves in the sandstone cliffs of Māhudi Hill, near Bādam.

(*d*) About 1670 the Karanpura Rājā transferred his residence from the fine new house at Bādam to Rāmgarh, thirty miles eastward, and separated from it by a very difficult stretch of country.

It would appear that it was between 1642 and 1670 that the pressure of the Muhammadans in the west of Karanpura first became serious and that the move to Rāmgarh was due to a desire to put as wide an interval as possible between the two parties.

In 1669 A.D., the Muhammadans were in a position to compel the Kunda chieftain to take a *sanad* from them "to guard the four passes of Babaltar, Pinjri, Banwadih and Nagdarra from the inroads of the Mārāthas, Bargis and Pindāris". In 1724 the Subadar of Patna marched against the Rājā of Chota Nāgpur, from whom he exacted a large *nazarana* in cash and diamonds. This appears to have encouraged a second expedition in 1731, which was cut short by the intervention of the Rājā of Rāmgarh, who paid Rs. 12,000 on account of his southern neighbour; and from this time onwards, till the British occupation, the tribute of the latter continued to be paid through Rāmgarh. Doubtless the passage of the Muhammadan expeditions, even though they touched merely the western fringe of his country, was injurious to the Rāmgarh Rājā. In 1740 the latter had become so powerful that a special expedition was sent under the command of Hidāyat Ali Khān, which captured Rāmgarh fort, but returned at the news of a Mārātha invasion of Bengal; and Rājā Makund Singh thirty years later was powerful enough to conquer Chhāi Pargana.

Kendi and Chhāi.

Kendi is situated in thana Chatra at the head of Dhangāin Pass which leads down to the Gaya plain. To the west it is bounded by Pargana Dantār, which was in the possession of the Rāmgarh Rajas in the seventeenth century, and to the east by Chhāi. Apparently some time about 1700 A.D., Kendi was reduced by the Muhammadans to the position of a zamindāri; and the earliest available information shows that one Nahir Singh was the proprietor at the beginning of the eighteenth century and his son Fateh Singh was making a *khorposh* (maintenance) grant in 1728. Chhāi lies at the top of the present Danua Pass, and at the time of its subjection by Makund Singh of Rāmgarh, about 1770, it was divided between five chieftains of whom apparently four paid tribute to the fifth, Raja Lāl Khān of Jāgodih. Eastward of Chhāi was Kodarma, a *gādi* of Kharagdiha, in which the Muhammadans do not appear to have acquired any special influence. In the Ain-i-Akbari Chhāi Champa is entered as assessed to revenue as a part of subah Bihar; but perhaps this merely indicated Kendi.

Kharagdiha.

In the north-east the Bābhan Rājās of Kharagdiha held also coterminous lands in Gayā district, the whole forming a revenue-paying estate under the name of Siwar Muhammadābād.

It has been stated above that the supremacy of this family in Kharagdiha probably began in the fifteenth century. The road from Nawāda up the valley of the Sakri passed through the north of the pargana to the south of Ghoranji Hill on to the Saiva temples at Deoghar, and probably served as a door to Hindu influence from Bihar. The allegiance of the Ghātwārs to the Rājā appears to have been very light. Direct interference by the Muhammadans in the internal affairs of the pargana is not heard of prior to 1765, in which year Akbār Ali Khān, a son of Kāmgār Khān, zamindar of Narhat in eastern Gaya, carried the attack on Rājā Mod Nārāyan Deo into his last possessions in Hazāribāgh district, and expelled him from Kharagdiha. Mod Narayan and his son died in exile at Rāmgarh, but in 1774 his grand-son Girwar Nārāyan Deo assisted the British in the expulsion of Akbar Ali Khān.

With the exception of these three areas there is no part of Hazāribāgh which was subjected to Muhammadan interference, so far as is known ; and the uniform distribution of the present Muhammadan population seems to be inconsistent with the exercise of any special local authority in the past.

THE ESTABLISHMENT OF BRITISH AUTHORITY.

With the grant of the Diwāni of Bengal, Bihar and Orissa, which was made by the Emperor Shāh Alam, the subah of Bihar passed to the East India Company, and with it passed the right to receive the tribute of Rāmgarh, the land revenue of Kharagdiha and Kendi, and the services of Kunda. It was not however till four years later that the British first came into contact with the district, and not till 1772 that its reduction was seriously taken in hand. The first approach was on the side of Kharagdiha, east of which Captain Camac was engaged in 1769 in establishing some sort of order in the 'Junglebury district'; but nothing of importance was then done, for it was not until 1774 that Akbār Ali Khān was ejected.

Kunda.

Captain Camac's next appearance was at Kunda, on his way to Palāmau, to restore Rājā Gopāl Rāi to the position from which he had been driven by his Thākur. He took along with him the chief, Dhrija Nārāyan Singh, the fourth in succession from that Ram Singh with whom the officers of Aurangzeb had made the settlement of Kunda ; and in the storming of the

Palāmau fort four of the Chief's relatives were killed. In return for his conduct in this matter Captain Camac renewed with him the old agreement, and up to this day Kunda is free from the payment of land revenue.

Rāmgarh. During the operations in Palāmau in 1772 Captain Camac received a visit from Rājā Durpnāth Sahi of Chota Nāgpur, and also obtained some useful aid from him, whilst on the other hand Mukund Singh of Rāmgarh had intrigued to thwart him. Consequently Rājā Durpnāth Sahi had no difficulty in persuading the British to terminate the arrangement whereby his tribute was being paid through the Rāmgarh chief. Either previous to this, or after it—the time, though important, is obscure—Tej Singh, whose alleged genealogy has been given above, appeared at Patna, and set up a claim to the Rāmgarh Rāj on the strength of the alleged seniority of Singdeo to Bāgdeo. On the bare materials available it does not appear that the claim had much substance. In any case it would be barred by, the limitation of some hundreds of years; and on the claimant's own showing the estate was acquired by Bāgdeo Singh, and not inherited from a common ancestor. The genealogical trees themselves are suspicious in showing an exact parallel of generations, and apparently, an unbroken succession from father to son which is in marked contrast to the fortunes of the family in the last hundred years. It would appear that Tej Singh's claim was accepted by the British with more readiness by reason of the impracticable conduct of Mukund Singh; who probably had inflated ideas of his military strength, based on the Muhammadan retreat in 1740 and his recent conquest of Chhāi. In the intrigue with the British Tej Singh was assisted by a resident of Gayā called Lāl Bahādur Singh, said to have been a *chaprasi*, whose family was rewarded later with the grant rent free in perpetuity of twenty-four villages, all of which have been dissipated long ago. The attack on Mukund Singh was made in 1772, by a force under Lieutenant Goddard, who was accompanied by Tej Singh. Simultaneously it appears that some pressure was applied on the south by the Rājā of Chota Nāgpur. There was no serious resistance; Mukund Singh fled and Tej Singh was installed, not however at first as raja but as *mustajir*. Lieutenant Goddard did not apparently take formal possession of the territory thus won, nor did his expedition extend to Kharagdiha.

Kharagdiha.

Raja Mod Nārāyan Deo had taken refuge at Rāmgarh when expelled in 1765 by Akbār Ali Khān, but by 1772 both he and his son were dead. The head of the family was his grandson, Girwar Nārāyan Deo; and it was arranged that the *tikāits* or chiefs of the thirty-eight *gādis* of Kharagdiha should be invited to assist in the expulsion of the Muhammadans. This was effected in 1774 by a force under Captain James Browne working from South Monghyr (the Junglebury district) with the active co-operation of twenty-six of the *tikāits* and against the opposition of two, ten remaining neutral. After this no further military action was needed in the district and the task of civil administration commenced.

ADMINISTRATIVE ARRANGEMENTS.

The district of Rāmgarh.

By 1780 Captain Camac's authority was replaced by that of Mr. Chapman, who was the first civilian administrator of Chota Nagpur. The "conquered provinces," as they were called, were formed into a British district, which included Rāmgarh, Kendi, Kunda and Kharagdiha (which together constitute the present Hazāribāgh), the whole of Palāmau, Chakāi on the east of Kharagdiha and Pānchet on the east of Rāmgarh, and the area round Sherghāti. The present district of Rānchi was added under the designation of the tributary mahāl of Chota Nāgpur. Mr. Chapman held his court alternately at Sherghāti and Chatra, and his authority was enforced by the newly-formed Rāmgarh Battalion, which was stationed at Hazāribāgh.

Headquarters.

Rāmgarh battalion.

District officer.

Mr. Chapman's official functions were divided into three branches: he dealt out both civil and criminal justice, and administered the revenue regulations, and he appears to have had no European assistant in these various tasks. The field of his labours was approximately 18,000 square miles in area; and in Rennell's map of "the conquered provinces on the south of Bihar containing Rāmgur, Palāmau and Chota Nāgpur with their dependencies, inscribed to Major Jacob Camac" the whole centre of Rānchi, is marked as "part not surveyed" and a great block of Hazāribāgh is 'woods' between the Dāmodar and Barākar from the west of Pālganj to the Hazāribāgh-Barhi road. It is obvious that Mr. Chapman's aim must have been not at efficient administration, but, as regards the remoter areas at least, at the slightest semblance of any administration at all; and that this limited task demanded great courage, activity and

Appeal.

versatility. From his civil and criminal judgments an appeal lay to the Governor General, and in revenue matters his authority was supervised by a Committee of Revenue in Calcutta. In 1793 civil and criminal appeals were transferred to a Provincial Court of Appeal in Patna, and from 1817 to 1829 the supervision of revenue vested in a Commissioner for the Superintendence of Revenue and Circuit for the Division of Patna. The "Statistical Account" of 1875 from which this account is taken proceeds concisely as follows :—

Failure of the early administration.

"During the period that elapsed from 1780 to 1833 the district was governed in general accord with the ordinary Regulations. An exception indeed was made in favour of the custom of primogeniture, by the special Regulation X of 1800; and even before that year I have been unable to discover any cases of estates being subjected to the law of partition. The sale of estates for arrears of land revenue was however occasionally resorted to, the action of the civil court was generally in favour of the foreign money-lenders, rather than of the old-standing landholders of the division; and it is clear that in both civil and criminal business equitable considerations were everywhere outweighed by legal ones. In short, the administration of Rāmgarh had all the faults of a rigidly legal system, applied unscrupulously over an unwieldy extent of country, by officials who had the scantiest knowledge of the people with whom they were dealing." [The writer forgets that equity is not at the command of ignorance; whose refuge is pedantic legality.] "British rule was made peculiarly distasteful to the aboriginal races, by the fact that all the native subordinates were foreigners from Bihar and Bengal; and the smouldering discontent of the tribes broke out on two occasions, in 1820 and 1831, into open revolt [not however in Hazāribāgh]. The great Kol insurrection of 1831 was followed by an entire change in the administrative system. By Regulation XIII of 1833 the districts of Rāmgarh and the Jungle Mahāls, with the estates of Dhalbhum, till then included in Midnapore, were exempted from the operation of the Regulations; and every branch of government within these tracts was vested in an officer appointed by the Supreme Government, styled the Agent to the Governor General. The Parganas of Rāmgarh, Kharagdiha, Kendi and Kunda, which compose the present area of the district, thus became part

The "Kol" rebellion.

Abolition of Regulations.

Creation of the South-West Frontier Agency.

of the South-West Frontier Agency, and were formed into a Division under the name of Hazāribāgh. The administrative headquarters, which had formerly been alternately at Sherghāti and Chatra, were transferred to Hazāribāgh, where the troops of the Rāmgarh Battalion had been stationed since the end of the last century. The chief executive officer was now styled the Principal Assistant to the Governor General's Agent, and he was guided in his administration by a series of rules for criminal justice prescribed by the Governor General in Council, under the provisions of section 5 of Regulation XIII of 1833. These criminal rules continued in force till they were superseded by the Criminal Procedure Code (Act XXV of 1861), which was immediately extended to the districts of the Chota Nagpur Division. As regards the administration of civil justice, a set of rules was proposed by the Agent at the same time that the criminal rules were laid before Government, but orders on those were suspended pending the promulgation of a Bill on the subject then under preparation. This Bill was never passed; and till Act VIII of 1859 was extended to the division, there was no specific law or rule to guide the procedure of the Civil Courts in the province; but they followed the Regulations, except in points where some order of the Agent interposed.

Formation of Hazāribāgh District.

Criminal Justice under Regulation XIII.

Civil Justice under Regulation XIII.

"From the first creation of the Agency the ordinary laws for the sale of land for debt or arrears of rent were regarded as inapplicable to the Province, and the rules proposed by Captain Wilkinson [the Agent] provided that no sale or alienation, or even mortgage of hereditary or immovable property was to take place without the sanction of the Agent. This rule has always been acted on as regards sales, and forms one of the most peculiar features of the administration of the Division, and in extending the Civil Procedure Code to the districts of Hazāribāgh, Lohardaga and Mānbhum a proviso to this effect was added to the notification * * * * By Act XX of 1854 the designation of the Province was changed to Chutia (Chota) Nāgpur, and it has been administered since that date as a non-regulation province under the Lieutenant-Governor of Bengal. At the same time the title of the chief executive officer was changed from Governor General's Agent to Commissioner." The Kol insurrection of 1831, as stated

Alienation of immovable property.

Inclusion in Bengal.

above, did not extend to Hazāribāgh, in which district there were very few members of those aboriginal races who took the leading part, and there was no disturbance of the public peace until the Mutiny of 1857, of which the following account is taken from the Settlement Report :—

The Mutiny of 1857.

"The sepoy mutiny in Chota Nāgpur started in and ended in Hazāribāgh district. At the beginning of August 1857 the Hazāribāgh detachment of the Rāmgarh Battalion consisting of two companies of the 8th Regiment mutinied. News of their revolt was sent to Rānchi, and Lieutenant Graham was sent from there with a detachment of the Rāmgarh Light Infantry to disarm them. His detachment mutinied on the road, and joined the Hazāribāgh detachment which was marching on Rānchi, at Burmu. The combined force continued to march on Rānchi, and Captain Dalton, the Commissioner, after ascertaining that the remainder of the native troops at Doranda were not loyal, withdrew with all the Europeans by the Rāmgarh road to Hazāribāgh and from there retired to Bagodar to await supports coming along the Grand Trunk Road. As soon as a guard of Rattray's Sikhs was put at his disposal Colonel Dalton reoccupied Hazāribāgh, and from there kept under observation the movements of the mutineers. The mutinous troops had received no support in Hazāribāgh, and very little in Rānchi. They stayed in Rānchi for over a month, and then moved westward, with the idea of joining another body of sepoys under Kunwar Singh near Rohtāsgarh. Their advance was opposed at two of the ghāts by loyal zamindars, but after forcing the breast-works with their cannon they marched through Chandwa and Bālumath in Palāmau to the town of Chatra. While they were looting there they were surprised and attacked by a much smaller mixed force consisting of 320 men, and completely defeated : their guns and all their ammunition were captured, 150 were killed, and the remainder fled in the direction of Sherghāti and dispersed.

* * * *

Santāls' unrest.

"While there was no sympathy with the mutineers in Hazāribāgh the Santāls not unnaturally became excited by the weakening of authority and thought the occasion opportune for squaring accounts with oppressive money-lenders and others. Several bands of Santāls collected for marauding purposes and were joined by the local bad characters, and a certain amount of plundering occurred between Gola and Chās (i.e. thana Petarbār) in Kharagdiha, at Kuju on the Rāmgarh road and at Jharpo near Bagodar. At Māndu they were instigated by three local landholders to commit murder as well as plunder the village. The landholders instigating the murder were subsequently caught and hanged. A small punitive expedition of Sikhs was sent to Gola, and the excitement died out immediately. The disturbances were only sporadic; there was no organized movement among the Santāls as a whole, and no special measures against them were considered necessary after the risings had subsided. Instead, it was decided shortly after the mutiny to raise a levy of Kols and Santals for military police, and a body of 500 of the more ardent aboriginals was enlisted for this work. Similarly in the north of the district the news of the sepoy rising evoked some small uprising among the dispossessed Bhuiya *tikāits*, who considered the opportunity suitable for recovering their lands from the purchasers then occupying them; and they received some support from their tenantry."

Since the suppression of these disorders the district has been tranquil, and the only event of more than passing importance has been the cadastral survey of the district and the preparation of a detailed record-of-rights, which began in 1908 and ended in 1915. During almost all this period Mr. J. D. Sifton, I.C.S., was Settlement Officer and responsible for the efficiency of the machinery of settlement. This costly and laborious work was undertaken in order to give to the general body of landlords and tenants clear and definite knowledge of their respective rights and obligations; and in conjunction with the new agrarian law of 1908 (the Chota Nāgpur Tenancy Act) it holds out the hope of a new era of peace and modest prosperity. Later History.

CHAPTER IV.

THE PEOPLE.

Growth of population

The first census was made in 1872 and disclosed a population of 771,875 living in 150,493 houses; the methods of enumeration were however experimental and the results unreliable. The first accurate census was made in 1881. The figures of this and later enumerations are as follows :—

1881	1,104,742		
1891	1,164,321,	variation	+5·4 per cent.
1901	1,177,961	,,	+1·17 per cent.
1911	1,288,609	,,	+9·39 per cent.

The increase of population between 1881 and 1891 occurred chiefly in the Giridih subdivision where coal mines were being developed : in Chaupāran and Chatra there was a serious decrease. In the next decade there was severe scarcity amounting to famine, which caused a greatly increased emigration and a high death-rate. The decrease in population was shared by Hazāribāgh, Chatra, Barkāgāon, Gumia, Barhi and Bagodar. Between 1901 and 1911 there was only one year of bad crops, in 1907, but its effect on the birth and death-rates was very severe. The rate of increase during these ten years was 9·39 per cent, being highest in the southern thanas. In the census of 1881 the district was divided into sixteen thanas, of which Jagesar was subsequently partitioned between Gumia and Māndu, and Kharagdiha lost the western portion now called Dhanwār. There appears to have been little alteration in the boundaries of these units, and it is possible to compare their populations in 1881 with those of 1911—after an interval of thirty years. Giridih has gained fifty per cent owing to the development of the Giridih coal-field and the growth of the new town which is the present subdivisional headquarters. There is a considerable aboriginal element in the east of this thana. Petarbār in the south has gained forty-nine per cent, Dumri thirty-eight, Gumia and Māndu thirty-four and Rāmgarh thirty-one. These are all in the Dāmodar valley, in the south and south-east of the district, and have a very considerable aboriginal element. Much of the area is hilly, and forest is fairly abundant ; but it is apparently the fecundity of the aboriginal races and the comparative absence of emigration which have led to this great increase. Bagodar comes next with twenty-two per cent, much of which has been gained in the last ten years, and is perhaps due in part to the opening of the Grand Chord Railway ; but it has a fair proportion of aboriginals, and the south of the thana is composed of jungle-covered uplands. Gāwān occupies the north-eastern corner of the district, where the lower plateau is broken down to the Gayā plain by the Sakri river. The population in the east is Santāl, but elsewhere it includes large numbers of Goālas, Bhuiyas and Rājputs. The increase has been twenty per cent, and is due in part to immigration from Gayā. The increase in Kodarma is nineteen per cent, and is due in part to the development of mica, which has kept the poorer classes at home. In Hunterganj, which somewhat resembles Gāwān in its physical characteristics, the increase of nineteen per cent is explained in part by immigration from Gayā and in part by the rigid suppression of emigration. The *kamiauti* system prevails in this area, and the landlords do not allow the landless serfs to leave the district. In Kharagdiha and Dhanwār the increase has been nine per cent. The country is bare of forests, and the density of the population is higher than elsewhere. There is no virgin land to bring under cultivation, and much of the lowest class of rice land is so high that it receives only the rain which falls from the sky. Such lands fail two years in five and under present agricultural conditions an increase in the population is undesirable : the natural excess can and should move away to the coal-fields or Assam. The same conditions are found in Barhi (2) and Chaupāran (—11) , but with an exaggeration increasing as one goes westward. These two thanas, in their more level and cultivated portions, are on the watershed between the Barākar and Mohani rivers, towards the east, and much of Chatra (—14) lies immediately to the west. This area has an arid appearance which is scarcely confirmed by the rainfall statistics, but is borne out by the census and by popular reputation. In addition to the unfavourable agricultural conditions to the east the urban portion of Chatra has suffered by the gradual curtailment of its trade, as a consequence of the advance of railways, and by the ravages of two severe epidemics of plague. Simaria is, for the most part, suited only for grazing; and where it broadens into rice lands the Bábhan landlords have worked the *kamiauti* system in such a manner that the serfs have fled in great numbers. Barkāgāon has increased by ten per cent only in thirty years. It suffered badly in the famine of 1897, and much of its eastern area is made up of precarious third-class rice lands. The sadr thana has decreased by two per cent, in spite of the increase of the urban population. Agriculturally it has little waste land fit for cultivation, and the practice of temporary emigration has increased considerably. The opening of the new coal mines in South Dumri (police-station Nawādih), and the possibility of similar developments in Gumia and Barkāgāon may result in large displacements of population similar to that which has occurred at Giridih. So far, however, the local people have shown no partiality for coal-mining in general, and under-ground working in particular; and the greater portion of the 1,500 labourers at the Bokāro (Joint Railways) colliery has been imported from outside.

Density of population. In the Giridih subdivision there are 226 people to the square mile, in the sadr 177, in Chatra 143, and for the district as a whole 186. For British territory in the province as a whole the number is 415: and the only other districts analogous to Hazāribāgh are Sambalpur (195), Rānchi (195), Singhbhum (178), Palāmau (140), and Angul (119). Of the total area of the district 3,004 square miles are permanently unfit for cultivation; but there remain 1,924 square miles which are cultivable but uncultivated. At first sight it would seem that much agricultural development remains to be carried out and that the population is capable of a large increase. It is however certain that the soil is for the most part inherently infertile. Moreover there are abundant traces in most parts of the district of unsuccessful cultivation, for which failure the ravages of wild animals may perhaps take the responsibility in some cases, but a more common reason is the inadequacy of moisture or inability to control flood water. Extensive irrigation works of a character beyond the means and equipment of local agriculturists might render some of the waste land cultivable; but the poverty of the soil and the irregularity of the surface make the chances of profit very doubtful. The extent to which the people resort to temporary emigration is a clear indication of the present agricultural poverty, and the absence of a local remedy: and the indefinite increase of the population would be a doubtful gain, unless new sources of income were developed in mines or manufactures.

In the census of 1911 there were found to be 41,631 persons residing in the district who had been born outside it, of whom 34,000 came from contiguous districts, 3,000 from other parts of the province and 4,000 from other provinces. There were 144,541 natives of the district residing outside it, of whom approximately 53,000 were in contiguous districts, 3,000 in other parts of the province and 88,000 in other provinces. From the figures on each side have to be deducted the brides and their first-born children along the border villages. There is much of this intermarriage, for the district boundaries in many places do not coincide with serious physical obstacles such as wide rivers or high hills; and it is a well-known custom among all castes to avoid the undue propinquity of the parents of bride and bridegroom. Also the young wife usually proceeds to her parents' home for the birth of her first child. After these allowances are made the balance of immigrants from contiguous districts is probably made up of old settlers from Gayā, and peons, *barahils* and other servants of landlords. From further afield came the Bengali residents of Giridih and Hazāribāgh, miners in Kodarma, and Mārwāris and other traders throughout the larger bazars. The largest number of emigrants in contiguous districts was found in Mānbhum (28,000), and a few had gone to work in the *rabi* harvest of Gayā. There were 56,000 Hazāribāgh-born persons in Assam and about 1,500 in the Duārs and Chittagong tea gardens, many of whom had probably settled there permanently. There is a fairly large annual migration to Calcutta, especially for conservancy work, and further east for agricultural earthwork. A curious sense of shame leads these people to conceal their resort to the coal-fields and conservancy work: when questioned their almost invariable answer, even with the coal grit still on their persons, is that they have been to "Sirāsganj to dig earth". There is one small field of employment under the Survey and Forest Departments which the people of the higher plateau monopolize. Each year some two

Migration.

or three thousand go to Burma, Eastern Bengal, Assam and Madras for this special work; and quite a number have earned gratuities for more than twenty years of such service. They go in the end of October and return in April or May with enough money saved to pay the rent, and to vary the task of preparing the ricefields with a modest indulgence in the pleasures of country spirits and the nocturnal drum.

Emigration to the tea districts.

Of an entirely distinct character from the temporary migration described above is the emigration to Assam for a term of years which usually ends in permanent residence. This emigration has been going on for a long time, for as early as 1865 it is noted that 1,200 people went there in that year, and there were 1,420 in 1866. The agencies for recruitment changed from time to time, and with them the methods; but of recent years the annual number of recruits has rarely exceeded 2,000. At present the only authorized agency is the Tea Districts Labour Supply Association, which has a Local Agent at Hazāribāgh; and instances of objectionable recruitment are now extremely rare. The recruits are drawn mainly from the aboriginal and lower Hindu elements, men who have failed in the struggle to keep their petty holdings together, or landless labourers discouraged by the hopelessness of their prospects at home. They are encouraged to take with them all their dependents, either at the time of recruitment, or after a year's experience of conditions at the tea gardens; and they usually visit their former homes at frequent intervals. To these classes the Assam tea gardens under present conditions provide immediate comfort, and the possibility of acquiring modest holdings of their own after a reasonably brief interval.

TOWNS AND VILLAGES.

For the purposes of the census the district was divided into four towns and 8,399 villages. In the recent record-of-rights, however, the units of the settlement record were 7,007 in number. This would suggest that the census figures relate to natural aggregations of houses; and in this interpretation it seems that these are unusually small. Out of the whole number 8,101 have less than 500 inhabitants each, and average only 124. There are 250 villages with from five hundred to a thousand people, forty-one with from one to two thousand, and eight exceed two thousand but have less than five thousand.

The following were treated as towns :—

Hazāribāgh (17,900), Giridih (10,665), Chatra (9,222), Ichak (4,995).

LANGUAGE.

In the census report of 1911 the distribution of the population by language was approximately as follows :—

Hindi and Urdu	1,184,100
Munda languages	95,000
Kurmāli	7,700
Dravidian languages	1,400
Others	1,200

The Hindi spoken by the great bulk of the population is Magahi : in the south-east corner to the east of Gola it is Kurmāli, as in western Manbhum. This language is sometimes described as Het Gola and is stated by Grierson to be essentially Bihāri in its nature with a curious Bengali colouring. The Santāls are practically the only people who habitually use a Mundā language, for the Mundās, most of whom live in Rāmgarh, will not ordinarily speak anything but Hindi to outsiders. There are 4,814 Orāons in the district ; but the majority of them are returned as Hindi-speaking, only about 1,400 using the tribal Dravidian language. It is to be noted that the local Hindi is spoken as a second language by all these people.

Religion.

The Hindus numbered 1,066,067 in the census of 1911 or 82·7 of the whole population. In the absence of a religious survey it is difficult to particularize regarding the character of the religious beliefs and practices of this heterogeneous body, whose members are drawn mainly from the lower strata of Hinduism. It is however to be expected that such a survey would disclose the extensive persistence of elements derived from aboriginal sources, in view of the inclusion of such races as the Bhuiyas, Bhogtas and Kurmis. The following extract from casual entries in the Deputy Commissioner's diary for December 1915 will illustrate the complexity of the religious beliefs in this district: (Near Lugu Hill in Mandu.) "There was a little *mandap* further on the road, with an earthen floor. On the beams were a pair of *kharoms* (wooden slippers), and a wooden box-lid studded with projecting nails with somewhat blunted points. The Kurmi stated that these were used by the worshippers of Kapsa, who is the *sipāhi* of Debi, and that when the worship of Debi was completed a subsidiary worship of her *sipāhi*

Mixed character of Hinduism.

was held, the officiating party putting on the *kharoms* and taking his seat on the iron points of the nails. A Santāl, however, who lives close by, and who was accustomed to take this active part in the performance, said that it was not in honour of any Kapsa, or any *sipāhi* of Debi, but of a brother of Lugu, the hill god. The Santāls however appear to be comparatively new comers to these parts ; and it is probable that the hill really belongs to an older race. The *pāhān* (village sacrificer) of Loiyo is a Bhogta, and Loiyo is probably a very old village, so that it is not unlikely that the gods of Lugu Hill belong to the Bhogta legends and beliefs."

Again in February 1916 is noted 'Visited Dungo on the road to Atka. It is a small village of fifteen houses, of Goālas, Chamārs, Telis, Bhogtas and Nauas. There are four deities—(1) Debi or Kali, (2) Kallian Kumār, (3) Bān Singh, (4) Gānwa Deoti. The second is the special god of the Goālas, and his province is the cattle and jungle grazing, and the dangers incident thereto. Bān Singh is a god of the Bhogtas. Regarding the fourth, the village goddess, I could get no information, except that things did not go well if sacrifice was not offered. But it is significant that this *Ganwa deoti* is the only one of the four to whom offerings are made of pigs and spirituous liquors."

Persistence of the local gods.

Even where the landlord, and the majority of the tenants are Hindus it is still the custom to employ as the *pāhān* or sacrificer one of the race of the original clearers of the village, or at least of an earlier dispossessed race. The idea underlying this is a belief in the existence of local spirits who must be propitiated by sacrifices, lest their anger vent itself on the fruits of the fields and cattle and the fertility of the women, or in the stirring up of disease for men and beasts. The jurisdiction of these spirits usually stops short at the village boundary; and it is therefore obvious that their peculiarities require the most intimate local experience. This is naturally found in the descendants of the original clearers: and so the Brahman or Bābhan grantee or purchaser of a jungle village considers it a matter of mere common sense to retain by the attraction of rent-free land the Mundāri or Bhogta *pāhān* whose brethren have long since been expelled, that he may perform the customary sacrifices and placate the spirits when some unintended or even unknown injury has aroused their anger. The belief that a village can become unlucky is sometimes the cause of serious loss to the landlord. When this reputation has been gained the village is said to be *mahanans*; no one will live in it; and only with great reluctance, and at a great reduction of the usual rates of rent will neighbouring villagers take the lands for cultivation. The reputation need not be ancient; all that is required for its acquisition is unusual sickness or mortality.

The Muhammadans were 133,328 in number, or 10·3 per cent of the district population. This is approximately the same proportion as in Gaya, and far in excess of that of Rānchi and Mānbhum. The numerically important castes are Jolahas (87,211), Shekhs (21,152), Kalāls (7,279), and Pathāns (3,634). The first-named are fairly evenly spread over the whole district, but are thickest in the Giridih Subdivision. There is a tendency here as elsewhere to avoid the designation of Jolāhā, and a man will usually begin by giving his caste as Shaikh, which, under pressure, becomes Shaikh Momin: and doubtless many Jolāhās were returned as Shaikhs in the census. It is not obvious why there should be so many of these humble Muhammadans, as there were no important Musalman landlords or officials, and the rule of the Bādshāhs pressed very lightly on the district. Muhammadans.

There are now some Pathān tenure-holders in Hunterganj, who have come from Gayā, when there was long a colony of Rohillas near Kothi. There are also a few in Kodarma thana, near Jainagar, who obtained grants for services rendered to a former chief of Rāmgarh. In each of these two groups it is still easy to detect traces of that old disregard of law and of the rights of others which ought by now to be an anachronism.

The 86,706 people returned as Animists in the census of 1911 were made up almost entirely from three castes—Santāls (77,000), Mundās (4,500) and Orāons (2,600). The border line between Animism and Hinduism is notoriously difficult to draw, and it would be unsafe to conclude much more than this, that the Santāls are not moving much towards Hinduism, and that the isolation of the small Mundāri and Orāon communities appears to promote the abandonment of their old tribal beliefs and practices. Animists.

Christians.

The Christians of the district numbered 1,786 in 1911, out of whom 210 were returned as Santāls, 126 as Mundās and 14 as Orāons. Of the remainder 1,201 were merely described as Indian Christians and 245 as Europeans and Anglo-Indians.

Up till 1914 there were three Christian missions at work in the district, but since then one (the Lutheran Mission) has been closed. So far their medical and educational activities have been more clearly fruitful than their proselytizing work.

The following account of the Dublin University Mission has been contributed by the Reverend J. C. Forrester, the head of that body :—

Dublin University Mission.

In the year 1890 several members of the Dublin University offered themselves for service abroad as a community in connexion with the Society for the Propagation of the Gospel. It was decided that a brotherhood should be founded which should look to the University for its supply of men and to the Society for the Propagation of the Gospel for part of its support, and that its sphere of work should be the district of Hazāribāgh in the diocese of Chota Nāgpur, of which the late Rev. J. C. Whitley was the Bishop. The members of the mission were to be graduates of the Dublin University, unmarried, and to lead a community life, receiving no salary apart from a small sum (Rs. 300 per annum) for personal expenses. The first members, the Revs. Eyre Chatterton, Head of the Mission (now Bishop of Nagpur), C. W. Darling, K. W. S. Kennedy, J. A. Murray, and G. F. Hamilton, arrived in Hazāribāgh in March 1892 and took over the remains of the old military hospitals and their compound which Bishop Whitley had obtained for the Mission from Government. The two main buildings were in process of demolition, and had to be entirely rebuilt with the exception of the plinth and a foot or so of the walls. With the first missionaries came Miss Fanny Hassard, and after a year Miss Richardson arrived; these were the first two ladies associate of the Mission. The ladies associate live a community life and undertake all women's work in connexion with the Mission. In 1900 the Rev. J. G. F. Hearn, M.D., was elected head of the Mission. He resigned in March 1912, and died very shortly after. The Rev. J. C. Forrester, M.A., was elected head in 1912, by the Mission chapter, which consists of all the members of the brotherhood, and is the supreme authority of the Mission. The bishop of the diocese is *ex-officio* Visitor of the Mission.

Medical Work.—In 1893 a dispensary and hospital for men were started in Hazaribagh under Drs. Hearn and Kennedy. Shortly afterwards a female dispensary and hospital were opened under the care of Miss Hassard, the dispensary being held in the verandah of the ladies' bungalow. On the arrival of Dr. Eva Jellett in 1906 efforts were made to build a zanāna hospital: the foundation-stone of St. Columba's Zenana Hospital was laid in 1907 and it was opened in 1913. It contains accommodation for forty in-patients, and a private ward is available for better-class Indian patients; and in cases of necessity accommodation can be provided for local European patients. The hospital receives a Government grant of Rs. 4,000 per annum. There are eight Indian nurses in training, two Indian certificated nurses, one Indian female compounder in training, two European nurses, and two European doctors.

In Chitarpur there are male and female hospitals, with outdoor dispensaries attached; there is accommodation for about thirty male and ten female in-patients. A sub-assistant surgeon is in charge and there is one fully-qualified compounder and dresser. In Rāmgarh and Petarbār are branch dispensaries, the average daily attendance at the former (new patients) being eleven and the latter twenty.

The male hospital in Hazaribagh was closed in 1913. There is now an outdoor dispensary for male patients, with a branch dispensary at Ichak. In Hazāribāgh there are a sub-assistant surgeon and a fully-qualified compounder and dresser, and there is a resident compounder at Ichak, which is visited once a week by a European lady doctor and also by the sub-assistant surgeon.

Education.—St. Columba's College was founded in 1899, the Rev J. A. Murray being the first Principal. Classes were opened in the central part of the present Post Office bungalow. A donation of Rs. 3,000 was given by Rājā Ram Narayan Singh of the Rāmgarh estate. The college opened with twenty-three students, most of whom had failed at other colleges. In 1904 the college was raised to the first grade (B. A. standard) and after several changes of location was removed to the old Mess House, part of the Post Office bungalow being obtained for a students' hostel, and the Rev. S. L. Thompson became Principal. In 1906 the building of the new college was commenced and its foundation-stone was laid in 1907. In November 1908 the college entered into possession of its new buildings which then consisted of the centre block with two wings serving as a hostel. Each student had a room to himself, an arrangement which was then unique. In 1909 the Bishop Whitley Memorial Hall was built, and in 1915-16 large chemical, botanical and physical laboratories were erected, towards the cost of which Government made a grant of Rs. 50,000. In 1912 a grant of Rs. 30,000 was made by Government for the erection of additional hostel accommodation, and accordingly a new block of thirty-four rooms with Principal's office and room was erected and opened in 1913. By special permission of His Majesty it is called "The King-Emperor's Block". In the same year the foundation-stone of the new science laboratories was laid. Towards the erection of the first block of college buildings Government contributed Rs. 27,000, the Society for the Propagation of the Gospel £1,500, and £1,000 were given from private sources in England. The college is lighted with electricity. It is now (1915) affiliated to the Calcutta University for the B. A. and Int. Sc. Examinations. The Rev. F. W. H. Kerr is Principal and the Rev. H. G. S. Kennedy, Vice-Principal. There are three Irish professors (members of the brotherhood), and eight Indian professors. There are 170 students on the roll, 100 of whom are resident in the hostel. There are three resident Superintendents, all members of the Mission. The college receives a monthly grant of Rs. 1,000 from Government. It publishes a magazine, and a Social Service Guild carries on vigorous Social Service work, including two night schools.

High School.—St. Columba's Collegiate School was opened in 1895, the Rev. C. W. Darling being the first Principal and the Rev. P. L. Singh, M.A., the head master, the Rev. J. A. Murray very shortly afterwards succeeded Mr. Darling as Principal. The school opened with seven boys on the roll. In 1912 Mr. Singh was appointed Principal. There are now (1916) 290 boys on the roll of whom about 120 are Christians, 150 Hindus and twenty Muhammadans. Two members of the

Mission are on the teaching staff, and there are seventeen Indian masters. The school receives a grant of Rs. 250 per month from Government and Rs. 175 from the Mission, which has also provided the school buildings and the Principal's quarters with the exception of two class rooms (of which half the cost was paid by Government).

From the beginning there has been a hostel attached to the school for Christian boys. The senior boarders live in one end of the Mission bungalow, while the juniors live in a new hostel to the south of the school, and adjoining it, which was completed in 1912. Government contributed Rs. 20,000 towards its cost, and the rest was raised from private sources. A sick-room was built in 1912, and its cost was given by a lady in England. The Warden of the hostel is a member of the Mission. To the hostel Government grants Rs. 50 a month, and the mission Rs. 4,750 per annum, the fees amounting to Rs. 2,370 per annum. As almost all the boarders are aboriginals the fees must be low, the seniors paying Rs. 4-8 a month and the juniors Rs. 3-8 a month, and these fees include tuition charges. There are 103 boys in the hostel, of whom forty are in part or wholly supported by the Mission. There are three Bengali Christians, who pay double fees.

Primary Schools.—In Hazāribāgh town there is an upper primary school, with 100 boys on the roll. Within the municipal area there are four lower primary day schools and four night schools. In Hazāribāgh and Māndu thanas there are three lower primary schools. In Chitarpur and the neighbourhood there are a lower primary boarding school, and three lower primary day schools. There are three night schools.

In Hazāribāgh town there is an upper primary school for Bengali girls and a lower primary school for Hindi-speaking girls. In Korra, Seotāgarha, Ichak and Singhāni there are lower primary schools. There is also an infants' school in connexion with the Mission Orphanage. In Chitarpur and the neighbourhood there are four girls' schools and one in Petarbār.

All the mission primary schools with the exception of three are aided either by Municipal or District Board grants, and the Mission contributes a substantial share of the expense. The male schools are under the direct supervision of one of the members of the Mission, and the female schools are looked after by the ladies associate.

A considerable amount of evangelistic work is carried on in the villages. Many of the *zananas* are visited by the ladies associate and bible women.

Near the College is a model Christian village, named Hearnganj, in memory of the Rev. J. G. F. Hearn. The land has been leased to the Mission by Government, and the Mission has issued sub-leases to Christians.

A printing press and a workshop have been established in Hāzāribāgh, and a lace class is carried on by the ladies associate.

There are Indian Christian congregations of the Church of England in Hazāribāgh, Seotāgarha, Dumar, Chitarpur and Jobla. The European congregations in Hazāribāgh, Giridih and Kodarma are served by members of the Mission, as are also the Indian congregations of Dumar and Seotāgarha; an Indian priest is in charge of Chitarpur and Jobla. There are masonry churches in Hazāribāgh (completed in 1842), Kodarma (consecrated in 1909) and in Chitarpur (dedicated 1901).

United Free Church of Scotland.

The following account of the United Free Church of Scotland Mission has been contributed by the Rev. Dr. Dyer of Pachamba :—

"The Santāl Mission of the United Free Church of Scotland was commenced as 'a new off-shoot from the Bengal Mission' according to its first report, issued in the year 1870. It was begun through the efforts of the late Rev. Dr. Murray Mitchell, when acting Principal of the Duff Institution in Calcutta; and was supported by contributions received in India. The first Superintendent was the late Mr. Verniew of Calcutta. In the report for 1872 the following statement of agents and work was submitted by the Rev. Dr. Templeton, an ordained Medical Missionary, who arrived from Scotland in 1871 :—

"*Christian Agency.*—One ordained European missionary, one native doctor, three native male teachers.

Dispensary, open daily; one boarding school; two village schools; thirty-five scholars on the roll. Contributions received locally amounted to £15."

Until the year 1878 the Mission report was issued as a part of the Bengal Mission report; but from that year it has been issued separately. By this time the Mission staff had been increased to three European missionaries. In the report of 1879 it was stated that "the work of extending the mission has been prosecuted during the year. A lease of land has been secured in a Santāl village in the district of Chakāi (i. e. in Monghyr), thirty miles north of Pachamba: Mr. Campbell undertook to extend the work by opening another station, and has been engaged for some time surveying the district of Tundi (i.e. in Mānbhum) which lies in a south-easterly direction about thirty miles from Pachamba". Thus by the year 1880 the Mission was working in the districts of Hazāribāgh, Monghyr and Manbhum, and was doing so in three languages, Hindi, Bengali and Santāli. In the same year the Presbytery of Calcutta, under which the Mission was being carried on, ordained the three missionaries as elders, and formed the "adherents and members of the Church" into a congregation under the name of a preaching station. The Mission belongs to a Presbyterian church, and Presbyterian law and order had to be kept in view and followed. There was no ordained minister in the Mission until 1881, when the convener of the Mission Committee was the Rev. A. Campbell. Dr. Dyer was ordained in 1886, the late Mr. Stevenson in 1887 (he died from cholera in the next year). Dr. Macphail joined the staff in 1889 and was posted to Chaḳai, and another station was opened at Tisri (thana Gāwān) by Dr. Kitchin in 1904. There are now four stations, in three of which are ordained medical missionaries with hospitals and dispensaries. In Tundi station there is a dispensary, and there are seven out-stations.

According to the latest report issued by the Mission Council for 1915 the numbers connected with the Santāl Church are as follows:—

Communicants	425
Baptized adherents	1,473
Scholars in 152 schools	2,765
Evangelists	30
Christian school teachers	71
Medical assistants	12

In the hospitals and dispensaries connected with the various principal stations about 25,000 new patients were treated. The European doctors are assisted in various capacities by thirteen Santāl agents. Medical fees and payments for medicines amounted to Rs. 5,700, and in two of the stations the receipts far exceeded the expenditure on the medical work. Surgical operations numbered 4,458, of which about 1,507 were eye operations, and of these 1,100 were cataract extractions.

It is scarcely possible to collect from these bald accounts an adequate impression of the true value of the services which are being rendered to the people of Hazāribāgh, and of a still wider sphere, by the disinterested philanthrophy of these two missionary bodies.

CASTES AND TRIBES.

In the census of 1911 there were separately enumerated sixteen castes of Muhammadans and eighty-six castes and tribes of Hindus and aboriginals. The remainder were entered under the head of 'Others'. In addition various nationalities of Christians were distinguished. Of the Muhammadans only one caste, the Jolāhās (87,211), exceeds 25,000, as against eleven Hindu castes—Goalās (149,740), Telis (54,347), Koiris (52,817), Chamārs (49,503), Brāhmans (35,558), Kahārs (31,747), Barhis (29,564), Rājputs (29,100), Hajjāms (27,533), Dusādhs (26,958) and Kumhārs (26,211) and five aboriginal castes—Santāls (93,059), Bhuiyas (89,682), Kurmis (84,589), Ghātwārs (54,509) and Bhogtās (36,984). Between them these seventeen castes account for about seventy-five per cent of the population; but inasmuch as they are fairly widely distributed the general impression left in the case of this district, as compared with its neighbours, is that of a very mixed population.

GOĀLAS.

The Goālas are found in the northern half of the district, their comparative insignificance in the whole of the Dāmodar valley being very striking. In the neighbouring district of Gayā they form nearly one-seventh of the total population, and it is probable that they have reached Hazāribāgh mainly from that district. They occupy tracts which possess a comparatively limited range of pastures, and are mostly engaged on agriculture. Unlike their neighbours in Gayā they are generally regarded as quiet and law-abiding people. Their panchāyats appear to possess considerable influence, and the head panch of Jainagar exercises an authority from Gayā to the north edge of the higher plateau and from the east of Kodarma to the west of Chauparan which has proved useful, specially in keeping down the price of brides.

Functional castes.

Of the remaining Hindu castes specified above the functional castes, as might be expected, are distributed fairly evenly over the district, with a tendency to thin out towards the south and east. These are the Telis, Brāhmans, Hajjāms and Kumhārs. Rājputs and Dusadhs are also widely diffused, except in Gumia. They are numerous in Gāwān, and though this might be due to a special immigration up the Sakri river it is more probably explained by the social ambition of the local Ghātwāls. The distribution of the Koiris, Chamārs, Kahārs and Barhis is almost identical with that of the Goālas. There have apparently been two distinct streams of immigrants, one through the Sakri valley to Kharagdiha and Kodarma, which halted on the south at the Barākar river, and the other from the Lilājān valley and Danua and Dhangāin *ghāts*, which spread over Hunterganj, Chatra, Chauparan and the region now traversed by the Grand Trunk Road to the neighbourhood of Dumri. Each stream seems to have failed to penetrate the hilly country round Pārasnāth Hill and the broken country that divides the watersheds of the Barākar and Dāmodar. The valley of the latter river was scarcely affected, though there is perhaps a slightly stronger Hindu element in the population of Karanpura, at the western end of the Dāmodar valley, which is possibly due to the situation in that valley of the old headquarters of the Rāmgarh Raj.

Other Hindu castes.

Santāls.

The distribution of the Santāls appears to be in two groups. The first occupies the east of Gāwān, Kharagdiha and Giridih, the whole of Pirtānr police-station and the north of Dumri police-station (both in thana Dumri) with a slight extension into the east of Bagodar. This group keeps up a close connexion with the Santāl Parganas and Mānbhum. The second group occupies the broken and wooded country which commences in the east in Gumia and the south of Bagodar and runs south to eastern Rāmgarh and Petarbār and west through Māndu into the eastern hills of Barkāgāon. This country is also the home of the Kurmis.

Bhuiyas.

The distribution of the Bhuiya-Ghātwāl caste is peculiar. They are dense in the compact block of Hunterganj, Chatra, Chaupāran, Simaria and Hazāribāgh thanas, and numerous elsewhere, except in Rāmgarh, Gumia, and Petarbār.

Bhogtas.

The Bhogtas are thick in Simaria, Hunterganj, Barkāgāon and Chatra, elsewhere they are few and they are scarcely found in the Giridih Subdivision.

Other castes.

The examination of the distribution of the less numerous castes gives the same result of a distinctively preponderating aboriginal element in the Dāmodar valley, and of a similar Hindu element in the north and centre of the district. The boundary line runs a few miles inside the eastern border of the district down to Sirāmpur, thence up the Barākar river to the boundary of Bagodar thana, southward to the Jamunia river, thence due west to the edge of the higher plateau, and then along the north of Māndu across the plateau to the north side of Simaria, which it leaves to meet the Gayā border north of Partābpur in the Hunterganj thana. This boundary coincides roughly with the growth of population in the district in recent years, the area to the south and east being the more prolific.

Santāls.

Of the tribes mentioned above the origin, history and institutions of the Santāls alone have been subjected to any scientific scrutiny, and they have been described at length in Risley's 'People of India'. Their early associations with this district have been referred to in Chapter III but more investigation is needed before their association with Chhāi and the fort at that place can be accepted. In Hazāribāgh they have shown themselves a somewhat volatile race and far less tenacious of their rights than the Mundās of Rānchi. The Settlement Officer reports that sometimes the mere advent of an unpopular *thikadar* has sufficed to lead them to abandon their holdings. There has in recent years been only one serious approach to organized agitation, when the injudicious interference of the zamindār of Pālganj with their forest rights excited such discontent as made it necessary for Government to intervene.

Bhuiyas and Ghātwārs.

It is now generally held that the name of Ghātwār or Ghātwāl was assumed by Bhuiya tribal chiefs, and adopted by their families; and that there is no distinction in race between Ghātwārs and Bhuiyas. The Tikāits (chiefs) of the Ghātwār *gadis* would now prefer to be described as Chhatris (Rājputs). The Ghātwārs have a reputation for courage which sometimes degenerates into ferocity. From time to time the aggression of Bābhan or Mahuri money-lenders is avenged by brutal murders; and the recent scarcity in 1914-15 promptly led to an outbreak of dacoities under the leadership of descendants of the old border marauders. The Bhuiyas are considered to be a Dravidian race, and it has been seen that their comparatively regular and even distribution in the district differs materially from that of the Santāls and Kurmis, between whom the evidence of a close connexion is very strong. They are numerous in Gaya and Palāmau, but thin out rapidly to the south (Rānchi) and south-east (Mānbhum). Eastward they are numerous in the Santāl Parganas. Further to the south they reappear in the Orissa Feudatory States and Singhbhum. Nothing is known of their historical relations with the Mundā-speaking tribes, whose supposed route from the north and west intersects that of the Bhuiyas from the south, more particularly in Hazāribāgh.

Bhogtas.

The Bhogtās are mainly occupied in this district with the herding of cattle. They are regarded as a branch of the Kharwārs, who again are considered to be a Dravidian race akin to the Mundās and Santāls and now greatly Hinduized. (Dravidian is used in this chapter as a common *racial* description of both Mundā and Dravidian-speaking tribes.) Their dwelling place in the west of the district contains numerous Mundā place names, such as Hisātu (Hesābatu) and Lowālāng, and numerous grave-stones of the same kind as are found in Rānchi. There are Kharwār *digwars* in the north of Chatra who claim to be the *khuntkatti* colonizers of the Hunterganj jungles; and the leading zamindari families of Rāmgarh and Kunda are probably Kharwārs.

Kurmis.

It would appear that Dalton had no doubt that the Kurmis of Chota Nāgpur were a non-aboriginal Hindu caste: but it is now generally considered that there is a wide difference between the Kurmis of Bihar stock and others. In this district the latter call themselves Kurmbi simply; the former use the terms 'Kurmi Mahto', and warmly repudiate kinship with the Kurmbis. Here the distribution of the Kurmbis is practically the same as that of the Santāls, and this may perhaps be deemed to support a kindred origin of the tribe of which traces appear in Santāl legends. At the same time it must be admitted that it has travelled a long way from Santāl habits, and that the ordinary native would scarcely class Kurmbis with aboriginals like Mundās. They make their living by agriculture, and occupy a humble position, though a few in Rāmgarh have enriched themselves by money-lending.

Other notable castes. Turis.

The Turis are nearly 24,000 in number, and are now found mainly in the Giridih subdivision. They are a branch of the Doms, and support themselves by making baskets, and also by day labour, particularly in the Giridih coal-field.

Mundāris.

The number of Mundās was 13,654 in 1891, 15,022 in 1901 and 16,568 in 1911. They are now found mainly in thānā Rāmgarh. A full account of the Mundās is contained in the Gazetteer of Rānchi. In this district there is no organization in *pattis* or *parhas* now surviving; but up to a comparatively short time ago there was a *manki patti* round about Laranga to the south of Tandwa, on the east of the Satpahri Hills, west of, and near the old road which runs from Tandwa to Bahera. Here there are some conspicuous *bid diris* (erect memorial stones); and to the west there is a tola which is still called Mankidih. The Settlement Officer records the existence of a Mundāri *khuntkatti* family at Korāmbe in thana Rāmgarh. With these two exceptions there are no other traces of any special organization or status in this district; but it is tempting to assign to the Mundās the Mundāri place names and the grave-stones and memorial stones which are found in the west and south of the district, and to speculate that the Mundās were temporary sojourners on a journey to the district of Rānchi which the Kharwārs helped to hasten.

Bedias.

The Bedias numbered 12,668 in the census of 1911. They are confined practically to the Rāmgarh thana, where they are mainly respectable cultivators. In the Santāl tradition given in Chapter II they appear as the descendants of those Santāls who were too faint-hearted to flee from the social outrages threatened by Mādho Singh Birhor. On the other hand, it is stated emphatically in the 'Statistical Account' that they are pure Mundās, a fact said to be placed beyond dispute by the character of their features, the existence among them of the *pāhān* as a village official, their practice of smelting iron, and the similarity of the names of their *killis* (exogamous subdivisions) with those of the Mundās. Whatever is the truth of this matter, they appear to be near in race to the Mundās and Santāls, and in any case have no connexion whatever with the wandering gipsy Bediyas.

There were about 8,000 Karmālis in 1911 mainly in Rāmgarh and Petarbār. They speak a dialect of Santāli, and in race are probably Dravidian. Their main occupation used to be iron-smelting and blacksmithy; and they had an evil reputation as robbers and dacoits. Now they have become agricultural labourers. Karmālis.

The number of Orāons decreased from 6,350 in 1901 to 4,814 in 1911. They are found in the tracts nearest the Orāon country of Rānchi and Palāmau, and maintain a very close connexion with their kindred there. They are fully described in the Gazetteer of Rānchi. Orāons.

The Mahalis numbered 3,692 in 1911, and make their living mainly by working up materials of bamboo. Dalton merely records that the name is an alternative appellation of the gipsy Bediyas: in Rānchi, however, they are found in close association with the more jungly Mundāris especially in the west of Tamār, where they perform subsidiary services in the primitive village life of those parts; and in Hazāribāgh they can scarcely be characterized as gipsy folk. Mahalis.

In the census of 1911 there were 1,024 Birhors in Hazāribāgh, 927 in Rānchi, and a total for the province of 2,340 souls. The word means 'jungle man', the language is very closely akin to Mundāri, and the race is Dravidian. Formerly without settled homes and winning a scanty subsistence from the products of the jungle, they have now fallen on evil times with the gradual extension of cultivation and the greater drain on the forests from the presence of a thicker population; and they are taking up settled work as landless labourers, living in permanent dwellings on the outskirts of villages, but still expert in discovering wild honey and making ropes of *chop*. The latest account of this unfortunate race is contained in an article Birhors.

by Babu S. C. Ray in the number for September 1916 of the Journal of the Bihar and Orissa Research Society.

Bābhans.

There were about 21,000 Bābhans in the district in 1911 as compared with about 26,000 in 1901. They are numerous and influential in Dhanwār, Kharagdiha and Giridih, and few but important in Chatra, Simaria and the west of Barkāgāon. If generalizations are permissible in discussing the qualities of a caste, it may be said that the Bābhans are mentally and physically vigorous, but that they are extremely unpopular with other castes ; and have the reputation of pressing their superiority of mind and body to the extreme limits that are permitted by the executive and judicial officers for the time being in authority, without much regard to law or prevailing moral standards of conduct.

Sokiārs.

The 13,982 Sokiārs of the census of 1911 were mainly concentrated round Ichāk, in the north of Hazāribāgh thana. They are skilful cultivators of much the same social status as Koiris, and are noteworthy for their unscrupulous litigiousness. As they are near neighbours of the Hazāribāgh courts of justice this quality wins for them a perhaps disproportionate amount of attention.

Patwas.

The Patwas were hereditary rearers and spinners of silk, but are now engaged in cultivation. In 1911 they numbered just under 2,000 but make an entirely unreasonable stir, like the Sokiārs, by the conspicuous faithlessness of their quarrels. They trouble Hosir-Sāram and Petarbār, but have now begun to emigrate.

Bandāwats.

The Bandāwats numbered 6,294 in 1911 and were almost exclusively confined to Chāupāran. There are, however, still about 200 in Kharagdiha thana, perhaps descendants of the Bandawat Rājā, who, it is said, preceded the Kharagdiha Chiefs. In Chāupāran they call themselves Rājputs from the United Provinces. They resemble the Bābhans in their sturdy physical virility, and in a certain strain of cruelty which makes them dreaded by their neighbours. In the Hazāribāgh Settlement Report is given a very interesting description of a form of subordinate village proprietorship which they still maintain.

Village officials.

Village officials are now of little importance in the conduct of affairs in Hazāribāgh—a fact for which there are two adequate explanations ready to hand. In the first place there are very few areas in which the village population is homogeneous; and in the second there has been an excessive delegation of the rights of the proprietor by sub-infeudation. In the 'Statistical Account' it was remarked that "This system of sub-letting every two or three villages to small under-farmers or *thikādārs* must be fatal to the existence of the ancient tribal headman. The small size of holding enables the former to deal with individual raiyats, thus rendering unnecessary the headman's peculiar function of representing the villagers to their superior landlord. Nor can the *thikādārs* tolerate a rival authority in the village, and the old headman sooner or later sinks into the position of an ordinary cultivator."

Formerly the same functionary, called sometimes the *gorāit*, sometimes the chaukidār, used to perform the duties both of watch and ward and also of landlord's messenger; but everywhere these have now been divorced, with the result that this State servant tends to be less and less an instrument of oppressive interference with the villagers. The amendment of the Rural Police Act has permitted the equalization of the burden of his support, and it is now possible to pay him a reasonable wage without serious hardship to the villagers. The number of villages in which the landlord finds it necessary to retain a *gorāit* at his own expense is limited, and in such cases the remuneration takes the form of a parcel of rent-free lands. Chaukidār.

The *pāhān* may perhaps be described as a village official, for it is his duty to keep in good humour those spirits of the jungle and rice lands and sacred groves to whose petulance is ascribed all unusual sickness of man or beast. These are the gods of an earlier race who do not enter into the worship of the ordinary villager; and if possible a member of that earlier race is charged with this duty of propitiation. In return he is the tenant for life or good conduct of the village *pāhānāi* lands, which he may not alienate or charge; and when he passes away the lands go without alteration or encumbrance to his successor in office. Pāhān.

The dress, the fashion of the houses, the festivals and pastimes of the heterogeneous elements who make up the ordinary village in Hazāribāgh do not present unique features, and the description given in Mr. Coupland's Gazetteer of Mānbhum Village social life.

is applicable with slight alterations to this district. It may be noted that the hook-swinging festival is scarcely found, except in the extreme east; and cock-fighting is not a popular amusement. The pilgrimage to Pārasnāth is scarcely a concern of this district; and the only resort of more than local dignity is Kuluha Hill, about six miles from Hunterganj. This was formerly held in great respect by the Jains, being the reputed birthplace of the tenth Tirthankara Sitala Swāmin; and Sir M. A. Stein, who visited the place in 1900, found there remains of Jain origin (which were of no architectural importance). It has for many years been completely abandoned by that sect, and is now associated by the local Hindus with the Pāndava brothers.

Pilgrimages.

Witchcraft.

It would be misleading in an account of the people of this district to omit mention of the belief in witchcraft, though the subject might perhaps with equal propriety be discussed under the head of crime. The belief that evils of every kind are caused by spirits is practically universal. These spirits are set in motion either by accidental causes or by the volition of those individuals who have acquired the power to do so. The following are illustrations of the working of the superstition.

In one case the spirit in question was the shade of the original founder of the village. He was irritated by some unknown and unintentional act of two substantial cultivators of the village, and he caused an outbreak of fever. Two professional detectives (*deonras*, or *deoklis*) were consulted independently, and each denounced these two men, though they were unable to give any indication of the nature of the offence. The only matter open for controversy was the value of the propitiatory offerings; and this was finally fixed, by friendly mediation, at fifteen rupees. Throughout there was no suggestion of bad faith on any one's part.

In another case a cultivator had an attack of indigestion which ordinary medicine failed to cure. He therefore consulted the nearest *deokli* who explained that a neighbour's wife had "set a *bhut*" on him. Accordingly he went to his neighbour and told him the facts; but the wife, who was present, denied the allegation with some warmth, and the husband refused to give him the satisfaction of taking her to the *deokli*. The next morning the dispute was revived at the ploughing: and the wife, taking her husband's 'drinking' to him, saw him being beaten and fall dead. She and her son-in-law, who was chaukidār of the next village, went off and told the police, and the inquiry then made left no doubt about the facts; but no one would agree to give evidence, and even the son-in-law drew back. The case came on for trial with the widow as sole witness, and even she deliberately contradicted herself, obviously under tuition: and it transpired that she had come to headquarters in the company of the accused for the trial, and they were staying together as guests of the lessee of the village, whose house was there.

In yet another case a young married girl was found dead with her throat cut; and it was established that she had been killed by her young husband and her father-in-law. She was a strong and healthy girl of seventeen, for whom a substantial bride price had just before been paid, and the only reason for the murder was the fact that she had said at the village well that her mother-in-law was a witch. Father and son—the sole child—thought that the only way to save the mother was by putting an end to such rumours with the death of the daughter.

A very detestable abuse of this wide-spread superstition is the practice of bribing the *deokli* to denounce as a witch a person whom he has no reason to believe to be such. For example, when other means have failed of evicting a man from his land, an unscrupulous landlord has been known to adopt this means of effecting the ruin of his tenant.

CHAPTER V.

PUBLIC HEALTH.

BIRTHS AND DEATHS.

THE decennial averages of births and deaths from 1901 to 1910 were calculated on the census population of 1901, which had increased by ten per cent. in 1911. To ignore this progressive growth has the effect of unduly increasing the percentages which were 46·6 and 32·2 respectively, as compared with provincial averages of 42·1 and 36·1. Since 1911 the averages for five years have been 46·8 and 28·1 respectively. In these sixteen years the highest birth-rate was 56·5, reported in 1904, and the lowest 37·1 in 1908; the highest death-rate was 53·9 in 1908, and the lowest 23·5 in 1913. The abnormal figures of 1908 were due to the serious distress which prevailed in that year, of which an account is given in Chapter VII below.

The comparatively high death-rates of 1911 and 1916 were due to virulent epidemics of fever probably consequent on the abnormal distribution of the monsoon rains, as they began in August and persisted till the end of October.

There is a large aboriginal element in the population, and this probably explains the comparatively high birth-rate. The district as a whole is well drained, and the climate temperate.

Reporting agency.

Outside the municipalities the reporting agent is the village chaukidār, whose work is checked firstly by the local Sub-Inspectors of Police, and secondly by the vaccination officers. It must be admitted that the results are usually markedly uniform for those police-stations which are exposed to similar conditions, and the reporting appears to be done fairly well. The chaukidār may delay the reporting slightly, though this scarcely disturbs annual statistics; and he is perhaps inclined to question the utility of reporting the birth of a child which lives for only a few minutes; but with this exception the statistics are fairly good and quite sufficient to afford a reliable basis of comparison from year to year. When the figures of a new census are obtained it is interesting to compare them with the balance of births and deaths during the preceding ten years; but there is so much movement of the people that no conclusions can be drawn about the merits of reporting. The excess of reported births over deaths between 1901 and 1911 was 170,221; and the increase in the resident population according to the census was 110,648.

Diseases.

The chaukidār is naturally not at his best in the diagnosis of the diseases which prove fatal to his parishioners, and he is inclined to return under the head of 'fever' all except a few unmistakeable causes of death. The decennial average was 23·2 out of 32·2, the balance consisting of 'all other causes' 6, cholera 1·65, injuries ·5, dysentery ·3, small-pox ·3, plague ·16 and respiratory diseases ·02. The district has escaped any serious visitation of plague, from which disease the highest mortality occurred in 1901. Cholera caused 6·6 deaths per thousand in 1908, but has been less active since. The general belief is that it is imported by returning emigrants, often from Jharia, and ordinarily it makes its appearance in the hot weather and dies out after the first heavy rain of the monsoon. Small-pox, if one may judge from the small proportion of cases which end fatally, is of a mild type, and is not regarded with the apprehension that is caused by an outbreak of cholera.

Infirmities.

Leprosy and elephantiasis are uncommon, and the former disease is rarely seen except in the neighbourhood of Hunterganj where a number of lepers have congregated from Gayā.

SANITATION.

Hazāribāgh town.

Urban conditions are found to some extent in the three municipalities and two large villages. The largest town is Hazāribāgh. It owes its existence to the fact that it was the headquarters of the Rāmgarh battalion and later on of the district administration. The present planning of the town was made after 1865, in which year a large area was added to the cantonment with the avowed object of improving its sanitation. Most of the old bazars were pulled down and a spacious area known as Boddam bazar was laid out with wide roads which cross one another at right angles. At the same time the ditch in the middle of the town was pitched with stone and brick and carefully plastered, so as to make a capacious and easily cleansed main drain. The one bazar left was what is called the Bara Bazar and this is practically the only congested area. The surface drainage of a large part of the town has recently been completed by the Municipality and is working satisfactorily. The removal of night-soil and its trenching are effected in the ordinary fashion; but steps are being taken to improve it by increasing the number of depôts and trenching-grounds. The great drawback is the dependence of the town for its drinking water on wells scattered over the urban area; but an experiment is being made with the water in the sandy bed of the Konār river, and if the supply proves adequate in quantity and quality the town will have little to complain of in comparison with similar Indian municipalities.

Chatra town. Chatra has for the last thirty years been losing ground steadily, and expensive schemes of improvement are not suitable for its impoverished and decreasing population. The town is built along several main roads, and the great majority of the houses have the road in front and the open ground in the rear. There is therefore no congestion, and rural practices in sanitary matters are not so objectionable as would otherwise be the case. The principal concern of sanitary inspection in this town is to prevent the accumulation of rubbish and the growth of thick vegetation near the houses.

Giridih town. Giridih is a comparatively new town. In 1871 the branch railway line from Madhupur was made for the benefit of the coal mines and the present town grew up at the rail head, three miles from the important trade centre of Pachamba. It was made into a municipality in 1902 and at the present time is contemplating an extension of its boundaries which will absorb Pachamba. Its streets have been encroached on rather badly in the neighbourhood of the station road; but it has good natural drainage and the newer parts consist largely of bungalows with spacious compounds. The town is very healthy and is popular with Indians both for permanent residence and for temporary sojourn. Recently the water-supply has been improved by sinking a number of good wells, and there is reason to hope that a disused coal mine at Kuldiha will yield a copious supply of pure water which may make more ambitious schemes unnecessary.

Pachamba. Pachamba is a small but closely packed bazar with a large number of Mārwāri and Mahuri merchants, many of them prosperous but careless of all sanitary principles, whether indigenous or exotic. For some years an attempt was made to keep up an elementary system of sweeping and conservancy by voluntary association; but it has now broken down, and it is proposed to include the place in the municipality of Giridih.

Ichak. Ichak had close on 9,000 people in 1872 but now it has less than 5,000. The town came into existence as such when in 1772 the Rāmgarh Chief built his residence there, and logically it should have ceased to exist when the succession passed in 1867 to the branch of the family which resides at Padma. Much of it is packed between two parallel roads; and in the building and drainage of the houses the guiding principles, so far as they can be discerned, were to utilize the site to the utmost without regard to the convenience of neighbours, and to pass on to them both rain water and other drainage without regard to their health. At this late stage and in so much decay it is difficult to make any sanitary improvement at a reasonable cost.

Ordinary villages. There are a few large villages like Mirzāganj, Dhanwār, Chitarpur, Bagodar and Gola where houses are crowded together to some extent; but in the typical village there is no such concentration, and the ordinary dwelling has a border of *bāri* lands on two sides at least. The water-supply is generally obtained from wells; and for bathing and washing cooking pots *ahars* or tanks are usually available. The washing of clothes is ordinarily done in rivers or water-holes; but among the humbler classes scrupulous cleanliness of clothing is not conspicuous. The neighbouring field serves the purposes of a latrine, and the use for that purpose of the village paths is confined to small children and decrepit invalids. In more fastidious villages the sweepings and cow-dung are stored in deep holes outside the *basti*. A Sanitary Inspector is employed by the District Board to discourage the less desirable of the practices indicated above; and he usually obtains an assent to his arguments, which is merely intellectual. The suggestion to isolate small-pox patients is unsuccessful. It is only when cholera breaks out and he begins to disinfect the wells and clean up the village that he can rely on energetic support.

Wells. The District Board has in recent years spent large sums in making wells along the main roads at convenient intervals; and now that this task is fairly complete, it is somewhat difficult to select fresh sites. Comparatively few villages are lacking wells of a kind, though all welcome an addition.

Vaccination.

The average number of successful vaccinations for the ten years ending in March 1911 was 37·36 per thousand. In 1915-16 the number was 36·24 per thousand. Vaccination is compulsory in the municipalities and also in Padma, where opposition to the practice has hitherto been somewhat persistent.

MEDICAL INSTITUTIONS.

The Dublin University Mission maintains a large and well-equipped female hospital at Hazāribāgh, with two European lady doctors, two European lady nurses, and a staff of Indian nurses fully trained or undergoing training. There are beds for forty patients and a private ward for better class Indian in-patients. A grant-in-aid of Rs. 4,000 is made annually by Government.

The same Mission has a hospital at Chitarpur in Rāmgarh thana in the charge of a competent Indian doctor with in-door accommodation for thirty males and ten females. In 1915 there was a daily average of thirty in-patients and forty-two out-patients; and much valuable work was done, specially in eye cases.

There are also out-door dispensaries at Rāmgarh, Petarbār and Ichak, and an out-door dispensary for males only at Hazāribāgh.

The United Free Church of Scotland Mission has two main stations in the district at Pachamba and Tisri, which are usually in the charge of European Medical Missionaries, and it also employs a number of Indian assistants. The hospital at Pachamba is widely known among the Jain pilgrims; patients come for eye operations from as far afield as Rājputāna, and the hospital is more than self-supporting. The separate figures for Hazāribāgh district have not been communicated; but the four hospitals between them, including one in Monghyr, and another in Mānbhum, treated about 25,000 new patients in 1915 and performed 4,458 surgical operations of which 1,100 were cataract cases. The proprietor of Dhanwār has for some years past maintained a charitable dispensary at that place which renders very useful assistance to the local public. The East Indian Railway Company takes full charge of the medical as well as the sanitary requirements of its Giridih collieries, and its arrangements are very complete. At the new colliery at Bokāro similar arrangements have been made, and in that remote place the general public is permitted to obtain medicine and advice free of cost. The Kodarma Hospital Committee has provided a very efficient hospital, with excellent rooms for in-door patients, male and female. The daily average of in-door patients in 1915 was four and of out-door patients thirty-one. The total expenditure was Rs. 4,347, of which Rs. 1,402 were contributed by local mine-owners.

At Barhi a local committee manages a small hospital which was established in 1868. The expenditure in 1915 was Rs. 1,971, of which Rs. 675 were subscribed privately. The daily average was two in-door and fifty-two out-door patients.

At Tandwa the District Board has recently built a hospital, but it was not working in 1915. Of the three municipalities, Hazāribāgh and Chatra take the responsibility for financing their local hospitals, but Giridih has so far been satisfied with an annual subscription. The Hazāribāgh Municipal Hospital has forty-three beds, and had a daily average in 1915 of fifteen in-door patients and one hundred and nineteen out-door patients. The expenditure, largely on construction, was Rs. 14,475, of which the municipality contributed Rs. 3,667.

The Chatra Municipal Commissioners are engaged on a building scheme, for which large funds have been raised, which will provide a new hospital of a modern type. The municipality is not well off, but it provided Rs. 1,185 from its resources in 1915, and has made substantial provision in 1916 also. The new hospital will be in the charge of the Government Assistant Surgeon, and it will be a valuable addition to the medical resources of the district.

The Giridih Rattray Dispensary has been hampered by poverty, but had a daily average of eleven in-door and fifty out-door patients in 1915. It is not likely that the Municipal Commissioners will be content much longer to lag behind Hazāribāgh and Chatra in so important a matter as its town hospital, but will undertake financial responsibility for its maintenance in a state of efficiency.

The expenditure of the District Board on medical and sanitary objects has averaged Rs. 17,000, in the last three years, compared with Rs. 4,000 in the corresponding three years from 1903-04. The amount is large, but the medical requirements of the district are very great; and there is ample room for the building of new hospitals and dispensaries, and for the improvement of old ones.

CHAPTER VI.

AGRICULTURE.

Statistics. The following statistics are taken from the settlement report. They exclude the Kodarma Government estate and the municipalities, but include the rest of the district, amounting to 6,878 square miles. The conditions in Kodarma are similar to those in the neighbouring tracts north of the Barākar river, and the conclusions to be drawn from the settlement report need no modification when applied to the district as a whole. This area of 6,878 square miles was found to contain 2,019 square miles of land under cultivation. Regarding the remainder it is classified into land fit for cultivation and land unfit for cultivation; and this is often a matter in which opinions may differ. Be this as it may, there were 1,895 square miles recorded as fit for cultivation and 2,948 as uncultivable, 16 square miles being current fallow. The corresponding figures for Kodarma were 17, 30, 7 and 2 square miles; and the reserved forest adds another 50 square miles of uncultivable land. Altogether over 3,000 square miles are declared to be permanently unfit for cultivation, and though these are large figures the general appearance of the country bears them out.

Cultivated area. The cultivated area was distributed as follows between the various classes of land:—

—	—	Giridih.	Sedr.	Chatra.	District.
1	2	3	4	5	6
Wet cultivation.	Dhankhet 1 percentage	7·04	5·79	0·63	5·44
	" 2 "	10·54	9·47	3·93	8·09
	" 3 "	19·65	22·94	36·05	23·83
Dry cultivation.	Tanr I "	7·73	5·78	8·31	6·82
	" II "	36·11	27·40	17·74	28·85
	" III "	18·18	28·27	33·33	26·04
		99·25	99·65	99·99	99·07

The system of classification of cultivated lands is common to the high lands of Chota Nāgpur: it is based on the outstanding fact that the most profitable staple crop is rice, and that the best crops of rice can be grown only on wet land. To keep land wet for an adequate time it must be levelled, and enclosed with a sufficiently high rim or *ail* of earth. But not all lands, if so prepared, would retain sufficient moisture to grow rice. The rain which falls thereon from the sky would in itself be quite inadequate; and so it has to be supplemented with water from outside. This can be obtained, either by the natural surface fall from higher lands, combined with percolation, or by irrigation from reservoirs. As the latter accounts for only about 14,000 acres in the whole district it may be ignored for the present purpose.

Pioneering.

When an enterprising cultivator seeks to make for himself a new home in the jungles, his first consideration must be the presence of a perennial supply of water for drinking and cooking, and this is usually found in some tiny spring. The next requisite is a valley which can be made into rice land, and for this purpose he must avoid a stream too copious and impetuous, whilst seeking one which will assist him by bringing down a sufficient quantity of silt. This being found, he selects a well-drained site near the spring, generally the crest of a gentle ridge, and clears from it the jungle growth, and builds himself a house; and in the ashes of the clearing he grows crops of *gangai* and *kurthi*, and fences with sal saplings a small enclosure in which maize is planted. These upland crops are his support till the rice lands are ready. Meantime he is making a dam across the valley to intercept the streamlet, and retain its sediment; and when the bed of this reservoir has silted to the top of the dam he cuts a channel by its side which he borders with a raised ridge of earth. His first rice field is now ready, with a rich soil of jungle humus; and a second dam is made across the valley above or below to form a second field. This is repeated until the original bed of the stream is occupied by a series of rice fields: and by enclosing these with embankments sufficiently high and solid he can force the stream higher up the sides of the valley and make a new parallel line of rice fields on either side. If the stream in the rains is only moderate it can be distributed over this wide stretch of land without serious risk;

but if it is considerable, a channel must finally be left for it, cut deep down in the hill side, and if possible over a rocky bed which it cannot scour too deeply. So far the fields have been made largely from sediment; but when nothing more can be done in that way, he begins to carve into the hill sides with his mattock, and by the borders of his larger fields he makes small terraces which receive a scanty contribution of surface water from the ground above, and may perhaps be assisted from the large fields higher up the valley. When the work is completed there are large fields at the bottom, and narrow terraces rising from them on either side. The first are naturally fertile, but the second have to depend for their productivity mainly on the inherent qualities of the soil from which they have been carved. The lowest fields receive most water in the rains, and bear the kinds of rice which mature last and give the heaviest yield. The intermediate terraces are intermediate also in their moisture and their yield, the highest are poorest in both respects; and the natural classification is apparent to a casual observer, though he may confirm his opinion by ascertaining the kind of rice which the cultivator has been growing in the field.

Classification of terraced land.

Privileges of pioneers.

The labour, and the weary waiting, which are involved in the making of rice lands in the jungle will be readily understood; and local custom amply recognizes the deserts of the jungle clearer. The first founders are the *khuntkattidars* of the village, and hold on privileged terms: and those who come later are still entitled to great concessions for the *khandwat* which they prepare.

Causes of failure.

Sometimes in the jungles are found such valleys, cleared of vegetation, levelled and embanked, but abandoned. Perhaps a huge scar explains that the force of a violent flood has broken through the successive embankments and scoured out the rich beds, leaving a long trail of heavy gravel on either side below. Or the deer and wild boars have plundered the annual yield; or sickness and death have proved the malevolence of the local spirits; or the oppression of the landlord has deprived the pioneer of the fruits of his labour, and reduced him to despair.

Such is the process of jungle clearing as one sees it at the present time; and doubtless the old cultivation was won in the same manner by hard toil and the endurance of much lonely danger. The Lilājān and Sakri alone among the rivers of Hazāribāgh have been bountiful with the gift of alluvial valleys.

Upland classification.

The division of the uplands between three classes is determined largely by proximity to the dwelling-place. The ground immediately round the homestead is fenced in at the opening of the rains. Throughout the year it receives the ashes, and sometimes the drain water of the house, and before a crop is sown it is manured with cow-dung. Sometimes too the silt from the tank is used as manure. It is usually sown with maize; and if there is a well or tank at hand the fence is kept up all through the cold weather and a crop of rape-seed or vegetables is grown. This homestead land is called *bāri*, and is the first class of upland. Beyond the *bāris* and still well under the eyes of the owner though unfenced are the second-class lands, the *marua bāri*. They are manured and grow a crop of *marua* and *urid*, and sometimes gram later on. The more distant uplands, exposed to pilfering and grazing, grow a precarious crop of *surguja* or *kurthi* after intervals which may be as long as five years.

The six classes of cultivated land are known by the following names:—

A. *Don, dhankhet*, terraced or wet lands—

1st class,—*gahera* or *gaira, bahiār*, and if the land is perennially wet, *jobi*. The total area is 70,366 acres.

2nd class,—*kanāli, dorāsa, kandi, singha*, and *gogri*. The area is 116,483 acres.

3rd class,—*baid* or *bād, tarkha, sāthin*, or *tānrkhet*. The area is 308,497 acres.

B. Uplands, *tanr*, dry cultivation. (*Tanr* as used in Hazāribāgh is more properly confined to the 3rd class.)

1st class,—*bāri, gharbāri*. (In this class are also included the few plots of land on the level of a river bed which grow sugarcane. They are called *tari kudar* or *pal*.)

The total area is 83,364 acres.

2nd class,—*marua bāri, chira bāri, bahir bāri* or *bhita*. The area is 373,435 acres.

3rd class,—*tanr*. The area is 337,146 acres.

CROP STATEMENT.

It is customary to divide the annual yield of agriculture between the *bhadai, aghani* and *rabi* harvests. In Hazāribāgh, however, the main crop is rice, grown in the terraced lands, of which the reaping is continuous from the end of October to early December, so that no clear distribution can be made between *bhadai* and *aghani*. It is least misleading to assign the 3rd class rice lands to the Bhado season and the 1st and 2nd to Agahan.

The combined area of the first two classes is 186,849 acres; and the winter rice crop may be taken to amount in a normal year to 1,636,000 maunds of clean rice or an average of 1·3 maunds per head of the district population. The 3rd class rice lands produce on an average 1,480,000 maunds of clean rice, or 1·1 maunds per head.

Rice (*gora*) is grown also on the uplands in the south of the district on an average annual net area of 5,716 acres. It is rather coarse, but it ripens early and is reaped at the end of September. In Ranchi it is an important crop, and the first new rice on sale in the Hazāribāgh market is *gora* rice imported from that district.

Gondli (*Panicum miliare*) occupies a net area of 67,378 acres. It is sown on 3rd class *tāar* which are fairly level and free from stones and has the great merit of ripening early in September. By the poorer classes of cultivators in the south the *gondli bhāt* is eagerly awaited, as it heralds the season of comparative plenty. The next important crop to mature is maize (80,795 acres), of which the cultivation is spread evenly over the whole district. Then follows *marua* (*Eleusine coracana*—53,919 acres) of which one variety is plucked in October, and another six weeks later. *Urid* (*Phaseolus mungo*—11,000 acres), *barāi mung* (*Phaseolus radiatus*) and *ghangra* (*Vigna catjang*) ripen about this same time, along with *kodo* (*Paspalum scrobiculatum*); and next the terraced rice lands are reaped. *Bajra* (*Pennisetum typhoeideum*—7,303 acres) and *gangai* (*Sorghum vulgare*—2,253 acres) are also harvested about November.

Kurthi (*Dolichos biflorus*), *masuri* (*lens esculenta*), *khesāri* (*Lathirus sativus*) and gram (*Cicer arietinum*—11,921 acres) ripen in January or February, and barley (11,591 acres) and wheat (5,427 acres) in February or March. Varieties of *rahar* are cut from

December to April. Potatoes (1,292 acres) are ripe from December to February and yams (560 acres) in February.

The area under the food-crops which has not been separately shown above is 168,355 acres. The total area of food-crops other than terraced rice is 427,403 acres, and the average outturn of these heterogeneous crops is extremely difficult to conjecture. If it is roundly assumed that three maunds an acre is the average the yield of 1,282,209 maunds of cleaned food-grain is equivalent to 1·2 maunds per head. At four maunds it would be 1·6 maunds. The rice crop from the terraced lands was calculated to be 2·4 maunds and the total district production of food-grains may perhaps be taken to vary between 3·6 and 4 maunds or between 6½ and 7 chitaks a day per head of the population.

The non-food-crops are linseed (17,032 acres), *til* (6,628 acres, *surguja* (31,914 acres) and other oil-seeds (55,701 acres). The latter are probably mainly rape and *colza* (*lotni* and *sarso*) which have taken the place of poppy for paying the rent.

Spices cover 3,267, cotton 1,092, other fibres 1,607, tea 81 and tobacco 407 acres.

The outturn per acre depends on the water-supply, the soil, the manures, and the character of the cultivation, after which the quality of the seed comes into play. FACTORS IN PRODUCTIVITY.

The rainfall has been described in Chapter 4, where the importance of its distribution has been duly emphasized. Cultivators time their operations according to the rising of various asterisms. The following list of those which are of agricultural importance has been supplied by Babu Bisheshvar Mukharji, the Government Pleader of Hazāribāgh, to whom a large part of the contents of this chapter are due:—

Kritika (Kartik)	... Pleiades	... 10th May 1916.
Rohan	... Aldebaran	... 24th ,, ,,
Mirgisra	... Orionis 1	... 7th June ,,
Adra	... Orionis A	... 24th ,, ,,
Punarbāsa	... Gemini	... 5th July ,,
Pukh	... Cancri D	... 19th ,, ,,
Aslesa	... Cancri A	... 2nd August ,,
Magaha (Singha)	... Regulus	... 16th ,, ,,
Purba	... Leonis D	... 30th ,, ,,
Utra (Kana)	... Leonis 1	... 12th September
Hasta	... Corvi	... 20th ,,
Chitra	... Spica	... 19th October
Sewāti	... Arcturus	... 23rd ,,

In Rohan the rice fields which have been prepared for the broadcast crop are sown, and seed beds are prepared for the transplanted area. If rain falls maize and *marua* are sown. In Mirgisra *gondli* is sown. The land should be cultivated very finely and reduced to powder, and be dry at the time of sowing. In Adra maize, *marua*, *gondli*, early *urid* and *bārāi* are sown. The transplantation of paddy may begin in Pukh and must end in Singha. In Purba, *kurthi*, late *urid*, *surguja*, and *til* are sown. In Hathia gram is sown. In Chitra *sarso*, *lotni*, gram, wheat and barley are sown.

It follows that rain towards the end of May is good for the broadcast rice, maize and *marua*. Towards the end of June it is needed for the upland *bhadai* crops, and heavy rain is necessary in July for transplanting *marua*. For transplanting rice the limits are the middle of July and the end of August; but in the latter case it is necessary for the rains to continue till the middle of October, and this will embarrass the reaping of the *bhadai* crops, and the sowing of the *rabi* crops. The Christmas rains are desirable for the rape seed and other *rabi* crops.

Irrigation. "Except in Gāwan, Sātgāwan and Hunterganj, where the riparian villages are irrigated from the Sakri and Lilājān rivers, there is no irrigation in the district except from *ahars* and wells. Irrigation from wells is confined to cultivation within the *bāri* lands adjacent to the village site, and to sugarcane. Irrigation from *ahars* is confined to the lower rice lands which are classed as *dhankhet* 1 and 2. The total area of land benefited directly by irrigation is 13,872 acres, which represents only 1·07 per cent of the cultivated area." (Settlement Report.)

The soil. Geologically the district is almost entirely Archaean, with isolated areas, chiefly in the Dāmodar valley, of Gondwana rocks, and the surface soil is the débris which has resulted from the decomposition of these rocks accompanied by most severe denudation. Where a stream has cut a deep bed in the soil this is usually seen to contain layers of boulders or bands of heavy gravel, showing how the lower-placed rocks after denudation have been covered afresh by materials washed down from higher ground. Only in the valleys of the Lilajān and Sakr is the gradient so low as to allow of the regular deposit of lighter sediment; for the greater part of the district the soil is composed of infertile débris, much of which is still in process of disintegration. The local classification of natural unimproved soils is given by Babu Bisheshvar Mukharji as follows :—

1. *Kewal*. These are lands of dark grey colour, and are naturally the most fertile in the district.

2. *Lālki māti*, or red soil, is a ferruginous loam and is most common in the district.

3. *Dudhia māti* is a white soil, the colour of which is due to excess of lime; by the addition of cow-dung and leaf mould it can be made fit for cultivation.

4. *Kankraili mati* is gravel or calcareous soil.

5. *Kāri māti* is black cotton soil, not uncommon in Gola, Karanpura and Ahuri. It has to be distinguished by the cultivator from another black soil which is gritty and worthless.

6. *Nagra* and *rekra* are names for the most inferior kinds of soil which cannot be improved by aeration or manuring.

When soils have been exposed to artificial improvement by cultivation they are locally known as—

1. *Kewal* as above.

2. *Gori mati* is the name given both to *lalki* and *dudhia* which have been aerated and heavily manured. The colour is changed to a greyish shade.

3. *Pondri* or *bhusri* is the final stage in the improvement of *gori*. It is sufficiently adhesive to be used for plastering walls.

4. *Maguhya* is used generally for good improved soil. It means as good as in Magaha (Gaya), from which country many of the Hindus originally came.

In most places wood is sufficiently abundant to allow of the use of cow-dung for manure. It is not ordinarily burnt, as is the practice in Rānchi. The common sweepings and ashes of the house are thrown on the *bāri* lands, and the house drainage usually finds its way there or to the neighbouring *chira* fields. Sometimes the terraced lands intended for rice nurseries are covered with cow-dung or sal branches, which are set on fire when dry. But the general impression left on the observer is that there is far too much waste of possible manures. For example, an abundance of leaves is usually obtainable, but the Manures.

same use is not made of this source of fertility as elsewhere. Artificial and mineral manures are unknown.

Seed.

So far there has been no attempt to improve seed by artificial selection; and there is no doubt that the higher price of seed so improved would prove a great obstacle to its general use.

Implements.

The implements now in use appear to be exactly the same as they were forty years ago when the Statistical Account was prepared, and it is scarcely necessary to repeat the list then given. The small size of the unit of cultivation is all against the economic employment of western implements, even if the first cost were not prohibitive, and the ordinary pair of oxen had the requisite strength to use them. The typical holding is the reverse of compact. Each raiyat usually has some portion of every class of land, and even that portion is not usually compact in the '*chuk.*' This fact is apparent from the number of separate plots, which in one season averaged 1,117 for every 640 acres, and that too after taking into account the large plots of jungle. For the district as a whole they averaged 786 per square mile. The plot often consists of more than one '*kiari,*' which is the unit of rice cultivation: and these latter are sometimes so small that the oxen can scarcely find room to turn within them.

Cattle.

Then the oxen are generally very feeble. Babu Bisheshvar Mukharji complains that the cultivator begins by buying the cheapest cattle obtainable, and these he feeds on grass so long as grazing is possible, and on leaves in the jungle during the hot weather. Straw lasts barely six months, and the raiyat will not trouble to chop it up for them. The milk cattle are similarly neglected, and it is a common practice among the Goālas to allow female calves to die for want of nourishment, and this great source of food is practically lost to the district. After struggling through the hot weather as best they may, the plough cattle are naturally unequal to the strain of anything but the merest scratching of the surface by a light plough, often guided by the feeble hands of a boy. Another result of the dispersal of the lands which make up the holding, and the excessive cost of fencing all but the *baris*, is the impracticability of independent action. The universal custom is that, when a crop has been cleared from a field, pasturage is open to all: and so each cultivator is compelled to grow the same crops as his neighbours, and at the same time. If they are left on the ground after those of his neighbours have been removed they are at the mercy of the cattle which by then are turned loose in the village. Only the Koiris have met the difficulty successfully. They build a high wall of earth round their land, dig one or more shallow wells, and grow irrigated garden crops till late into the hot weather.

Agricultural calendar.

The agricultural calendar of the year is as follows, according to Babu Bisheshvar Mukharji :—

Month.	Field work.	Subsidiary tasks.	Social occupations.
1	2	3	4
Chait 2nd half (March and April).	Ploughing *bari* lands in case of *rain*.	Collecting the *mahua* flowers. The ground must be kept clear beneath the trees.	
Baisākh (April and May).	Ditto ...	Drying the *mahua* in the sun, collecting edible roots, repairing houses, burning manure on the rice nurseries, cutting wood for fencing the *baris*.	Marriages.
Jeth (May and June).	Sowing seeds in the Rohan asterism for seedlings, and broadcast sowings in the terraces.	Repairing roofs ...	Ditto.
Asārh (June and July).	Sowing paddy seeds, *gondli*, *ghangra*, early *urid*, *rahar*, *marua* seedlings, maize, *barai*, beans to grow on fences, and pumpkins on the roofs.	Repairing rice-fields and weeding maize.	
Sāwan (July and August).	Transplantation of rice and *marua* seedlings.	Repairing rice-fields and weeding maize.	
Bhādo (August and September).	Transplantation of paddy, sowing *til*, beans, *kurthi*, late *urid*, *surguja*, harvesting maize, *barai*, *gondli* and early *urid*.	Weeding paddy-fields ...	*Jhumar* (dances and songs at night).
Āsin (September and October).	Sowing *surguja*, harvesting *gondli*, sowing gram, rape and colza.	Extending the terraced fields and making new terraces.	Quarrels followed by panchayats and litigation, consulting *deoklis* (witch-finders).

Month.	Field work.	Subsidiary tasks.	Social occupations.
1	2	3	4
Kārtik (October and November).	Sowing gram, rape, *colza*. Harvesting early rice.	Making *machāns* for straw.	
Agahan (November and December).	Harvesting late rice.		
Pus (December and January).	Pressing sugarcane.		
Māgh (January and February).	Pressing sugarcane, planting sugarcane, harvesting gram and barley, ploughing the rice-fields for broadcast sowing.		
Phālgun (February and March).	Harvesting barley and wheat and ploughing.	Cutting wood for fuel, *kher* for thatching, and building earth walls.	Marriages (after Phālgun badi 14th).
Chait, first half (March).	Harvesting barley and wheat.	Cutting wood for fuel and for repairing houses.	

It will be noticed that this calendar prescribes the month of Asin as appropriate for quarrelling and mischief-making generally. There is by then a reasonable abundance of food, and the severe labour of the rice cultivation is over, so that the season is opportune for pursuits that are by no means completely neglected during the remaining eleven months of the year.

Daily routine.

The same observer has prepared the following daily routine of the small cultivator:—

A. *Cultivation season*—

From 2 a.m. to 4 p.m. buffaloes are taken out to graze (*melan kholna*). Bullocks are usually taken out at sunrise.

7 to 10 a.m.—Ploughing.

10 a. m.—*Bhunja jalpān* or breakfast. As fried grain is usually eaten it is called *bhunja*. But gruel (*ghatta*) of maize, or cakes of *marua* are also taken.

10-30 a. m. to 12—Ploughing.

12 to 1 p. m.—Midday meal of maize gruel.

Afternoon—Fields and *ails* are repaired and fences made. Weeding and transplanting go on all day long.

7 to 8 p.m.—*Biāri*, or night meal, consisting of boiled rice if there is a stock of paddy. Otherwise *chikas* is eaten, i.e., marua and maize flour. After the *gondli* is cut it is boiled and served with vegetables, such as beans.

8 to 9 p.m.—Recreation—ordinarily repeating the events of the day or resuming the quarrels which through pressure of work could not be finished earlier in the day.

After 9 p.m.—Sleep. But in good seasons with a full *bhadoi* crop, and a promising crop of paddy, *jhumar* (songs and group dancing) is indulged in. Though the party usually consists of Bhuiyas, Dusādhs and Chamārs all castes encourage it, especially employers of *kamias* (serfs).

B. *Other seasons*—

5 to 6 a.m.—Taking out cattle to graze.

7 to 10 a.m.—Ploughing, if there has been rain.

10 a.m.—*Bhunja* (breakfast).

12—Midday meal.

12 to 6 a.m.—Intriguing, quarrelling, seeing landlords and landlords' agents.

7 to 8 p.m.—Evening meal.

8 to 9 p.m.—Quarrels and intrigues.

This daily programme is of course varied by frequently recurring festivals, by a weekly visit to the nearest market, and by domestic occurrences which usually involve at least the compensation of a meal above the average in quantity and quality.

Character of the cultivator.

Regarding the better class of cultivators, such as Koiris, Sokiārs, Suuris and Bābhans, Babu Bisheshvar Mukharji considers that they have an instinctive knowledge of things best suited for their purposes. They are skilful to select the best places for their *ahars* and *pāins* (reservoirs and irrigation channels). "They are ignorant of scientific discoveries, but the knowledge handed down by the practical experience of centuries does not leave them far behind in the art of agriculture. If they are not aware of the fact that *ghangra* has root nodules which carry nitrogen from the atmosphere to the soil, that does not affect their practice, as they know all the same that *ghangra* fertilizes the soil. They do not know that pulses of all kinds should be sown on newly-reclaimed lands, but they begin fertilizing by sowing *kurthi* seeds. They are not aware of the virtues of aeration, but they recognize the value of early ploughing, and exposing the ploughed fields during the hot weather."

This is not, on the whole, a very pleasing picture of the condition of agriculture in the district. But it has to be remembered that hitherto the peasant has had no real security, either in respect of his tenancy or in the matter of rent. The sheep grows its fleece again heedless of the future shearing, and the bees collect their honey without taking thought of the spoiler; but the peasant has in the past been sufficiently intelligent to doubt the wisdom of improving his lands solely for another's benefit. In Rānchi the settlement has created a new desire for improvement in the cultivators; and the magic of property may have the same effect in Hazāribāgh.

Improvement of agriculture.

It is difficult to see where any fundamental alterations in the agricultural methods of the district are likely to be made. That better results can be obtained even in present conditions is demonstrated by the Koiri cultivators; but the ordinary peasant is more ready to supplement his income by temporary emigration to the collieries, or Calcutta, where every one else is kept hard at work, than by voluntary persistence in similar toil in his own village. The physical peculiarities make grandiose schemes of irrigation impracticable, and without a reliable supply of water large areas which at first sight appear to be suitable for reclamation are by the texture of their soil so arid that they have been left aside. For example, from Pitij to Gidhaur, as a base, with Chatra as the apex, the enclosed triangle is fairly level but to a large extent waste in consequence of this aridity. Moreover, even if the higher reaches of the larger rivers could be dammed, the broken nature of the lower lands would make the work of distribution expensive, and the labour of levelling excessive. The area which even the largest *akars* can command is small, and they are unreliable because they depend for their store of water on the current season's rainfall. Altogether the prospects of any serious addition to the cultivated area by works of irrigation are not bright.

District statistics.

Total area in acres...	...	...	4,471,132 = 6,986	sq. miles.
Forests ...	...	...	2,524,590 = 3,945	"
Not available for cultivation (1)		...	365,298 = 571	"
Cultivable waste (other than fallow)		...	263,263 = 416	"
Current fallow (2)...	...	...	343,497 = 599	"
Net cropped area ...	...	...	931,542 = 1,455	"

(1) This area is exclusive of forest lands unfit for cultivation. If these be added, the total area permanently unfit for cultivation is 3,004 square miles.

(2) Current fallow includes—

(*a*) Land ordinarily cultivated each year but left uncultivated in the year of record.

(*b*) "It is the custom of the district to leave *tanr* lands fallow from time to time. The cycle of years according to which the lands are cropped has been recorded in the case of each field, and reckoning made accordingly. Thus a field of three acres only cropped once in three years, will appear as three acres in the gross column and as one acre in the net column." The balance of two acres is shown above as current fallow.

CHAPTER VII.

NATURAL CALAMITIES.

Income of the district.

It has been calculated in Chapter VI that in an average year the outturn of food-grains is made up of 1·1 maunds per head from the autumn terraced rice, 1·3 maunds per head from the winter terraced rice and from 1·2 to 1·6 maunds from the rest of the food-crops, according as the average outturn is taken to be three or four maunds. A large but indefinite income is derived from non-food-crops. The other serious income of the district is obtained from the following sources:—Mahua, lac, hides, jungle produce, service abroad and local mining and manufactures.

Mahua.

No reliable estimate can be made of the quantity of mahua which is collected in an ordinary year. In the record-of-rights such trees as grow in the cultivated lands and in the smaller wastes are recorded, though no total is made; but such as are in the jungle are not entered. There is no accurate knowledge of the amount of dried flowers or of fruit which an ordinary tree will produce in an average year; the crop is, however, very irregular. The buds begin to swell from the beginning of March, and from that time till the end of April, when the fall ceases, rain is undesirable, as it prevents the ripening of the buds and sometimes completely stops their development. With ordinary fortune, however, the mahua flower contributes very materially to the income of the people; and it has been conjectured that it makes an addition of two months' food, an estimate which must be far too high for any but specially-favoured tracts. Whatever it may be, it is as liable to fail as any ordinary field crop.

Lac.

There is equal uncertainty regarding the outturn and value of lac. In the first place, it is grown only in the Dāmodar valley, east of Rāmgarh, and in the west of the Chatra subdivision, the principal markets being at Chatra and Gola. Secondly, an exaggerated idea appears to prevail regarding the profits of lac cultivation. The fact that hundreds of thousands of *parās* trees are annually left vacant is in itself sufficient to indicate that there are grave drawbacks. The insect is very susceptible to disease, and sometimes the crop over an extensive tract is an almost complete failure. Moreover, prices fluctuate within very wide limits, and the dealers sometimes can afford to pay only a price which discourages the cultivators. Again, the cultivation is very irksome, owing to the necessity of watching the trees constantly in order to prevent theft. These objections go far to explain the lukewarm attitude of the people to the trade even in the tracts where lac is freely grown.

Hides and skins.

Most cattle die of disease or old age and owners rarely cause them to be killed: the price of the hide is therefore not so much a source of profit as a slight alleviation of misfortune. Goats are in a different position in this respect, and owners can make some sort of calculation of their profits in advance. The agricultural stock statement of the district as compiled during the Settlement operations (1908—1915) was as follows:—

Cows	212,277
Bullocks	213,881
Calves	171,903
Bulls	9,187
Total ...	607,248
Buffalo Cows	31,088
„ bullocks	71,681
„ Calves	26,887
„ Bulls	12,895
Total ...	142,551
Sheep	34,009
Goats	217,642
Total ...	251,651

The average duration of life of a goat must be very small; but sheep are rarely killed for food.

Jungle produce.

It is entirely impossible to estimate the food supplies and other products of value obtained from the jungles in an ordinary year, and still more so in a year of distress. There appears to be a general consensus that it is considerable; but the estimate of Mr. Ball, made in 1867, that throughout Hazāribāgh a considerable number of the poorer classes depend solely upon the jungle to supply them with the means of subsistence, for from two to three months of every year is probably not applicable to present conditions. Even in 1867 the jungles of Hazāribāgh did not extend into the north Barākar basin, and there are now large areas where what remains is of a character likely to yield very little of value. The domestic economy of the poor is not easy to learn even in ordinary times; but still it appears to be safe to say that where the jungle is abundant the supplement to ordinary food can be considerable in case of need.

Service abroad.

The income of the district which is derived from service abroad is difficult to ascertain because most emigrants are absent only for about six months in the year, and prefer to bring back their savings on their persons. The post offices of the district in the year 1915-16 paid money orders for Rs. 13,93,148 and issued money orders for Rs. 13,94,062. If these figures correctly include all transactions with other districts, wages earned abroad are not ordinarily remitted home by money order.

Local mines and manufactures.

Mica provides work for a small number of under-ground workers and a considerably larger number of women and children, who are employed to split the mineral. Altogether about 9,000 people are believed to obtain work. The mines are mostly in Kodarma and Gāwān thanas, but much of the splitting is done elsewhere, where labour is more easily obtainable, as at Giridih and Arkhango. The coal mines at Giridih employ about 9,000 workers, with a large body of dependants; but the employés in the Bokāro field are mainly immigrants without children. There are no other industries of importance.

Importance of the terraced rice.

This survey of the resources of the cultivating and landless classes discloses an excessive dependence in all but a few areas on the outturn of the crop of rice grown on the terraced lands. In the comparatively small valleys of the Lilājān and Sakri rivers the *rabi* crops are perhaps of more importance than the rice; and the mica industry affords protection to the remainder of Gāwān and to north Kodarma; but the rest of the district must have recourse to temporary emigration in case the rice crop fails, and this step is practically restricted to male adults. Irrigation is confined to about 14,000 acres, and the outturn of the terraced lands is annually dependent on the amount and distribution of the rains. These lands are either sown broadcast, or are planted from seed grown in nurseries. The former lands should, if possible, be ploughed in January or February; but the latter can wait until they are wet or even submerged, immediately before transplantation. With the rising of Rohan towards the end of May the broadcast rice must be sown in the terraces and the nurseries must be planted; and if there is rain the maize and *marua* are also sown. Light rains and an early and light monsoon favour these latter and other *bhadai* crops, and a heavy downpour is not needed till the middle of July or even the end of that month. When it arrives transplantation of the *marua* and rice seedlings is pushed on; and as the plants are weak from that operation they are in special need of good rain for a few days after. Right through September rain should fall at such intervals and in such quantities that the terraces will remain submerged, yet not so heavily and continuously as to break the *ails* or prevent the pollination of the *bhadai* crops and, later on, their harvesting. If, after this, the Hathiya rains fall in the first week in October and then cease, the maize and *marua* and other *bhadai* crops will be good, the rice crop will be full, and the soil will be fit to cultivate for the sowing of the *rabi* crops.

The ideal programme of the rains.

From this perfect programme the departure which causes most serious loss is the postponement of transplantation till the end of August and the cessation of the rains early in September. A break at that precise stage cannot be remedied for the third-class rice by subsequent rainfall. The *bhadai* crops, on the other hand, require light but fairly frequent rain till the beginning of August. If there is no rain in Rohan sowings are delayed and heavy rain in July will cause very great loss. A poor *bhadai* harvest is usually due to excessive rain in July.

Causes of crop failures.

The *rabi* crops are sown in October or early November; and rain continued till the end of October prevents the proper cultivation of the soil, and sowings cannot be made in sodden ground. They require one or two showers in the interval between the blade and the ear, but rain during flowering is very injurious.

The mahua crop dislikes rain in March, which often has the effect on a tree of completely stopping the development of the flower buds.

Famine and Scarcity. The rainfall in 1908 was as follows :—

April.	May.	June.	July.	August.	September.	October.
·66	·60	14·14	6·55	18·36	9·16	Nil.

1908. It will be obvious that transplantation was very late, and as the rains stopped abruptly after the first week of September the plants in their new soil never had a chance of thriving except in the lowest fields. The *bhadai* crops were drowned by the excessive rain of June and the *rabi* crops could not be sown for lack of moisture. The mahua crop did badly; and whilst the local outturn of lac was poor prices were very low. The worst tracts were thanas Barkāgāon, Simaria, Chatra and Hazāribāgh. The maximum number on test-works was about 1,000 and on gratuitous relief 5,000. Expenditure from public funds was, works, Rs. 10,400, food, Rs. 39,800, and *takavi* loans, Rs. 3,53,800. That in spite of these figures, there was very real distress, is proved by the vital statistics. The average death-rate is 32 per 1,000, and the average birth-rate is 47 per 1,000. In 1908 these rates were 53·8 and 37·1 respectively ; or, in other words, an average gain of 15 per thousand became a loss of 16·7 per thousand, and that calculated on the population not merely of the affected tracts, but of the entire district. The diminution in the birth-rate naturally continued into 1909, when it was 39·1 per thousand. Six people per thousand died of cholera.

1897. The next preceding year of distress was 1897. The rainfall at the sadr station in 1896-7 was as follows :—

April.	May.	June.	July.	August.	Sept.	Oct.	Nov.	Dec.	Jan.	Feb.	Mar.
0·15	1·60	11·00	13·12	9·30	8·10	0	0·25	0·59	0·28	2·16	2·01

The excessive rain in June was harmful to the *bhadai* crops, and the rather heavy rain in July increased the damage. The rice crop was injured by the insufficient fall in August, and the cessation of the monsoon by the middle of September made a poor outturn inevitable; and as it followed on a 10-anna crop in the previous year, local stocks of rice were very deficient. The absence of rain in October prevented the sowing of the *rabi* crop, and storms in March severely damaged the mahua.

Finally the lac crop was poor and prices unduly low. The tracts most seriously affected were Chaupāran, Barhi, Bagodar, Kodarma, Gumia, Māndu and Hazāribāgh. The price of rice rose to six seers a rupee against a normal price of 17 seers. The maximum number of workers was 2,152 and of gratuitous recipients 7,815; and expenditure was Rs. 73,000 from Government funds and Rs. 39,000 from charitable funds. Rs. 51,000 were advanced as *takavi* loans. The birth and death-rates were both adversely affected to a serious extent.

The information about the distress of 1874 is meagre. The rainfall of 1873 was as follows:— 1874.

April.	May.	June.	July.	August.	September.	October.
0·50	0·46	3·35	22·80	17·85	9·06	0·0

In the absence of more definite information about the distribution of the rain within weekly periods it is impossible to explain what happened. The *bhadai* crops must have failed, as they would be drowned out in July. The outturn is said to have been 4 annas. The rice crop is said to have been 8 annas, and this indicates an early cessation in September. *Rabi* was from 3 to 8 annas. The mahua crop was very good in 1874. No gratuitous relief was given. The highest number of workers was 16,303. The cash expenditure locally was Rs. 1,69,210, and in addition 1,261 tons of grain were imported at a cost of Rs. 1,70,235.

Since 1908 communications have been improved in the south of the district by the opening of the Rāmgarh-Bokāro Railway, the building of the Dāmodar bridge at Rāmgarh and the improvement of the Gola-Jhālda road. Between Chatra and the Railway the road has now only one gap unbridged and is metalled throughout. No tract is now liable to serious danger of isolation for more than a day or two. Local prices of food-grains are no longer determined by purely local conditions. Temporary emigration is on the increase, and local scarcity will doubtless swell its volume even more than on past occasions, with a consequent difficulty in gauging distress by test-works. Probably *takavi* loans coupled with a small amount of gratuitous relief will be sufficient to cope with the modified scarcity which alone is to be expected. The period of distribution should, however, be carefully selected. For buying plough bullocks Present conditions.

February is the latest opportunity, and for seed the end of April. The cattle must do much of their ploughing, if possible, in February; and most of the seed must be sown in Rohan (May-June).

Famine work programmes.

Elaborate programmes of famine relief works are in readiness; but it is improbable that they will ever be used. Adult male labour will wish to seek the coalfields; and private employment on productive work of that character is obviously preferable to state-managed employment on *bandhs* and roads.'

Floods.

The physical configuration of Hazāribāgh confers on the district immunity from floods, but makes it a source of danger to its neighbours. Excessive rain in Gāwān in September 1896 caused a flood in the Nawāda Subdivision of Gayā in which 34 people were drowned and 2,000 houses destroyed, while much rich land was made permanently useless by a heavy deposit of sand. Similarly, on the 8th of August 1913, heavy rain fell in the Dāmodar basin, and the rain gauge at Rāmgarh recorded 6·12 inches. The flood exceeded all previous experiences and the design of the bridge then under construction was revised. Beyond the district this flood caused extensive damage in the coalfields and lower down its course. An arrangement has since been made for giving timely information direct from Rāmgarh by telegram to the Collector of Bānkura in case five inches are measured in one day or eight in forty-eight hours, or if the water rises to a black band on the seventh pier 16 feet above the bed of the river.

Other calamities.

In respect of other natural calamities the district is comparatively immune. Locusts are not unknown, but they have so far done little damage. Earthquakes have been felt but buildings have not been destroyed; and even forest fires are small and unimportant.

CHAPTER VIII.

RENTS, WAGES AND PRICES.

Rents.

THE Hazāribāgh settlement was practically completed in 1915, and exact knowledge about the rents of the district has now been obtained for the first time. Prior to the settlement most cultivating tenancies were harassed, if not with dues, at least with demands, of a character which obscured the real burden of rent to the raiyat; and one of the chief objects of that settlement was to commute all praedial conditions and services, otherwise known as *abwāb* and *begāri*, into a cash equivalent which was consolidated with the rent. The history of these *abwāb* presents to the spectator, if not to the raiyat, a definitely humorous side; and students of the local civilization may with profit grope in the landlords' *jamabandis*, as in a Scandinavian kitchen-midden, for evidence of progressive culture in Chota Nāgpur. The first step in social progress was the keeping of a horse, if not for riding yet to be led at weddings, and this is duly registered by the cess of *ghora dānā*. With promotion to Hinduism and probably also to Rājputism, came the pilgrimage to Mathura or even further afield, and the promise of an annual contribution, which was forthwith embodied in a new *abwāb*. Usually, however, the custodians of these sacred shrines preferred the solid certainty of a grant of villages. The purchase of an elephant is indicated by the appearance of *hathi chāul;* and though the one and only elephant died, and was never replaced, the *abwāb* remained for a proof to the incredulous that the family had really at some time owned an elephant. The student will fix with approximate accuracy the date of the foundation of the district hospital by the "*aspatal ka chānda*", and the invention of the singing machine by the *gramophonāi*. With the passing of the Tenancy Act in 1908 the record ends abruptly; and the district has been deprived of the distinction of a *motokart-ka chānda*.

Abwāb and begāri.

Prohibition of new praedial conditions.

In addition to the abolition of existing praedial conditions and services it has been illegal since 1908 to create a new tenancy to which liability of *abwāb* and *begāri* are attached; and contravention of the law forbidding these services is punishable by a very heavy penalty. But the initiative in such cases must be taken by the aggrieved tenant, and this presupposes the existence of a degree of self-confidence which, in the opinion of the Settlement Officer, cannot yet be presumed with safety. He would accordingly assimilate the procedure in such cases to that which is prescribed for failure to give receipts for rent paid.

Danger of illicit restoration of *begari*.

There is no doubt that great care will be required to prevent the re-establishment of *begāri* for purposes of cultivation, a danger which is intimately connected with the position of the landless labourers discussed below.

Crop-cutting experiments.

The classification of land has been described in the chapter on agriculture. The classes differ very considerably not only in respect of their productiveness but also in their reliability; and it may perhaps be doubted whether crop-cutting experiments are so conducted as to give due emphasis to the latter factor, as they are ordinarily made in normal years only. There has been no continuous record of the produce of typical areas over even a brief term of years; and it is probable that such a record would considerably depreciate the credit of third-class rice lands. These are certain to fare badly in those years when the September rains cease at the middle of the month; and this usually happens two years in five.

Relative outturn of the six classes.

The crop-cutting experiments made during the course of settlement, together with careful inquiries regarding the value of upland crops, led to the adoption of the following estimate of average outturn and comparative value :—

	Mds.	srs.	ch.			Ratio.
Rice, first-class	21	32	2	...	...	25
„ second-class	14	32	4	...	...	18
„ third-class	9	24	8	...	...	12
Upland, first-class ...			...	...	...	25
„ second-class			...	...	...	6
„ third-class			...	...	...	2

The outturn is in *pakka* maunds of paddy, and is approximately double the amount of clean rice which would be obtained.

Cash-rents.

With the exception of the Government estates and Dhanwār, rents throughout the district are not based on classification, but are what are known as lump rents. It is often necessary, as in the case of land acquisition proceedings, to ascertain the rent which should be paid for a portion only of the tenancy; and the method by which this is done is explained in the following extract from the Settlement Report :—

"In the Rāmgarh area there are no recognized pargana or thana or estate rates of rent, and no standard rates of any sort. Accordingly, in order to determine the first question, whether the rents of a village or holding are relatively high or low, the Revenue Officer had first to ascertain what is the general rate of rent in the area treated. To do this he fixed after inquiry a table of multiple values of the various classes of land, as compared with third class *tānr*. Thus in thana Rāmgarh the relative values of the classes of land are :— Method of distribution of lump rents.

Dhānkhet.			Tānr.		
1	2	3	I	II	III
16	10	8	16	2	1

The total area of cultivated raiyati lands of all classes is reduced in accordance with this table to units of one acre of *tānr* III; and the rent paid for the lands is divided by the total number of units, and the existing unit rate of the village is thus ascertained. Having ascertained the unit rates of all the villages of the thana, the Revenue Officer examines them to find out the prevailing village rate, following the definition contained in section 31 (A) of the Bengal Tenancy Act. This prevailing rate is called the 'thana rate'. Unit rate. Thana rates.

The following are the thana rates so ascertained :—

Name of Thana and Police-station.	Terraced rice land.			Uplands.		
	1	2	3	I	II	III
	Rs. a. p.	Rs. a. p.	Rs. a. p.	Rs. a. p.	Rs. a. p.	Rs. a. p.
Hazāribāgh Sadr	3 12 0	2 5 6	1 14 0	3 12 0	0 7 6	0 3 9
" Ichāk	3 9 4	2 3 10	1 12 8	3 9 4	0 7 2	0 3 7
Gumia	3 0 0	1 14 0	1 8 0	3 0 0	0 6 0	0 3 0
Māndu	3 0 0	1 14 0	1 8 0	3 0 0	0 6 0	0 3 0
Petarbār Sadr	2 4 0	1 6 0	1 2 0	2 4 0	0 4 6	0 2 3
" Jaridih	2 0 0	1 4 0	1 0 0	2 0 0	0 4 0	0 2 0

Name of Thana and Police-station.	Terraced rice land. 1	2	3	Upland. I	II	III
	Rs. a. p.	Rs. a. p.	Rs. a. p.	Rs. a. p.	Rs. a. p.	Rs. a. p.
Rāmgarh Sadr	2 9 4	1 9 10	1 4 8	2 9 4	0 5 2	0 2 7
" Gola	2 4 0	1 6 0	1 2 0	2 4 0	0 4 6	0 2 3
Barkāgāon Sadr	3 15 0	2 10 0	1 8 6	3 4 6	0 14 0	0 3 6
" Tandwa	3 15 0	2 10 0	1 8 6	3 4 6	0 14 0	0 3 6
Barhi Sadr	5 0 0	3 0 0	{1 10 0* 2 0 0 2 4 0}	4 0 0	1 0 0	0 4 0
" Barahkatha	4 3 6	2 13 0	1 11 0	4 3 6	1 6 6	0 4 6
Bagodar	3 4 6	2 3 0	1 5 0	3 4 6	1 1 6	0 3 6
Kodarma Sadr†	5 5 6	3 4 3	2 1 3	4 4 6	0 14 3	0 4 6
" Jainagar	5 1 0	3 1 6	1 15 6	4 12 6	1 2 0	0 4 6
Chaupāran Sadr	3 15 9	2 9 3	1 6 6	3 8 3	0 15 0	0 3 9
" Itkhori	3 15 9	2 9 3	1 6 6	3 8 3	0 15 0	0 3 9
Chatra Sadr	...	...	...	...	...	...
" Gidhaur	5 8 0	3 7 0	2 1 0	4 2 0	1 0 6	0 5 6
Simaria	4 13 0	3 7 0	2 1 0	4 2 0	1 0 6	0 5 6
Hunterganj Sadr ... {River non-river}	5 0 0	3 12 0	2 8 0	5 0 0	3 7 0	0 10 0
" Partābpur	...	...	...	...	...	...
Giridih Sadr	...	...	...	...	...	...
" (a) Sirāmpur ...	3 8 0	2 2 0	1 5 0	2 2 0	0 7 0	{0 3 6 0 4 9
" (b) Gānde	3 4 0	2 0 6	1 3 6	2 0 6	0 6 6	0 3 3
" (c) Remainder ...	3 1 0	2 3 0	1 8 6	3 1 0	1 1 6	0 2 6
" Bengabād	3 0 0	2 0 0	1 0 0	0 12 0	0 2 0	0 1 0
Gāwān Sadr	3 15 0	2 7 0	1 8 6	3 8 0	0 10 6	0 3 6
" Sātgāwān‡	5 0 0	3 12 0	2 8 0	5 0 0	3 7 0	0 10 0
Kharagdiha	3 1 0	2 3 0	1 8 6	3 1 0	1 1 6	0 3 6
Dhanwār Sadr	3 1 0	2 3 0	1 8 6	3 1 0	1 1 6	0 3 6
" Birni E.	3 1 0	2 3 0	1 8 6	3 1 0	1 1 6	0 3 6
" Birni W.	3 0 9	2 0 6	1 3 6	3 0 9	1 0 3	0 3 6
Dumri Sadr	3 9 0	1 14 0	1 2 0	3 0 0	0 6 0	0 2 0
" Pirtānr	3 9 0	1 14 0	1 2 0	3 0 0	0 6 0	0 2 0
" Nawādih	2 12 0	1 11 6	1 6 0	2 12 0	0 5 6	0 2 9

* There are three rates for 3rd class *dhānkhet*. The first is for villages where no second crop is grown in them; the second is for villages where *rabi* crops also, are grown in them; the third is for villages where sugarcane and *rabi* can either be grown.

† Excluding the *khas mahal*.

‡ The river tract only pays these rates. The rates for the remainder are :—

Rs. a. p.	Rs. a. p.	Rs. a. p.	Rs. a. p.	Rs. a. p.	Rs. a. p.
3 15 0	2 10 0	1 8 6	3 8 0	0 10 6	0 3 6

The rates had not been determined by the end of 1916 for Chatra-Hunterganj non-river area, and Partabpur.

With these thana rates may be compared the rates adopted in the khas mahal settlements of Sarkāri Hāta (1904), Kodarma (1904), Kharagdiha khas mahal (1915) and Dhanwār (1915).

—	Terraced rice lands.			Uplands.		
	1	2	3	I	II	III
	Rs. a. p.	Rs. a. p.	Rs. a. p.	Rs. a. p.	Rs. a. p.	Rs. a. p.
Sarkāri Hāta ...	3 13 0	2 10 8	1 7 0	{ 3 4 0 { 2 5 0	} 1 5 4	0 6 8
Kodarma ...	2 11 0	2 0 3	1 5 6	1 5 6	} 0 10 9	0 5 4
Kharagdiha ...	3 0 0	2 0 0	1 0 0	1 4 0	0 4 0	0 1 0
Dhanwār ...	3 1 0	2 3 0	1 8 6	3 1 0	1 1 6	0 3 6

The rates for *korkar* terraced lands are much lower, in accordance with local custom.

The gross produce per acre of each class of rice land may be calculated for the district as a whole on the results of the crop-cutting experiments stated above; and in a matter where exactness is inherently unattainable (for these calculations are usually directed to future crops) this is probably a sufficiently accurate method. The average annual produce of a particular tenancy may also be calculated on that basis for the purpose of commuting produce-rent into cash, the thana rate being taken as the prevailing rate. In land acquisition proceedings, however, it is necessary to estimate the net annual profit to the cultivator, and for this purpose the cost of cultivation must be worked out. There have been no recent investigations of a sufficiently close character into this difficult problem, which is ripe for examination. For the purposes of the acquisition proceedings of the Rāmgarh-Bokāro Railway the following rates were adopted, after allowing for the rent payable to the landlord:—

Net profits.

Rates in land acquisition proceedings.

Rice, first class, annual profit Rs. 18-8-0, compensation per acre, Rs. 129-8-0.

		Rs.	a.	p.		Rs.	a.	p.
Rice, second-class	...	13	0	0	and	91	0	0
„ third-class	...	9	0	0	„	63	0	0
Upland, first-class	...	10	2	6	„	71	1	6
Do. second-class	...	2	0	0	„	14	0	0
Do. third-class	...	1	0	0	„	7	0	0

The price paid is seven years' purchase. The rates for uplands were suited to the circumstances of the area concerned; but except in the south-east of the district they are perhaps comparatively too low for first and second-class uplands.

Khandwat or *korkar*.

Khandwat lands are rice lands which a raiyat (or his ancestor) has reclaimed or terraced for himself. They may be made out of uplands already included in his holding, or out of jungle and waste lands not so included. In the former case the landlord's consent is not needed, and the Settlement Officer found that the custom in Hazāribāgh, differing from other districts, is that no additional rent is payable in respect of the improvement so effected, and the landlord cannot claim an enhanced rent, inasmuch as section 33 of the Tenancy Act is subject to custom. In waste and jungle lands it is a matter of local custom whether the consent of the landlord is necessary. In most villages it is now the rule to obtain his consent beforehand; but the custom of every village has been specifically recorded in a note made on each landlord's *gairmazrua malik* khatiān.

Rates of rent for *korkar*.

The custom about the rent to be paid for such reclaimed lands in waste and jungle is not uniform. "The maker is ordinarily allowed to hold it free of rent for three, four, or five years after the field is ready for cultivation, after which it may be assessed at half the rate at which other land of the same class is assessed. The fraction is generally one-half, but in some places it is three-eighths, and in others five-eighths. The period for which it is so held also varies. It is sometimes claimed by the raiyats to be privileged in perpetuity, but this would not be admitted by any landlord; landlords will often admit a period of twelve or fourteen years. The fact is that there is no definite period recognized for the lasting of the privilege. As a practical settlement both landlords and tenants are content that lands now found to be *khandwat* should be assessed at half rates for the next fifteen years and should be liable to full assessment after that period." (Settlement Report.)

Produce-rents.

The produce-rents which are ordinarily found in the district are *ādh-batāi* or *sajha* and *saika;* in Satgāwān, where agricultural conditions are like those of Gayā, the *dānabandi* or appraisement system was in force for some years before the settlement, but the rent has now been commuted into cash. In the case of *ādh-batai* the actual produce of the field is divided into equal portions, sometimes on or near the field, and sometimes at the landlord's threshing floor. In the case of *saika*, the cultivator merely pays instead of a cash-rent a fixed quantity of some particular grain. He is at liberty to grow that or any other kind of crop in the land, and the landlord has no more interest in the cultivation of the year than he has in that of a cash-rent holding. A half-produce-rent is very high indeed for a country generally infertile; but it has one advantage over a *saika* rent, that though the latter may be comparatively light—it very rarely is—it is bound to be ruinous to the ordinary hand-to-mouth tenant in a year of scarcity, when the yield of his land is less than the grain to be paid, and he has to make good the deficiency by buying the grain from others at an excessive price. *Adh-batai.* *Saika.*

Area held on produce-rents.

In the course of the settlement proceedings many of the raiyats applied for commutation of their produce-rents into cash, and a number of such cases has since been received in the ordinary revenue courts. The area in acres held on such rents according to the finally-published record-of-rights was as follows :—

Class of tenant.		Rice land.		Upland.
Khuntkattidars	...	29·15	...	25·83
Settled raiyats	...	9331·90	...	7934·20
Occupancy raiyats	...	452·89	...	694·94
Non-occupancy raiyats	...	815·87	...	1278·60
Total	...	10629·81		9933·70
Under-raiyats		2648·51		3223·89

Non-occupancy and under-raiyats are not entitled to apply for commutation of produce-rents.

Commutation.

In disposing of applications for commutation the revenue courts are now in a favourable position. The thana rates (which have been given above) furnish the prevailing rates for each class of land, the tenant's *khatiān* shows the area and class of land of his holding, and the crop-cutting experiments of the settlement department show the approximate quantity of *dhān* or its equivalent to be expected from each class. The mean between the thana rate and the value of half the average produce is usually fixed as the cash-rent in *adh-batai* cases, and that value is calculated from the retail selling price in January to March over a term of ten years at the nearest market, with a suitable allowance in respect of the distance from the market and the difference between wholesale and retail transactions. In the commutation of *saika* rents it is a necessary precaution to compare the proposed cash-rent with the value of the average gross outturn of the holding; for otherwise there is a danger of fixing an impossible proportion of the gross outturn.

Customary rights.

The rent paid by a settled raiyat entitles him not merely to cultivate certain parcels of land but also to enjoy numerous rights outside his holding, including rights to fuel, timber and other jungle produce for his domestic consumption (recorded in Khatian, Part II, of the record-of-rights), the right to make *khandwat*, the right of pasturage on jungle waste and cultivated lands, and other rights, whose extent and conditions are fixed by local custom. The aggregate of these rights affects his real welfare very considerably. Formerly there was no reliable information about their nature and extent and in consequence there was a serious danger that they would be ignored, both in executive action and in judicial decisions; but the preparation of the record-of-rights has done much to obviate this menace to the contentment of the cultivating classes. There may be customary rights which arise out of conditions which are merely transient, and their continued exercise after those conditions have changed may be injurious to the general welfare; but now the onus of proof is thrown on the innovator, and to the charge of confiscation the defence of ignorance is no longer admissible.

Transfer of holdings.

Since the passing of the Tenancy Act in 1908 a raiyat is forbidden permanently to alienate his holding or any portion of it. He may, however, grant a usufructuary mortgage for a period not exceeding five years, or a *bhugut bandha* for a period not exceeding seven. In the latter case both principal and interest are liquidated by the mere enjoyment of the land; but in the former it is only the interest that is so paid, and when the period of the mortgage has expired the borrower receives back his land, but is still burdened by the principal debt. The lender may not legally obtain an extension of his occupation of the land either directly or by any subterfuge; but it is open to him to recover his dues either from the voluntary payments of the borrower or after decree from his movable property. It has been suggested that this prohibition against alienation is being extensively evaded, either by the pretext of surrender, or by a direct transfer. The question, however, is purely one of fact, and must await the preparation of a fresh record-of-rights before an answer can be given.

After the cultivating tenants the most important element in the population is that made up of labourers. These include (1) ordinary day labourers known as *mazdurs or majurs*, (2) agricultural labourers hired by the year and (3) *kamias*. The first-named are usually fully aware of the demand for labour which exists outside the district, whether in the coalfields, in Calcutta, or in the agricultural districts of Bengal; and they have little reluctance to move about freely in search of the employment which is for the time being the most attractive. In comparison with labourers from some other districts they cannot properly be described as hard-working, or intelligent, or frugal; and usually they remain just so long in their employment abroad as will suffice to put them in funds for a long holiday at home. So much having been saved they will not respond to an increase in wages, and in consequence they are an insecure foundation for industries in which a continuous and equal production is essential. In the district, wages for men run from two to four annas, the highest rates being paid in urban areas, or in the neighbourhood of the coalfields. Women earn from one and a half to two and a half annas and boys from one to one and a half annas. **Landless labourers.** ***Majurs.***

Agricultural labourers hired by the year are not usually paid in cash, and the variety of their allowances makes it difficult to express the real wages with accuracy in terms of money. A man's wage may be four to six seers of *dhān* or *gondli*, or three seers of maize or *marua*, the seer being about three-fifths of the standard seer. In addition he receives the *jalpan* or drinking at 10 o'clock consisting of *marwa* bread, or parched grain, worth half an anna. Between June and September he also has a full meal at midday of rice or maize, which may cost as much as six pice.

The *kamias*, and the *kamiauti* system, have attracted the attention of local officials for many years past. The first District Officer of Hazāribāgh, Dr. John Davidson, was very much impressed with the evils of the system, which he roundly called slavery; and one of his earliest letters to Captain Wilkinson, the Governor General's Agent, was written in March 1834 with the object of remedying the evil. He differentiated between ***Kamias.***

ancestral slaves, and slaves who sold themselves or their children into slavery; and proposed the prohibition of the latter practice. As regards ancestral slaves he thought it sufficient to await the issue of general orders for giving effect to the then recent determination of the British Parliament to abolish slavery in India. Forty years later no improvement had been effected, if one may judge from the statements in the "Statistical Account"; and the recent settlement report discloses the persistence of some of the worst features in the west of the district after the lapse of another forty years. A new factor has recently been introduced by the abolition of compulsory labour from tenants; and many landlords who cultivate large areas of land now find it specially necessary to command the services of hired labourers, more particularly in the early rains. It is probable that they will attempt to obtain that command by undesirable practices; and legislation may be necessary to put an end to existing abuses, and prevent the growth of new ones. In England the regulation of agricultural labour was for many generations one of the most important tasks of Parliament, and it is only the industrial revolution in the last century which has obscured the gravity of this matter in all agricultural communities.

PRICE OF FOOD-GRAINS.

Roads and railways have made communication with the outside world so easy that the local price of food-grains is now largely independent of local stocks. As the district does not grow enough for its own consumption the price at any bazar is usually the price on the railway together with the cost of conveyance from the railway. In 1855 a maund of common rice cost a rupee, and by 1870 it still cost only Re. 1-10-0. In 1904 it cost Rs. 2-15-0, after which the price has fluctuated as follows:—

	Rs.	a.	p.
1905	3	14	0
1906	3	9	0
1907	4	5	0
1908	6	2	0
1909	4	11	0
1910	3	9	0
1911	3	5	0
1912	3	10	0
1913	5	2	0
1914	5	0	0
1915	5	0	0
1916	5	5	0

In 1870 the cash wage of a day labourer was one and a half to two annas and his grain wage was 2 seers of rice or 5 of *marua*. In 1911 the grain wage had fallen to 1¼ to 1¾ seers, and the cash wage had failed to rise above two and a half to three annas Since 1911 the price of rice has risen considerably and the wages of labour have not kept pace with this increase. The comparative figures of the wage census are as follows :— Wages.

Year.	Unskilled labourer.			Black-smith.	Car-penter.	*Gha-rami.*	Ploughman.	
	Cash in annas.	Grain. Value in annas.	Grain. Weight.	Cash in annas.	Cash in annas.	Cash in annas.	Day in annas.	Month.
1	2	3	4	5	6	7	8	9
	A. p.	A. p.		A. p.	A. p.	A. p.	A. p.	Rs. a. p.
1911 ...	2 6 to 3 0	1 6 to 2 6	1 seer 4 ch. to 1 seer 12 ch.	2 0 to 2 6	3 0 to 5 0	2 0 to 3 6	2 0 to 2 6	3 8 0 to 4 0 0
1916 ...	2 6 to 3 6	3 0 to 3 9	Not reported.	3 3 to 4 0	3 3 to 4 0	3 3 to 3 9	Not exactly ascertainable.	Not exactly ascertainable.

If the district is regarded as a unit, this great increase in the price of food-grains is of no advantage, because a portion of the amount annually consumed has to be imported from outside. The individual cultivator is benefited thereby only to the extent that he grows so much grain as to leave a surplus for sale after feeding his family. As the ordinary holding does not suffice for this, it follows that the majority of the cultivating classes have been injured by the rise. The wages of artisans and labourers have failed to keep pace with the increased cost of food; and the widening gulf between production and consumption has been bridged mainly by increased emigration. The net import of food-grains so far as they are imported by rail cannot be ascertained from the annual reports, as the unit in these reports is now not the district but the block consisting of a number of districts. Effect of the rise in the price of food-grains.

Material condition of the people.

Indebtedness is undoubtedly widespread among every class of the population. At present there are no co-operative credit societies in existence; and the grant of *takāvi* loans is restricted to times of scarcity; so that the private *mahājan* enjoys a monopoly of the business of money-lending, and rates of interest of 75 per cent are not unusual for petty unsecured cash loans. It is questionable whether the economical condition of a large population can be ascertained by the method of general averages. The extent of cultivation is known, and the average annual production of food-grains therefrom can be calculated with some pretence to accuracy; but the validity of the inferences to be drawn from a mere division of the crop area by the number of holdings, and of the population by the number of houses is disturbed by numerous and irregular factors. Detailed investigation of the domestic economy of all the residents in a typical area is a method of inquiry which has not up till now been applied to Hazāribāgh. The general impression that is left is of a people unambitious, intolerant of hard or sustained labour, inefficient, and cursed with an improvidence that is content to be separated from want by the thinnest of partitions.

CHAPTER IX.

OCCUPATIONS, MANUFACTURES AND TRADE.

OUT of a total population of 1,288,609 in 1911 no less than 1,004,131, or 78 per cent, were dependent wholly or mainly on agriculture for their living. These were (including dependants) distributed as follows:— OCCUPATIONS. Ordinary cultivation.

Rent-receivers	...	...	...	35,085
Landlords' agents	...	...	...	4,104
Cultivators ...	...	...	...	784,499
Farm labourers	...	...	...	180,443

Of the cultivators about 74,000 had subsidiary occupations.

Cattle grazing provided a living for 16,000 people, and forest produce for another 4,000. Grazing.

The number of actual workers employed in coal mines was about 9,000, and the mica mining and splitting industry had also 9,000 workers. Mining.

Potters and their dependants were about 7,000, oil-pressers 2,500, grain-parchers 3,000, *darzis* 3,000, *chamars* 3,000, *dhobis* 4,000, *barhis* 4,500, masons 1,500 and silversmiths 1,300. Village arts and crafts.

Carters were 1,800, palki-bearers 1,300, bullock drivers 1,300, and railway employees 2,400. Transport.

Bankers and *mahājans* with their clerks and dependants were 3,600. Money-lending.

Dealers in piece-goods were 2,500, hides 1,400, timber 1,500 and liquor 1,500. Dealers.

Sellers of groceries (*nun tamāku*) were 8,000, of milk and ghee 2,300, of sweetmeats 2,300, of vegetables and betel-nut 2,200, of grain 7,500, of fuel 1,200 and of bangles 1,000. Petty vendors.

The police and chaukidars with their dependants were 7,100 and other public servants 2,500. Public services.

Priests numbered 4,500, lawyers 1,600, doctors 1,800 and teachers 1,300. Professions.

Domestic service. Domestic service found employment for 30,000 people.

Wastrels. Beggars, vagrants and prostitutes between them numbered 8,000.

MANUFACTURES. This list of the principal occupations of the district discloses the absence of any extensive manufactures. The simple requirements of the village, as elsewhere in the province, are met from local industries, with two notable exceptions. The first is clothing, which is very largely imported. The spinning of wool and silk is practically non-existent, for only 77 and 220 people respectively make their living by those trades; and the Jolahas who used to make the cotton cloth for the country-side have now largely abandoned their ancestral occupation for agriculture. The cloth they spin is strong and durable, and is useful in winter for those who cannot afford woollen blankets; but it is not really as economical as imported cotton cloth.

Lac. The contribution of lac to the annual income of the district has been referred to in Chapter VII. The life-history of the insect which produces lac, and the process of manufacture into shellac, are described in great detail in Sir George Watt's "Commercial Products of India". In Hazāribāgh it is grown to some extent round about Gola, and more largely in Hunterganj thana, and that portion of Simaria which adjoins it. In reply to inquiries which were made regarding the produce per tree it was stated in the Gola area that lac was grown there on *parās* trees only, and that a large tree would give five seers in the year with a superabundant crop, or three seers in a good year; but the average annual outturn was considerably less. The local price also might vary from two annas a seer to as much as five annas. Only one crop is reaped in that quarter, planted in Asin and cut in Baisākh, a few twigs being left uncut from which, in the second generation, the next year's crop is grown. In Hunterganj no lac is grown on *kusm*, a little on *bair*, and the bulk on *parās* trees. Here a full crop from an ordinary *parās* would be a *pakka* seer and from a *bair* five seers, in the month of Baisākh. If cropped in Kārtik the outturn would be one-quarter and one and a quarter seers respectively.

Chatra used to be a very important centre to which all kinds of country produce were collected before despatch to the plains, and it still has a large trade in lac, though even rough estimates cannot be obtained of the average annual amount of the imports and exports. The following rough calculations relating to the trade were made by the leading merchants of the town :—

Firstly, the quality varies according as the parent tree was *kusm, bair,* or *parās,* in the ratios of 8, 7 and 6. Secondly, in the quantity that reaches the market at Chatra the ratios are *parās* 5, *kusm* 2, and *bair* 1. Thirdly, as regards seasonal crops, the Baisākh (May) harvest is double that of Kārtik (November). It also exceeds it in quality in the ratio of sixteen to thirteen. The former crop is peculiarly liable to damage by frost in December and January and by hail later on. The chief danger to the latter is heavy rain in June and July when the broods are swarming over the young shoots and are then liable to be washed away: The effect of low prices is seen at once in a great reduction in the plantings, and the difference between a good and a bad season is expressed by the ratio of sixteen annas to four annas.

The grower disposes of the crop either in his own village or at the local bazar, to a petty trader, Bania or Musalman, who buys on his own account. The trader takes it to Chatra, and is brought into contact with the agent of a factory by a broker (*āratiya*), who receives a larger commission from the trader and a smaller from the agent. The great bulk of the lac is exported forthwith from the district, packed in sacks, and only a small quantity is locally manufactured into shellac, though in view of the proportion of refuse contained in stick lac and the cheapness of fuel it would at first sight appear to be profitable to do so. Out of two factories at Chatra and one at Hazāribāgh in 1916 only one was at work, and that too on only a small scale.

Cutch or Catechu is made from the wood of the *khair* tree, a kind of acacia which grows rather freely in the dry scrub jungles of the district. The usual process of manufacture is described in the "Commercial Products of India"; but the following account of a very primitive method is taken from the Deputy Commissioner's diary of 1915 : "On the road, at Digwār, a Mallah had put up a little enclosure for making *kath*. He had two furnaces of earth, each supporting six pairs of earthen pots. In one pot of the pair are put the chips of the heart-wood of the *khair* tree, and the pot is filled up with water. As it boils it overflows into the Cutch.

second pot. When the boiling is completed the chips are thrown away, and a fresh supply is put in the pot, and over them is poured not fresh water, but the liquid in which the first set of chips was boiled. The liquid from this second boiling, which contains the extract from two sets of chips, is then allowed to cool, and when cold is poured into a settling pot, where it forms a pinky drab slime. This is collected into a wickerwork creel, with so close a mesh that the water alone oozes out and leaves a semi-solid mass behind. The Mallah employed eight men to cut and chip the *khair*, and hoped to make fifteen maunds in the season from Agahan to Chait. He pays Rs. 2-8-0 per furnace to the Rāmgarh Estate, and bargains for the wood with the various tenure-holders. The produce is sold to a firm of Mārwāris in Hazāribāgh. The man could give no estimate of his profits, but obviously they were not great. The process differed from that followed near Partābpur, where the liquid obtained from each set of chips was removed and concentrated by a second boiling in a pan."

Mines.

An account of the mining industries is contained in Chapter II.

Trade.

In 1871 the nearest railway station to the district was at Barākar on the Grand Trunk Road in Mānbhum. Away to the south there was no railway until Madras was reached. The trade of western Rānchi and Palāmau, of Surguja, Jashpur, Gangpur and Singhbhum made its way to the Ganges and the outer world by Chatra. There were collected food-grains, oil-seeds, stick-lac, resin, gums, silk-cocoons and iron, which were exchanged for English cotton, salt, tobacco, household utensils and luxuries generally. Oil-seeds and ghi went to Burdwān and Rāniganj, the crude iron to Patna, the lac to Mirzapur and the other goods to Gayā and Shāhābad. There was a great cattle fair in November at Chatra, and another near Kunda, and the local trade was conducted not by means of village shops, which practically did not exist, but by weekly bazars. Goods were conveyed on *sagars*, carts of rough construction carrying about five maunds, or on pack bullocks which carried two maunds and marched from six to eight miles a day.

Early trade of Chatra.

Communications inside the district improved with the construction of the Grand Trunk and other provincial roads, and small two-wheeled carts carrying twelve maunds came into use; but the import and export trades continued to be carried on mainly by pack bullocks. Then came the new railways, the Bengal-Nāgpur, Daltonganj, Grand Chord and Lohārdaga lines, which have each filched a slice of Chatra's commercial territory; and with the construction of a railway through Karanpura which is now proposed, its trade will sink to purely local limits. As matters now stand the commerce of Rāmgarh and the eastern portion of the Dāmodar valley goes to Jhalda on the Purulia-Rānchi line; Hazāribāgh Road attracts the trade of the whole centre of the district, Pachamba-Giridih that of the north-east, and Kodarma Road that of the north-west. The Grand Trunk road has now ceased to carry traffic, whether of pilgrims or of goods. Weekly bazars still form the chief medium of local trade, though shops are beginning to increase in number; and the two cattle fairs of Chatra and Lowālāng are still held. Away from the railway station the chief markets are at Hazāribāgh, Ichāk, Mirzaganj, Tandwa, Hunterganj and Gola. The principal exports are coal and mica, timber, oilseeds, mahua, lac, and myrabolans; the chief imports are kerosene, cotton piece-goods, salt, rice, tobacco, spices, and wrought-iron.

Present trade routes. **Weekly bazars.** **Fairs.**

Except in the west of the district the currency in use in the district is the standard Government coinage. From Chaupāran to Simaria the copper coin in use is the Gorakhpuri *paisa*.

Currency.

The use of the *pakka* seer of 80 tolas has not made the progress that is desirable, and much petty cheating is done over the weighing of goods at the village markets. Grain is usually sold by weight, and not by the measure of the *paila* or cup. In all inquiries regarding prices it is necessary to ascertain clearly what is the precise weight in rupees of the unit which the informant is using. The *pakka* seer (i.e. 20 '*gandas*') weighs 80 rupees or tolas, and a *pakka* maund contains forty seers. The informant will talk about seers and *paseris* (five seers); but his seer may be anything from twelve *gandas* upwards and his *paseri* may contain other than five seers. Accordingly a small sum in arithmetic is necessary to reduce the *pakka* maund and the *kacha* maund or *kāt*, to common terms. In recording produce-rents the Settlement Department has taken the precaution of entering the quantity of grain not only in the village denomination but in *pakka* maunds and seers.

Weights and measures.

CHAPTER X.

MEANS OF COMMUNICATION.

EARLY ROADS. THE earliest maps of the district were published in England in 1779 by Major James Rennell, the first Surveyor-General of India. Rennell left India in 1776, and in view of the long time then required for communication between the two countries it is probable that the materials utilized by him in the preparation of the maps were obtained mainly before his departure. As Rāmgarh was reduced only in 1772, and Kharagdiha two years later, the time allowed for the collection of those materials must have been very short.

Rennell's No. IX. The first map which concerns this district is a congregated map of Bengal and Bihar. The scale is small and probably the roads shown therein were primarily of military importance. Accordingly in Hazāribāgh there appear only four roads, as follows:—

1. The road from Patna to Doisanagar, where the Rājā of Chota Nāgpur resided, passed through Gayā and Sherghāti. It entered Hazāribāgh by the Lilājan valley and climbed up Jori Ghāt to Chatra, whence it proceeded through Jabra to Tori in Palāmau. From Jori to Jabra its course probably coincided with the present Bālumath-Sherghāti road.

2. The road from Bihār to Nawāda led ultimately to Bishnupur and Calcutta. It entered Hazāribāgh by the Sakri valley, passed through thānā Gāwān and reached the plateau north of Kharagdiha whence it proceeded south-east to Sirāmpur and Tundi. It corresponds with the present roads from Satgāwān to Giridih and Giridih to Tundi, except for slight modern diversions.

3. Another road is shown as leading from Nawāda to Rāmgarh and thence south through Chutia (Rānchi) to Doisanagar. There is some reason to believe that it was little known to the British, for the map is strikingly inaccurate between Kodarma and Ichāk, and south of the Chutupālu Pass it traverses an avowedly unsurveyed country. Moreover, even in 1837, it had no

place in the district list of roads. It entered Hazāribāgh by the pass between Rajauli and Kodarma.

4. A cross road runs from Rāmgarh through Gola and Petarbār, leaving the district beyond Kasmār to join the Calcutta-Bishnupur road through Raghunāthpur. It corresponds closely with the existing road.

A map on twice the scale of the above, inscribed to Major Jacob Camac, is entitled "The conquered provinces on the south of Bahar, containing Rāmgar, Palamau, Chuta-Nāgpur with their dependencies." It excludes Kharagdiha, which was at that time more accessible to the military from the side of Monghyr. In this map there are shown quite a large number of routes; but many of them can have been only the merest tracks. For example, no less than seven radiate from Kundi, which even up to the present day is with difficulty accessible to any kind of wheeled cart. The most striking features in the map are as follows :— Rennell's No. VIII.

(1) There was no road at all along the country now served by the Grand Trunk Road. There is a great square of jungle country corresponding to the present thānās of Māndu Bagodar Gumia, and police station Nawādih of thānā Dumri, which has no roads at all, except one track from Ichāk to Mokamo, south of Bharkatta, and thence to Bāraganda, where the copper mines were.

(2) Hazāribāgh appears as Ocunhazari, near to Makundganj on the Barhi-Rāmgarh road. The present road to Chatra by Damol Ichāk and Katkamsānri are represented in essentials, but Kendi was the immediate objective of the latter.

(3) The road centre of Chauparan was then a mile to the south-west at Bigha, from which place one could go north through the Champa pass to the Gayā plain, or west through Itkhori to Kendi, or south-west to what is now Padma but finds no place in the map, and thence to Ichāk, or east through Rāmpur to Gumo. From Itkhori, which has ruins of a Hindu temple, one could go north by the "Donoh" pass to meet the other road down the Champa pass.

(4) Gumo was another important centre. There were roads north to Rajauli and south to Rāmgarh (described above), and north-east to Kodarma and Domchānch. Another went south-east to Jainagar and Markacho, and then entered Kharagdiha and passed through Birni Bharkatta and Leda to Pālmo and Sirāmpur. From Pālmo a route led across the Barākar to Pālganj.

(5) From Pālganj there was a short road to Madhuban, where the Jain pilgrims now assemble to climb Pārasnāth ; and another circuitous road led westward to Bāraganda, where the copper mines were situated. It may be surmised that the road which was continued north through Mokamo and Saranda to Doranda owed its existence to the mines, for now that the latter are unworked it has disappeared from modern maps.

(6) Another road from Pālganj passed south to Nāwāgarh traversing the difficult spurs of Pārasnāth and went south to Jaipur in Mānbhum. From Nāwāgarh, the traveller could proceed first to Pālganj and thence to Nawāda either by Kharagdiha or by Kodarma and Rajauli. This is interesting in the light of a theory of Mr. Beglar (page 50, Vol. VIII, Archæological Survey of India Reports) that in early times there was a road across Hazāribāgh from Patna to Tamluk. "It would cross . . . the Barākar close to Pālganj, the range of hills near Rajauli . . . This road would be a great thoroughfare, and we see that at every obstacle large cities sprang up as attested by the remains about . . . Pālganj and near Rajauli." The existence of such a road would throw a very important light on the early history of the district if it could be established and if any approximate dates could be fixed. But the records of the Archæological Department contain no further reference to ruins of arhæological interest at Pālganj, or at any place intermediate between Pālganj and Rajauli ; and what meagre mention

of the country is found in pre-modern records does not suggest that wayfarers would be safe on such a road. Until further evidence is forthcoming along the route the theory, so far as it concerns Hazāribāgh, can scarcely be entertained.

The third of Rennell's maps includes Kharagdiha. It is entitled "The Jungleterry District . . . . comprehending the countries situated between Moorshedabad and Bahar." The scale is the same as in No. VIII. Kharagdiha is shown as a part of Monghyr, the boundary between being indicated by a dotted line with "Sarhaut" to the east and "Ghidore" to the north-east. The additional roads shown in this map are:— Rennell's No. II.

(1) The continuation of the Gumo-Domchānch road to Khesmi and "Taranaka" (probably Doranda) east of which it joined the main road north of Kharagdiha to Nawāda.

(2) A road from Kharagdiha which led north to Gidhaur and threw off a branch to the east to Chakai.

(3) From Sirāmpur a direct road north to Chakai, a second to Deoghar and a third eastward to Deopur. There is little room for doubt that there was at the time when Rennell's map was made a direct pilgrim road from Nawāda through Gāwān to Deoghar, and the route which led through Kharagdiha to Tundi and Mānbhum was not the main road but merely a branch from the pilgrim road.

From a report submitted in 1837 it appears that the roads of the district were then as follows:— Roads in 1837.

A. First class roads—

1. Shorghāti-Hunterganj-Jori-Chatra.
2. Chatra-Jabra-Lohārdaga.
3. Chatra-Sinduāri-Katkamsānri-Hazāribāgh.
4. Hazāribāgh-Chandauri-Balia-Jainagar-Kishenpur (i. e. Rānchi).
5. Bishungarh-Jharpo-Ichāk.
6. Gobindpur-Nasirganj-Manjhne-Gāwān-Ghoranji to Baidyanāth (Deoghar).
7. From Kharagdiha to Chakai and Bhāgalpur.

8. Kharagdiha-Sirāmpur-Pālganj-Mānbhum district.
9. Chatro-Gumia-Chitarpur-Gola-Kasmār-" Rugoah"-Jhalda.

B. Third class roads—

10. Chatra-Kanha-chatti-Debipur-Danua.
11. Chaupāran-Pathra-Padma-Icbāk-Hazāribāgh.
12. Hazāribāgh-Indra-Jabra-Rāmgarh-Chitarpur-Gola-Nawadih-Silli.
13. Hazāribāgh to Chatro.
14. Kharagdiha, south-west to Bishungarh and Chatro.

In the above list No. 4 is the military road through Bādam and Pithauria between Hazāribāgh and Rānchi, now abandoned. No. 6 is the Nawāda-Deoghar pilgrim road, Chatro was a police thānā on the old military road, about 23 miles east of Hazāribāgh.

The old Benares Road.

Shortly after the entry of the British into Hazāribāgh a new road was constructed for improving military communications with the United Provinces along which semaphore towers were placed at suitable intervals and in commanding positions. This road was not metalled, and with the construction of the Grand Trunk Road it ceased to be of military importance. As it had been made irrespective of local needs it rapidly passed from neglect into complete decay, and it is not now always easy to follow its exact alignment, though the semaphore towers are conspicuous landmarks across the district. From the west of Chās in Mānbhum it passed through Angwāli, Gumia, Chatro, Hazāribāgh, Katkamsānri and Kanhachatti near Kendi, and down the Dhangain pass into Gayā. The construction of the road was commenced in 1782 and its usefulness ended with the opening of the Grand Trunk Road.

The Grand Trunk Road.

This road enters the district at the 193rd mile about 10 miles east of Dumri and leaves it at the foot of the Danua Ghāt by the Guāri river at the 268th milestone. It was completed in this district in 1838 and was being bridged at Barahkatha in 1848 when Dr. Hooker visited Pārasnāth. It is metalled and planted with road-side trees and has dāk bungalows at Dumri and Bagodar, with rest-houses at frequent intervals; but its importance has naturally decreased since the construction successively of the East Indian Railway main (loop) line, the Chord line and finally the almost parallel Grand Chord line. It is, however, still used in the cold weather for the passage of troops, who usually halt at Dumri, Bagodar, Barahkatha, Barhi and Chauparan, where spacious camping grounds are maintained for their use.

Other provincial roads are (1) Giridih-Dumri road, 26 miles long, connecting the Grand Trunk Road with Giridih. Its importance has been reduced by the construction of the Grand Chord Railway, as goods no longer cross the unbridged Barākar river, and the pilgrim traffic to Pārasnāth tends to come by Isri station on the Grand Chord. Between Dumri and the Barākar the lower spurs of Pārasnāth are finely wooded. Other provincial roads.

(2) Hazāribāgh-Rānchi, of which the first 41 miles are in Hazāribāgh district. At the Marāngi and Chutupālu Ghāts the scenery is very fine.

(3) Hazāribāgh-Bagodar, 33 miles long, and Bagodar-Hazāribāgh Road station 8 miles long. These together connect the district headquarters with the railway, and

(4) Hazāribāgh-Barhi 22 miles.

These provincial roads are all first-class metalled roads, of a total length of 203 miles, and are excellent for motoring.

District Board Roads.

The District Board maintains a large number of roads of various classes. In the Chatra subdivision the Hunterganj-Chatra-Simaria road is badly interrupted in its northern section by the Jori Ghāt, too steep for wheeled traffic and by the sandy bed of the Lilajān river. This historical road is unsuited to modern conditions, and no practicable realignment has so far been discovered. From Simaria its proceeds south to Tandwa, below which it has been abandoned for the last four years, as there is no local cart-traffic, and its upkeep was very expensive.

The Chatra-Chaupāran road is a metalled road, 30 miles long, giving access for the goods of Chatra to the Grand Trunk Road and Kodarma Railway Station. It is seriously interrupted by the Mohani river at Itkhori.

The Hazāribāgh-Simaria road is a good gravelled road but unbridged.

In the Sadr Subdivision the main roads are:—

(1) Rāmgarh-Gola, a metalled road partially bridged.

(2) Gola to Dākagarha on the way to Jhālda, a station on the Purulia-Rānchi railway, a gravelled road partially bridged.

(3) Gola-Mānjhidih, a gravelled road, unbridged.

(4) Petarbār-Gumia-Bishungarh, a gravelled road badly intersected by the Dāmodar, Bokāro and Konār rivers.

(5) Singhrāwān-Kodarma-Domchānch, a metalled and bridged road.

(6) Hazāribāgh Road-Dhanwār, a metalled road intersected by the Barākar, Baretto and Arga rivers.

(7) Kodarma-Markacho-Kowar, a partly gravelled road, unbridged and intersected by several large rivers.

In the Giridih Subdivision are :—

(1) Giridih-Kowār, metalled and bridged.

(2) Kowār-Kharagdiha, gravelled and bridged.

(3) Kharagdiha-Dhanwār, an earth road and unbridged.

(4) Kharagdiha-Gāwān, gravelled and partially bridged, with one large unbridged river.

(5) Gāwān-Sātgāwān, an earth road badly intersected by large rivers.

Urgent needs. The maintenance of the existing roads is almost beyond the financial ability of the District Board, and the construction of new roads is under present conditions impossible. The most important of the immediate needs of the district are the bridging of the Mohani and Barākar, the construction of practicable roads to Hunterganj, Partābpur, Kunda, and Lowālāng in the Chatra Subdivision and the construction of a good road in the mica country from Domchānch round to Tisri. The development of the Bokāro and Karanpura coalfields will create new and heavy demands of which the precise character cannot yet be foreseen.

The total length of roads maintained by the District Board is as follows :—

Metalled, bridged and drained ...	45	miles.
Unmetalled, bridged and drained ...	46	„
Metalled, partially bridged and drained ...	33	„
Unmetalled, partially bridged and drained	301	„
Banked and gravelled, but not drained ...	80	„
Banked, partially bridged, and drained ...	154	„
Cleared, partially bridged and drained ...	25	„
Total ...	684	„

RAILWAYS.

There are at present (1916) three railway lines in the district, of which the oldest is the branch from Madhupur on the Chord line to Giridih. This was made in 1871, simultaneously with the Chord line, for the sake of the railway's colliery at Giridih. Prior to 1871 the rail-head since 1858 had been at Barākar on the Grand Trunk Road. Giridih remained the railway station for Hazāribāgh for no less than 36 years; and it was not till February 1907 that the Grand Chord Line was opened for traffic. As the headquarters station is 72 miles from Giridih, the journey, which was ordinarily made in *push-pushes* was very trying, in spite of two excellent provincial roads, of which the first connected that station with the Grand Trunk Road at Bagodar, and the second connected Dumri on the Grand Trunk Road with Giridih. The latter road was without a bridge at the Barākar river, and the crossing is dangerous when the river is in flood.

The Grand Chord Railway enters the district near Nimia Ghāt station, close by Pārasnāth, and leaves it west of Gajhandi by a rather severe pass from the lower plateau to the Gayā plains. The total length in the district is about 60 miles.

There are two important stations, at Hazāribāgh Road and Kodarma, each of which is connected with Hazāribāgh by metalled roads and they are about equally distant from the district headquarters. Hazāribāgh Road is, however, the station ordinarily used, as it is considerably nearer Calcutta, whither both goods and passengers ordinarily proceed. Kodarma is the station for Chatra, from which town a considerable traffic is received.

The third railway runs from Mahudā in Mānbhum to Bermo, at the Bokāro Colliery of the joint E. I. and B. N. Railways. Its future extension will depend on the precise determination of the position and value of the coal beds in the Bokāro and Karanpura fields. A reconnaisance survey was made some 20 years ago as far as the Daltonganj line in Palāmau.

The question of connecting the town of Hazāribāgh with the Grand Chord Railway has received attention, and the routes to Kodarma and Hazāribāgh Road have been surveyed, but for financial reasons the project has been temporarily shelved.

River communications.

The Lilājān river is used for [floating down bamboos to the Gayā plain; but with this exception no use is made of the rivers for transport or communication, for which purposes they are entirely unsuited.

Ferries.

One ferry is maintained on the Barākar river between Giridih and Pārasnāth. Formerly there was considerable traffic to and fro, but the opening of the Grand Chord Railway has reduced it to unimportance.

Staging and inspection bungalows.

A detailed list of staging and inspection bungalows is contained in table XXX of Part II. Food and lodging for Europeans and Indians are procurable at Dumri and Bagodar on the Grand Trunk Road, at Rāmgarh on the Hazāribāgh-Rānchi road, at Giridih dāk bungalow and at Hazāribāgh staging bungalow. There is a staging bungalow for Indians at Hazāribāgh Road; and there are numerous inspection bungalows on all the principal roads, where however no meals are supplied.

POSTAL COMMUNICATIONS.

In 1916 there were 40 post offices in the district, and 588 miles of postal communication. The average weekly number of postal articles was delivered 17,467. The value of money orders paid is reported to have been Rs. 13,93,148 in the year 1915-16, and the value of those issued Rs. 13,94,062. The difference is less than Rs. 1,000, and it is not easy to understand, in view of the large volume of temporary emigration from the district, why there was a practical equality between issues and payments. In Rānchi and the Santāl Parganas, the other two emigrant districts the value of the money orders issued very largely exceeds that of money orders paid. There were 3,568 savings Bank accounts open on the 31st March 1916; and the amount of deposits during the year was Rs. 1,28,148. There were 13 postal telegraph offices and 53,827 messages were issued.

CHAPTER XI.

LAND REVENUE ADMINISTRATION.

NUMBER OF ESTATES.

If the *mukarraris* of Kharagdiba be given brevet rank there were in 1915-16 seventy revenue-paying estates, one temporarily settled estate (Karharbāri Colliery), four Government estates and 272 revenue-free estates. The land revenue payable is Rs. 47,260 in respect of the first class, Rs. 59,729 in respect of the second, and Rs. 37,538 in respect of the third.

Amount of revenue.

Original number of estates.

When the British took over the *diwāni* of the three provinces in 1765, the area of the district was distributed between three estates, Rāmgarh, Kendi and Kharagdiha and one "*thānādāri jāgir*" of Kunda, on which no revenue was assessed. The early history of these four divisions has been given in Chapter III.

Kunda.

From the settlement report it appears that the question of resuming the Kunda service *jāgir* was raised in 1797, but it was considered that there was a probability of causing thereby such disturbances as would cost more to quiet than the revenue would be worth. In 1823, when Mr. Cuthbert, Collector of Rāmgarh, reported that the Chief was not guarding the ghats or securing the roads, and therefore should be deprived of his *jāgir*, the proposal was rejected on the same grounds. At that time Mr. Cuthbert found that it cost the *jāgirdar* only Rs. 370 a year to keep up the police. The proprietor now pays Rs. 600 a year as contribution to the cost of the police, and *digwāri* dues of Rs. 213-5-6 a year.

Kendi.

The land revenue of Kendi was fixed at Rs. 2,030-9-0, and no liability was imposed in respect of either police or *digwāri*. This anomaly is explained as due to the fact that the estate was traversed by the military road which had been made in 1782, and was guarded by Government police, stationed at Kanha Chatti. As a consequence of successive alienations, first by the transfer of full proprietary right in portions of the estate and later on by means of similar transfers disguised as *mukarrari* tenures at low rates of rent, and by *jāgir, khairāt* and *khorposh* grants, the family of the original proprietor is reported to have for its support at the present time practically the produce of only one *thika* village.

Rāmgarh.

Later family history.

After the death in 1772 of Tej Singh, Chief of Rāmgarh, who removed the headquarters to Ichāk, he was succeeded by his son Maninäth Singh, who was the first chief to repudiate the supremacy of the Mahārājā of Chota Nāgpur by refusing to receive investiture from him. This used to be given by the Mahārājā smearing his own big toe with sandal wood and placing it on the forehead of the recipient.

Maninäth was succeeded in 1812 by his son Sidhnāth, after whose death in 1822 three sons in succession inherited the property, viz., Lachhmināth (died in 1842), Sambhunāth (died in 1862) and Rāmnāth (died in 1866). The succession was then disputed, for a posthumous son Tilaknāth, who was born in 1867, died in the following year. A decree of the Privy Council awarded the estate to a younger branch of the family, the maintenance-holder of Padma, of whom the head (Barm Nārāyan Singh) was fourth in descent from Tej Singh by a second wife; but before the decision Barm Nārāyan had died, and his son Nām Nārāyan Singh (later Mahārājā) took possession of the estate. He died in 1899, and his son Rām Nārāyan Singh (later Rājā) died in 1911. The present owner is his only son Lachmi Nārāyan Singh, at present a minor under the Court of Wards.

Assessment of land revenue, 1770 A. D.

In 1770 the revenue stood at Rs. 27,000; but out of this Rs. 4,000 were paid in respect of the Mahārājā of Chota Nāgpur (as explained in Chapter III). In addition Rs. 9,001 were paid under a separate *patta* which gave the following details (which, however, total Rs. 9,503):—

Jāgodih, Rāmpur, Parwaria	Rs. 5,501.	Champa, Rāmpur Buzurg, Gumo, Markacho, Barsot	Rs. 2,000.
Kodarma	... Rs. 401.		
Itkhori, Daihar	Rs. 1,601.		

Shāmilāt or Shikmi tāluks.

Rāmpur. Parwaria. Jāgodih. Itkhori.

Of these Jāgodih, Rāmpur, Parwaria and Itkhori, with Pitij, had made up pargana Chhāi, which was reduced to subjection, shortly before the arrival of the British, by Mukund Singh of Rāmgarh. The chiefs had previously been paying a tribute to Rājā Lāl Khān, who appears to have been one of themselves (chief of Jāgodih); but in what way if at all Rājā Lāl Khān had been included in the Muhammadan revenue system does not appear. Mukund Singh, it is said, gave Rājā Lāl Khān a *nānkār* of Rs. 1,200, and took for himself the tributes of the Chhāi chieftains. As this arrangement was quite recent, the latter tried to make settlements directly with the British and not through Rāmgarh, but they were unsuccessful; the tributes were converted into fixed rents, and they were ordered to pay them to Rāmgarh. One of them, the owner of Pitij, who was a resident of Gayā, refused, and made over his property to the proprietor of Kendi, in whose estate it merged. Of the remaining four, three made over a number of villages to Rāmgarh, of which the profits were to pay the rent of their respective *tāluks*, so that they should hold the remainder rent-free.

Barsot.

Kodarma.

In a similar way the Chief of Barsot succeeded in saving his property from being merged into Rāmgarh and it was made a *Shāmilāt tāluk*. Kodarma was at first treated in similar fashion, but the proprietor Braja Mohan Sāhi obtained a decree from the Sadr Diwāni Adālat in 1804, in execution of which his pargana was assessed separately from Rāmgarh at Rs. 315-0-10 land revenue, with the liability to maintain the police establishment of Kodarma, and eight *digwārs* to guard the passes of the estate and eight *barkandāzes* for escort duty between thānā Kodarma and the sadr station. This estate later on passed into the direct ownership of Government, as explained below.

1772.

The immediate consequence of the submission of the Mahārājā of Chota Nāgpur to Captain Camac in Palāmau was the discontinuance of the arrangement whereby the tribute of Rs. 4,000 had been paid through Rāmgarh; and upon the installation of Tej Singh at Rāmgarh the revenue was fixed at Rs. 30,000, to which in 1777 a *nazarāna* of Rs. 10,000 was added. Preliminary to the decennial settlement a *jamābandi* was submitted by the proprietor (of which particulars are given in paragraph 66 of the Settlement Report); but it was apparently disregarded, and the sum actually assessed was as follows :—

		Rs.	a.	p.
Annual amount, as in the past	...	40,001	13	4
Deduct 6 per cent. ...	...	2,300	0	9
		37,701	12	7
Deduct for *sayer* ...	...	9,500	0	0
		28,201	12	7

The six per cent. deduction is explained as due to conversion into *sicca* rupees.

1790. The "Statistical Account" states that the revenue was fixed at *sicca* Rs. 28,100-15-3, and that in 1791 further reduc-
1791. tions were made in respect of *sayer*, viz., *abkāri* or excise Rs. 800-5-6 and *hāts* or markets Rs. 377-11-6. Again in 1792 a further reduction was granted of Rs. 347-11-4, being the rent
1792. of certain lands taken up for the formation of cantonments. Since then lands have from time to time been taken up by Government (especially for the new cantonments at Hazāribāgh), and the land revenue now payable for this estate of 4,425 square miles is Rs. 22,988-6-7. In addition Rs. 11,396 are paid as *digwāri* contribution, and Rs. 2,592 as Police contribution. The

Sayer. question of "*sayer*" will be found discussed in paragraphs 68 to 70 of the Settlement Report.

Kharagdiha. The history of the Kharagdiha estate has been given in Chapter II. The following is the account of the subsequent revenue settlement contained in the "Statistical Account".

"The portion of the *zamindāri* of which Mod Nārāyan Deo was deprived which lay in Hazāribāgh consisted of thirty-eight *ghātwāli* tenures. Each of these tenures was held by a head *ghātwāl* called *tikāit*, who, on succeeding to the tenure, received the *tilak* of *tikāit* from the Mahārājā (of Kharagdiha), and agreed to pay rent for the holding. These *tikāits* appear to have been semi-independent. All that was required of them then was, on succession to the *gādi*, to acknowledge the supremacy of the Mahārājā, and annually to pay him a small sum of money as rent. Mod Nārāyan Deo and his son died in exile and when the English entered Rāmgarh the grandson, by name Girwar Nārāyan Deo, represented the family. After the conquest of Rāmgarh was secured attention was turned to that of Kharagdiha. Girwar Nārāyan Deo assisted the English heartily, and his influence was of immense importance. Of the thirty-eight *ghātwāls* twenty-six were induced to take up his cause, and ten remained neutral, while only two, Sātgāwān and Kargāli, showed themselves entirely hostile. Akbār Ali Khān was in his turn driven out of Kharagdiha. It was found that during his government he had held direct possession of seventeen villages, the assets of which he had expended on his household expenses under the name of *nānkār*. These seventeen villages were at once made over to Girwar Nārāyan Deo rent-free in perpetuity, as some acknowledgment of his services, and they now form the nucleus of the present Dhanwār estate. The twenty-six *gādis* held by the *tikāits*, who took the side of the British Government, were settled with the holders as *mukarraris*, in accordance with the orders of the Governor-General in Council in 1780. The *ghātwāls* of Sātgāwān and Kargāli, who had resisted the English forces, were dispossessed, and their *gādis* settled in the same year (1780) in *mukarrari*, with two newly-installed *tikāits*. Twelve farmers or *ijāradārs* of Akbār Ali Khān, who had also rendered assistance to the British, had their holdings converted into *mukararis* under the Governor-General's orders in 1783. After these forty *mukarraris* had been settled, an offer was made to Girwar Nārāyan Deo to settle with him the remainder of Kharagdiha, consisting of ten *gādis* and fifty-four villages; but he refused to accept this arrangement, maintaining that he was entitled to a settlement of the whole of Kharagdiha—a request with which it was impossible to comply, seeing that Government had already entered into direct agreements with so many other persons. The ten *tikāits* who had remained neutral were permitted to hold their *gādis* as farmers; while the rest of Kharagdiha, consisting of fifty-four villages, was let in farm on temporary leases to different parties. In the year 1800 the ten *gādis* hitherto held on temporary leases were given in *mukārrari* to their respective *tikāits*; and the fifty-four villages termed *khālsa* were again resettled for a term of years, yielding a revenue of Rs. 5,226 per annum to Government. In 1808 Girwar Nārāyan Deo offered to take a permanent settlement of these fifty-four villages on an annual rent of Rs. 6,334; and his application was sanctioned in 1809. This completed

Nankar or revenue-free estate of Argāli.

The *mukarraris*.

The permanently-settled estate of Dhanwar.

the settlement of Kharagdiha by creating fifty *mukarrari* tenures, one permanently-settled estate paying revenue to Government, and one rent-free (*nānkār*) estate. It will be noticed that the *gādis* never came under the purview of the Permanent Settlement. The *tikāits* have been called *ghātwāls*, but there is no mention of this title in their *sanads*, nor in the *kabuliyats* given by them ".

The permanently-settled estate is called Bangaro Dhanwār and extends over 69 square miles in thānās Dhanwār, Kharagdiha and Giridih. Its present land revenue is Rs. 6,756. It pays no police contribution, but is liable for a *digwāri* contribution of Rs. 288. The revenue-free estate is called Argāli and has an area of 108 square miles. It pays neither police nor *digwāri* contribution.

Status of the mukarraridars.

The question of the precise status of these Kharagdiha *mukarraris* is discussed at length in paragraphs 81 to 94 of the Settlement Report. For the purposes of land revenue accounts the rent payable is treated as land revenue.

The Kharagdiha Khās mahāl.

"Since the settlement of 1809 various changes have taken place. *Gādi* Bagridih was purchased by the Raja of Kodarma; and was in his possession when in 1841-42, on his being convicted of harbouring dacoits the whole of his estate was escheated to Government. This *gādi* is now the property of Government; it consists of only three villages. The holder of *Gadi* Kargāli sold the entire estate to eleven persons. This sale was held to be a contravention of the conditions of the original settlement, and Government took possession of the estate in 1848. The purchasers sued Government for possession, but as they did not bring this suit till more than twelve years had elapsed since the resumption of the estate, their claim was held to be barred by limitation. In 1860 the *gādi* was settled for twenty years, and was then found to contain forty-two villages, which were leased out in seventeen lots ...... In 1847-48 resumption proceedings under Regulation II of 1819 were commenced in this district and continued up to the year 1856, when they were summarily stopped, and orders were passed that all the villages of which the proceedings had not finally closed should at once be made over to the parties in whose possession they had been found. During the above period, however, Government obtained possession of 151 villages, viz., 149 in

(1) Gadi Bagridih.

(2) Gadi Kargāli.

(3) The *taufir* villages.

pargana Kharagdiha, one in pargana Chhāi and one in pargana Kendi. In 1860 all the villages resumed as *taufir* in Kharagdiha were settled in fifty-two lots. .... Thus in 1861 there were seventy revenue-paying estates in pargana Kharagdiha over and above the fifty-one estates of 1809."

Present revenue.

In the recent fair rent settlement of the government villages of Kharagdiha which are now treated as a single estate, the total rent has been fixed at Rs. 11,578. The unit which constitutes a village has been changed since the Statistical Account of 1875 was written, and the number of villages is now 150, of which a detailed list is given in Appendix L of the Settlement Report. The new settlement has been made as far as possible *raiyatwari*.

Kodarma Government Estate.

The Kodarma Government estate extends over about 108 square miles, of which about 50 square miles are Reserved or Protected Forest. It is situated in the north of the thānā of the same name. Its early revenue history has been given above, in connection with the *shāmilāt* tāluks. In 1841 the proprietor, Tej Nārāyan Sahi was implicated in a dacoity, and in the following year Government ordered the confiscation of his property, which consisted of twelve villages in Gayā known now as the Dabaur estate, and in Hazāribāgh of the remainder of *gādi* Kodarma as well as the contiguous *gādi* of Bagridih. The last settlement of the estate was made with effect from 1904, when a rent of Rs. 15,217 was fixed. The settlement was originally for twelve years, but it has been extended and will expire in 1918. The reserved forest is rich in mica, and the mining and splitting of mica provide employment for the surplus workers of the estate.

Sarkāri hātā.

The establishment of a cantonment at what is now the town of Hazāribāgh made it necessary to acquire lands for military purposes from the proprietor, the owner of the Rāmgarh estate, and to these lands known as the Sarkāri Hātā Government Estate, additions were from time to time made, of which the details were :—

				Rs.
1790	465 bighas,	revenue abatement	...	371
1819	188 ,,	rent of ...	...	203
1838	496 ,,	rent of ...	...	879

In 1842 the cantonment was abolished, only to be restored in 1859, when the total area held by Government was 1,400 bighas and the rent Rs. 1,357, besides the original abatement of Rs. 371 allowed in 1790.

In 1865 4,462 bighas were taken up to improve the sanitary condition of the cantonment, for which a rent of Rs. 2,600 was fixed; and in 1871 all the rent payable was converted into a reduction of revenue. The total reduction so allowed in respect of the entire cantonment is Rs. 4,328, and the area as measured in 1904 was 7,273 acres. The rent then settled was Rs. 9,157, and the settlement will expire in 1918. The establishment of the cantonment and later on of the public offices, at Hazāribāgh has led to a great increase in the value of land for building purposes, of which the advantage will for the first time accrue in the approaching settlement. It is fortunate that practically the whole of the increment due to these state activities will go into the public treasury.

Partābpur transferred estates.

In 1875 the boundaries of the revenue jurisdiction of Hazāribāgh and Gayā were re-arranged in the west of Hunterganj thānā, and an area of six square miles was transferred to the former district, divided between sixteen revenue-paying estates, and assessed at Rs. 754-3-0. (These bear tauzi numbers 35, and 52 to 66 inclusive.) They were originally a part of the Kunda *jāgir*, and were resumed in 1847 in the Gayā district, probably because they had been improperly alienated by the *Jāgirdar*. At first they were included in the district of Gayā for revenue purposes, though in respect of criminal jurisdiction they belonged to Hazāribāgh, and this anomaly was removed in 1875.

Nimādih.

The estate bearing tauzi number 339 and the name of Nimādih is half a village in Kharagdiha which was resumed as *taufir* in 1836 and included in the Kharagdiha Government estate until 1895, when it was sold with a revenue fixed in perpetuity of Rs. 10-3-8. The other half of the village is included in the *gādi* of Bairia.

Barhi Chatti.

Barhi Chatti was the site of the jail building at Barhi, and was sold like Nimādih in 1895. It is now permanently settled on a revenue of Rs. 3-2-8.

REVENUE FREE ESTATES.

There are in all 274 revenue-free estates, of which Argāli has been described above in connection with the history of Kharagdiha. Kunda is really a revenue-free service *jāgir*

Amnāri was created in 1772 by a sanad granted by Tej Singh in favour of Lāl Bahādur Singh, who had been the intermediary in the communications with Major Camac which led to the expulsion from Rāmgarh of Makund Singh. The grantee is said to have been a chaprāsi. The grant was confirmed in favour of his son by the Governor-General in 1780. The Kodarma and Khurchuta reserved forests are entered in the register of revenue-free estates, though they are in the direct possession of Government in the Forest Department. The former was a part of the confiscated estate of Kodarma and the latter was a portion of the ninety-two villages which were resumed from Rohan Narāyān Singh, *tikāit* of Khurchuta in 1847, on the ground that they had not been included in the *sarsikan* lists filed by his predecessors. The remaining estates are petty charitable and religious endowments which escaped resumption by the production of valid sanads about 1795 and 1796. It is curious that none are within the sphere of the Rāmgarh estate. Amnāri.

The origin of the three large estates of Rāmgarh, Kunda, and Kharagdiha explains the existing custom whereby the next male succeeds to the entire estate, and younger members of the family are entitled to maintenance only. Kunda is now a service tenure, but originally the holder was a Kharwar chief who established his power by force of arms and maintained it by a vigorous personal rule. He is now *de facto* a Rājput; but the conditions of his tenure were obviously not of a kind to admit of subdivision. The origin of the Rāmgarh estate is analogous. The founder of the Kharagdiha estate was an armed invader from outside the district, who established a direct ownership over a comparatively small area, and a loose authority over the far-spread *tikāits*, which he could enforce only so long as his resources enabled him to maintain an adequate force. The subdivision of the *khas* property would have impaired these, and the allegiance of the *ghātwāls* was obviously a personal relation incapable of subdivision. Primogeniture in estates.

The corollary of the custom of primogeniture is the grant of tenures adequate to the respectable maintenance of junior members of the family. In the case of Rāmgarh these are not resumable in whole or part so long as a legitimate male descendant of the original grantee survives; but in default of such heirs they are resumed free of all encumbrances. *Khorposh* grants in estates. Resumability.

The magnitude of such a grant appears to depend on the benevolence of the head of the family; and in theory the only legitimate consideration to which he need have regard is the honour of his house. There is, however, a tendency to increase the grants to an extent which might impair the principle of primogeniture, and this is probably due to the influence of Hindu ideas of inheritance.

Among these maintenance-holders (or *khorposhdārs*) of the Rāmgarh estate the influence of these Hindu ideas has even gone so far as to lead in some cases to claims to partition. Thus recently in the case of Kapka upon the death of the head of the family and the succession of his second brother, the younger brothers sued for partition. Their claim was dismissed.

Protection of estates and tenures against sale.

In Chapter III is reproduced a passage from the 'Statistical Account' in which are described the evils which after the British occupation resulted from disregard of local peculiarities, among which one of the most considerable was the extensive transfer of immovable property by the action of the Courts from the possession of the old landlords to undesirable new-comers. One of the immediate results of the great insurrection of 1831 was the modification of the civil law so as to provide a remedy against this evil. This was effected by a set of rules for the guidance of his subordinates which Captain Wilkinson, the wise and sympathetic peace-maker of Chota Nāgpur, issued after he had suppressed the disorders. These rules, though they never received the explicit confirmation of Government, were generally followed throughout the province. That portion which relates to the sale of landed properties is quoted by Mr. Reid in his Settlement Report of Rānchi in paragraph 57, and in succeeding paragraphs the later developments are explained. The general effect was to make it necessary to obtain the sanction of the Commissioner prior to any sale; and such sanction was given very rarely. In consequence the old families were preserved from ruin, at a period when their disappearance would have provoked grave discontent among their tenants. A special side of the general question was developed in the Encumbered Estates Act (VI of 1876), regarding which reference is again desirable to Mr. Reid's report (para. 85). The latest alteration in the Act was made by Bengal Act

Encumbered Estates Act.

IV of 1911, which empowered the Commissioner, after the receipt of an application for protection under the Act, to prohibit the sale of the applicant's immovable property, or any portion of it, in execution of a decree or order of a Civil or Revenue Court, until the passing of final orders on the application. If the prayer is granted the property is vested in a manager and sale is prevented.

The question whether the retention of the Act is necessary has recently been agitated. Mr. Reid considered that as regards Ranchi there were two new factors which were of very great importance. The first was the preparation of a record-of-rights for the entire district, and the second the presence throughout the district of Christian missionaries. The first showed to all concerned what their rights were, and left little room for honest dispute: the second constituted an effective if unofficial body of advisers and guides to the peasantry. For both these reasons he considered that there would be little danger to the interests of the cultivators by the abolition of the Act. In Hazāribāgh Mr. Sifton, the Settlement Officer, considered that it is premature to hold that the mere existence of a record-of-rights will in itself serve to protect the cultivators, whose history discloses a much lower degree of self-reliance than is possessed by their neighbours in Rānchi; and he thought that the Act should be retained for the present. There appears to be no objection to its retention on the statute book; for that in itself acts as a deterrent to alien exploiters. But its application in any particular case, except where the estate is of genuine historical importance and high local prestige, should be carefully scrutinized with reference to the probable effect on the tenantry; and protection should be afforded only when their interests are likely to be seriously prejudiced by alienation. In any case there is little to be said for bolstering up under the provisions of this Act alien landlords whose ancestors acquired their property by the exercise of those same arts from which they now seek to be protected.

The number of properties enjoying protection under the Act has been as follows; in 1881 eleven, in 1891 eleven, in 1901 seventeen, in 1911 twenty-two, and at the end of 1916 fifteen.

Detailed information regarding the various kinds of subordinate tenures in the district is contained in Chapter VII of SUBORDINATE TENURES.

the Settlement Report, and the following remarks are in the nature of an epitome of much of what is there explained at length.

Shamilat taluks. Khorposh grants.

The *shamilāt tāluks* have already been described.

Khorposh grants are tenures intended for the maintenance of members of a landlord's family. They have been referred to above in connection with the Rāmgarh estate; and in addition to the ordinary type described there the Settlement Officer refers to two special kinds, of which one is known as *hin hayati* and the other as *sindurtari*. The former is given for the life of the grantee. *Sindurtari* is given on marriage, as a dowry, or provision for pin money. In the case of the Rāmgarh estate it is known as *deorhi*. Sometimes such a grant is for life, but others are only during the continuance of the status, the death of the husband having the effect of transferring the tenure to the wife of his successor. As regards succession to *khorposh* tenures generally the Settlement Officer found that in about half the *khorposh* villages primogeniture is not the rule; and that family custom, and not any well-defined local law governs succession.

Digwāri

Digwāri tenures were originally service tenures of which the services have now been commuted into cash. In origin some of these properties were without doubt created for the specific purpose of watch and ward; but others, in the opinion of the Settlement Officer, were in existence prior to the attachment of such obligations, and in fact prior to the extension to the locality of the authority of the Rāmgarh estate. "As the minor chiefs of the jungle tracts submitted to the Rāmgarh chief and were absorbed into his estate they were allowed to retain some portion of their old property, and had assigned to them the duty of guarding the roads and jungly passes; and for this purpose they had to support a number of retainers as road patrols." The instances given by him are the Kharwār chiefs of north Chatra, and the Mundāri *khuntkatlidars* of Korāmbe, on whom *digwar* duties were foisted. With the commutation of personal service into a cash rent these tenures came to be treated as transferable properties, and in consequence they have to a large extent passed into the hands of aliens.

Jagirs.

"The term *jagir*, originally applied to the assignment of villages made to military retainers for the upkeep of a military force, came to be used almost as loosely as the term *thika,* and covers any land given by a zamindar as a reward or a present. The purchaser of a tenure consisting of a large block of villages is called the *jāgirdar* of those villages, the *khuntkatti* tenure of a Goala, who obtained a reclaiming lease of jungle, is called a *jāgir ;* even the petty service holdings of the *Pāhān* and *Kumhār* are called *jāgirs ;* and all the service lands assigned by landlords to their servants, whether permanently or temporarily are called *jāgir* lands. *Jāgirs* proper are of various descriptions :—

Masruti, which is said to mean 'conditional' upon the continued rendering of services.

Khairkhahi khidmati, for good-will and services.

Baiswan, which apparently means "assigned for a particular service".

Baksh pikhdān, a gift confirmed by the grantor spitting on the *sanad.*

Maurusi murkatti, given to a retainer who killed the Chief's enemies.

Sirkatti, given to the family of a retainer who had been killed in the Chief's service.

The question whether such grants are resumable, and if so, in what circumstances, or are non-resumable and transferable, has been greatly disputed, and is not yet finally decided.

Partibility of *jagirs.*

It appears from the record-of-rights that in seventeen *jāgirs* the younger members of the family of the *jāgirdar* have maintenance grants (*khorposh*) ; in 279 cases there is a single holder, and in 613 shares have been recorded. "Kāyasths, Bābhans, Rājputs and Muhammadans coming from Bihar seem to have brought with them into the district the Hindu and Muhammadan ideas of partition, and the rights of younger brothers to a share in the family property; and most of the older autochthonous *jāgirdars* have now broken with the ancient custom and adopted partition." The incidents of a tenure cannot, however, be modified on the grantee's side so as to affect the rights of the grantor ; and in the case of those *jāgirs* which came into existence by the creation of the superior landlord (and were not confirmations of preexisting rights) the absence of recognition of the practice by the grantor or his successors would appear to be fatal to a claim of partibility as against him.

Khairats. *Khairāts* are grants made to Brāhmans either with or without conditions of service attached. *Kusbrit* is such a grant made on condition that the receiver maintains the worship at a particular temple; and is resumable if the condition is not fulfilled.

Debotar is a gift to an idol to be held by the *sebāit* for the time being: it is not in any way his property and cannot be alienated by him.

Brahmotar and *Gurutar* are lands made over as gifts to a Brahman or a *Guru* (spiritual guide).

Khairāts in general are not ordinarily resumable; but it has been held by the High Court that there is a local custom in Kunda whereby the grantor resumes when there are no male heirs of the grantee. In Rāmgarh these grants are assessed to a rent of two annas in the rupee of the original assets, but no rent is collected, and the demand is shown as temporarily excused.

Mukarrari istimrari. Rāmnath Singh was the holder of the Rāmgarh estate between 1862 and 1866. He had succeeded late in life, and had no child at the time of his death, though his widow bore a posthumous son later, who died in infancy. In the short period of four years he created no less than 644 tenures, in which the words *istimrāri mukarrari* occurred, without mention of heirs and successors. This was the beginning of great evils to his successors, to the grantees, and above all to the peasants of the villages which were so granted. For the real character of these grants has been the subject of litigation ever since his death, in which fortune has favoured first one side, and then the other; and the history of the dispute is of considerable interest to the student of the administration of the civil justice. The costs of tenure-holders have been reimbursed as far as possible at the expense of the cultivators in the affected villages. In 1875 the author of the 'Statistical Account' wrote that the grand father of the present proprietor had instituted a suit as a 'crucial test' which was then pending in the Civil Court. After the lapse of forty years a similar 'crucial test' is before the Privy Council.

Temporary tenures. In this district, as elsewhere in Chota Nāgpur, it is a common practice to use the word *thika* to express not only leases of a purely temporary character, but also any other kind of tenancy in which one special incident, namely, the amount or rent payable, is liable to alteration; and the Settlement Officer, who has discussed the question at considerable length (paragraphs 193 to

201), adverts to the risk of misunderstanding which has in the past attached to this ambiguity. As regards existing tenancies, which find entry in the record-of-rights, there is no room for mistake, for their true character has been duly recorded : but in the case of future tenancies it will be necessary equally as in the past to seek the nature of the contract beneath its verbal covering.

The delegation for a term of years, upon payment of a premium and the undertaking to pay an annual rent, of the landlord's right to collect the rents payable by the tenants, and to cultivate such lands as are at the landlord's disposal during that term, is a form of lease which a landlord in this province adopts usually for one of three reasons. He may be in urgent need of money, in which case the initial premium is the inducement ; or he may be unable for some reason or other to provide the ordinary machinery for collection or cultivation, which, in the case of large estates, is an admission of incompetence ; or he may, as sometimes happens, wish to pursue an aggressive policy against the pretensions, or even the rights, of other parties, not by recourse to the Courts but by other means which may involve personal responsibility to the Criminal Court, and this the *thikādār* undertakes. The economical unsoundness of temporary leases is obvious ; but the real gravamen of the case against them is based on the experience that the cultivators are even greater sufferers than the landlord. Such farming has been completely discarded in Government estates ; and in the management of wards and encumbered estates every opportunity is taken to abolish it. In the last few years some progress in this direction has been made in Rāmgarh and Pālganj ; but the proprietor of Kunda, on the contrary, has recently had recourse to this means of anticipating future income in order to meet pressing demands.

CULTIVATING TENANCIES.

Of cultivating as opposed to rent-collecting tenancies there are three main divisions,—tenure-holding cultivators, raiyats, and under-raiyats. This subject is treated in Chapter VI of the Settlement Report, with historical propriety, before that of tenures, where a full account is given of each class. Tenure-holding cultivators are either *khuntkattida's* or *doāmi thikadārs,* with the exception of one *Mundāri khuntkatti* tenure-holder in Gola.

Khuntkatti tenures

The character of the *khuntkatti* tenancies is explained by the circumstances in which villages are even now coming to birth. In the case of the *khuntkatti* tenures the descendents of the original founders still remain, and by a natural development have to the function of cultivating the lands which they originally added cleared in the jungle that of collecting the rents of relatives, or of the outsiders who from time to time have been admitted to their villages. The business of collecting these rents may have been retained in the hands of a single member, or divided with others and all such are technically tenure-holders by virtue of their function of receiving rent. Those who no longer discharge that function are technically *not* tenure-holders and are recorded as *khuntkatti* raiyats. There were 307 *khuntkatti* tenure-holders, and 2,956 *khuntkatti* raiyats recorded at the settlement.

Doāmi thikādārs.

Doāmi thikādārs are of two kinds. The first is distinguished from *khuntkatti* tenure-holders by the accident that the area in which he settled had been once before occupied by cultivators, but had been completely and finally abandoned by them, and to all intents and purposes his equitable claims are precisely the same as those of a *khuntkattidar*. The second class is found where the *khuntkatti* family has died out or abandoned the village, or its development has been taken over by a new head, not a member of the original founder's family. The character of the services which are requisite to establish such a title will appear from the following extract from a decision of the Judicial Commissioner in a suit brought by the superior landlord for resumption.

"The defendant's ancestor Udāy Rām came into possession fifty or sixty years ago; and that fact shows that Udāy had remained in possession for twenty years before the first *kabuliyat* was executed. Moreover at that very time Udāy Rām was admitted by the plaintiff to have been in possession of *khandwat* lands. He had therefore exercised a right to reclaim land and possessed an occupancy right in that land. He and the other defendants have continued to reclaim and to cultivate lands and to settle raiyats, and they have planted orchards, erected *bāndhs*, and effected such other improvements as go to indicate the permanency of their interest." He concluded that the defendants could not, as claimed by the landlord be ejected from their tenure upon notice.

The Settlement Officer records that among the incidents of these *doāmi thikās* are non-transferability, and resumability upon a decree for arrears of rent.

Mundāri khuntkatti.

There are thirty tenants recorded as *Mundāri khuntkattidars* in the district. The origin and incidents of this class of tenancy are described in Chapter V of the Settlement Report of Rānchi, in which district they are numerous and important.

Settled raiyats.

The great body of ordinary cultivators was recorded with the status of settled raiyats, the number of holdings with that status being 207,599. Occupancy rights which had not yet ripened into the higher status were held in 26,752 holdings. Non-occupancy raiyats held 5,335 tenancies, and there were 41,692 tenancies of under-raiyats. In the last ten years the land-owners and the tenants have received two great boons. The rights and obligations of every class of tenant have been codified in the Chota Nāgpur Tenancy Act of 1908; and the concrete material in which the individual enjoys his rights and discharges his obligations has been clearly defined in the record-of-rights. The two great trades of land-owning and cultivation can now demand from the State that its officers shall bear constantly in mind the supreme importance of maintaining the equilibrium in their relations which has now at length been won after so arduous and costly a quest.

Occupancy raiyats.

Non-occupancy raiyats.

Under-raiyats.

CHAPTER XII.

GENERAL ADMINISTRATION.

The non-regulation District.

THE districts of the Chota Nāgpur Division are known as non-regulation districts since 1834, when they were formed out of the old Rāmgarh district, and the ordinary regulations were declared to be without force in them. Very little is left now of the difference then established. A clause in the Encumbered Estates Act is the last survival of the old policy of preventing the sale of land for debt; and in the sphere of criminal justice the District Officer has certain extended powers of original jurisdiction: An agrarian law co-extensive with the Division imposes on his subordinate Deputy Collectors the duty of trying rent suits; and he decides the appeals where the value is less than Rs. 100. In Hazāribāgh his part in the administration of civil justice is confined to the execution of decrees of the Subordinate Judges, the grant of succession certificates, and the relief of insolvents. His official designation is Deputy Commissioner, instead of Collector-Magistrate.

Subdivisions.

The district is at present divided into three subdivisions. The sadr subdivision has an area of about 3,435 square miles, with 612,544 people. The staff usually consists of a Deputy Commissioner and four Deputy Collector-Magistrates, of whom one acts as Sadr Subdivisional Officer. There is also a Special Excise Deputy Collector for the entire district and a Manager for the encumbered estates. Occasionally a Joint or Assistant Magistrate or a Sub-Deputy Collector is attached to headquarters. There are also a Civil Surgeon, Executive Engineer, and District Engineer at headquarters. Giridih subdivision was formed in 1870, when it was centred at Karharbāri, about four miles west of Giridih. In 1871 it was moved two miles north to Pachamba, and the final transfer was made to Giridih in 1881. The staff at Giridih consists of a covenanted civilian as Subdivisional Officer, a Deputy Collector-Magistrate and a Sub-Deputy Collector. The area is 2,006 square miles and population 452,656. Chatra subdivision was opened in 1914, with its head quarters at the town which had been the capital of Chota Nāgpur from 1780 to 1834. The staff consists of a Deputy Collector-Magistrate as Subdivisional Officer, and a Sub-Deputy Collector. The area is 1,545 square miles, and the population 223,409. In 1870 there was a subdivision at Barhi, but it was abolished in 1872.

Revenue work.

Land registration, partition, excise, and the collection of land revenue and cess are done solely at the district headquarters, but the two Subdivisional Officers continue to do the minor Land Acquisition work of their subdivisions, the collection of all arrears under the Public Demands Recovery Act, and all Tenancy Act cases, including the trial of rent suits.

Rent suits.

Rent suits are tried at the sadr station by two Deputy Collectors, at Giridih by the Subdivisional Officer and the Munsif, who has been specially empowered, and at Chatra by the Subdivisional Officer.

REVENUE.

The revenue of the district in 1915-16 totalled Rs. 9,80,709, exclusive of a sum of Rs. 33,856 obtained from petty miscellaneous sources. In 1901 the respective amounts were Rs. 5,50,363 and Rs. 8,706.

LAND REVENUE.

The collections from land revenue necessarily fluctuate very little. The demand from the Government estates expands very slowly, for re-settlements occur only after long intervals, and meantime additions to the rent due to the extension of cultivation are small. The demand from the permanently-settled estates is very light and defaults are rare. The total demand of Rs. 1,35,527 in 1915-16 was made up of Rs. 47,260 due in respect of seventy permanently-settled estates, Rs. 50,729 from the Karharbāri colliery temporarily settled estate, and Rs. 37,538 from the three *khās mahāls* and the camping grounds. Collections totalled Rs. 1,35,444: The demand of Rs. 47,260 represents about seven rupees a square mile; and the cash rents alone which landlords receive are over twelve lakhs, on which sum the Government revenue is less than four per cent. Over and above the cash rent the landlords have extensive areas in their own cultivation, and also collect a considerable produce rent.

EXCISE.

The revenue from excise has undergone an extraordinary expansion, especially in the last few years. In 1835 *sayer* and *abkari*, as it was termed, brought in Rs. 23,471, and in 1850 Rs. 37,485. In 1870 the excise revenue was Rs. 48,770. By 1900 it had risen to Rs. 1,77,669, and in 1913, when the highest point was reached, it amounted to Rs. 6,24,381. When the war broke out in 1914 the trade in lac, mica and hides was temporarily dislocated, and the revenue fell to Rs. 5,15,019. The continued rise in the income from country spirits had, however, already led to the issue of orders to reduce facilities for drinking, and eighteen shops were closed in the last three years, mainly in areas where the aboriginal population is strongest. The average income of Government from excise per head of population rose from 2·4 annas in 1901 to 7·8 annas in 1913, and now stands at 6·4 annas. Though the real consumption at outstills is difficult to ascertain it is probable that the increase in the income of Government has corresponded with an increase in the consumption of spirits; and that emigrants to the coal-fields and elsewhere have brought back the drink habit.

Country Spirits

There are two classes of shops in the district for the sale of country spirits. In the neighbourhood of Giridih the contract supply system is in force. The manufacturers deliver the concentrated spirits to Government at Giridih warehouse, whence it is issued to the vendors on payment of excise. The consumption from this source is exactly known; but such is not the case in respect of the rest of the district, where the outstill system is in force. The lessee of an outstill pays a fixed monthly fee, and Government is not financially interested in the quantity of spirit which he distills or sells, and he falsifies his figures in order that reliable information of his profits may not reach either the Income Tax Department or possible competitors at the next auction. The spirit is distilled from dried *mahua* flowers, with a small quantity of *gur*, and three strengths of spirits are manufactured, of which the cheapest is usually about 88 under-proof and sells at an anna for a quart bottle. The outturn per maund of *mahua* of spirit of this strength is entered in the accounts at the lowest quantity which the lessee hopes will pass scrutiny, and one man will put down sixteen gallons per maund every day of the year, while another puts down twenty-two gallons. One of the most common offences is exchanging liquor for grain, and this is specially heinous in the case of the *Kamias*, who may be seen in the Kunda outstills after the day's work is over buying a temporary oblivion with their children's food. The extension of the contract supply system to the entire district has been sanctioned, but the war has necessitated a postponement. Out of the total revenue of Rs. 4,32,682 from country spirits outstills contributed Rs. 3,75,567.

Hemp drugs brought in Rs. 38,329, of which *ganja* produced Rs. 36,121 and *bhang* Rs. 2,208. The number of *ganja* shops has been reduced considerably in the last few years, but the habit of taking hemp drugs is widespread among the lower classes of Muhammadans in the towns. The revenue from opium is growing steadily since the abolition of poppy cultivation in 1911, and amounted to Rs. 33,691. This increase is probably due to the gradual exhaustion of the stocks which used to be held back illicitly. The fermented juice of the *tar* and *khajur* palms is sold under license by the name of *tari* and brought in Rs. 8,733. DRUGS.

The income from stamps in 1835 was Rs. 13,048, in 1850 Rs. 12,131 and in 1870 Rs. 31,775. Between 1901 and 1911 the average was Rs. 1,24,649, and in the five years ending 1915-16 this increased to Rs. 1,76,240. Judicial stamps in 1915-16 brought in Rs. 1,39,260 and non-judicial stamps Rs. 31,533. The costly litigation indicated by the increase in the last five years has been mainly in connexion with the mineral and *mukarrari* resumption suits of the Rāmgarh estate and disputes about Pārasnāth Hill. STAMPS.

The receipts from the tax on incomes have risen very little in the last sixteen years. In 1900-01 they were Rs. 27,165 and in 1915-16 they were Rs. 31,877. The greatest sum collected was Rs. 35,296 in 1902-03, after which the minimum assessible income was raised from Rs. 500 to Rs. 1,000. INCOME TAX.

The demand for cess amounted in 1915-16 to Rs. 1,33,172, and collections were Rs. 1,21,440. It is levied at the rate of an anna in the rupee on the rent of agricultural lands, in accordance with an assessment made at comparatively long intervals; and on the profits from mines and forests. This last cess is calculated annually on the profits of the three years immediately preceding, and in 1915-16 collections amounted to Rs. 8,093. A general revaluation for cess purposes is being delayed by the necessity of awaiting the completion of fair rent settlements in connexion with the district record-of-rights. CESS.

REGISTRATION.

There are five offices for the registration of assurances under Act XVI of 1908. At Hazāribāgh there is a District Sub-Registrar, who deals with the documents presented there, and assists the Deputy Commissioner, who is *ex officio* District Registrar, in supervising the proceedings of the Sub-Registrars who are in charge of the outlying offices. The average number of documents registered annually during the quinquennium ending in 1910 was 6,521 as compared with 4,847 in the succeeding five years.

The marginal statement shows the number of documents registered as well as the receipts and expenditure of each office for the year 1915.

Name.	Documents registered.	Receipts.	Expenditure.
1	2	3	4
		Rs.	Rs.
Hazāribāgh ...	1,717	5,843	4,056
Giridih ...	1,478	2,819	2,030
Chatra ...	482	725	2,064
Barhi ...	552	846	2,1(3
Gola ...	1,641	1,502	2,014
Total ...	5,870	11,735	12,267

Since the passing of the amending agrarian act in 1903 the transfer of raiyati lands has been greatly restricted, and great care is exercised to prevent the registration of deeds in contravention of the present law. Similar care is taken to ensure that all lands are duly described by their survey area plot numbers, village and thānā. The registration of *kamiauti* bonds has also been forbidden by executive order.

ADMINISTRATION OF CIVIL JUSTICE.

The Judicial staff entertained for the purposes of civil justice consists of the Judicial Commissioner of Chota Nāgpur, whose head-quarters are at Rānchi, the Deputy Commissioner Sub-Judge, who now deals only with the execution of decrees, and certain insolvency and succession cases, a special Subordinate Judge whose headquarters are at Rānchi, and Additional Sub-Judges sanctioned from time to time to cope with extra work. There are three Munsifs at Hazāribāgh, Chatra and Giridih, respectively, but the Munsif of Chatra is also the Subdivisional Officer; and the

Munsif of Giridih assists in the disposal of rent suits in his special character of Deputy Collector. The three munsifs originated in 1834, immediately after the creation of the district. The first officer to be placed in charge of the new district was Dr. John Davidson, who afterwards did most valuable work in different parts of what was then called the South-West Frontier Agency in association with the Governor General's Agent, Captain (later Sir Thomas) Wilkinson. In a letter to Captain Wilkinson, dated the 24th January 1834, he reported that there were five munsifs at Māyāpur, Chatra, Chhāi, Bishungarh and Kharagdiha, who were paid by the price of the stamp paper filed in their courts, and occasionally received fees for the attachment and sale of property in execution of decrees from the superior courts. With the exception of the munsif of Chatra they had a very indifferent character, and Dr. Davidson proposed their immediate dismissal, and the creation of three munsifs at Chatra, Hazāribāgh and Kharagdiha, of which the last was ultimately transferred to Giridih.

Statistics of civil justice for 1915 were as follows :—

Suits disposed of.	Munsifs.	Sub-Judges.	Judicial Commissioner.
1	2	3	4
(a) Ordinary procedure.	1,167	103	2
(b) Small Cause Court ,,	654	*Nil*	*Nil*

The Judicial Commissioner disposed of 366 appeals from the three districts of Rānchi, Hazāribāgh and Palāmau.

ADMINISTRATION OF CRIMINAL JUSTICE. Criminal justice is administered by the Judicial Commissioner of Chota Nāgpur, who visits the district from time to time on circuit as Sessions Judge, and also hears appeals from the decisions of magistrates of the first class; by the Deputy Commissioner, who is vested with extended powers under section 30 of the Criminal Procedure Code, and also hears appeals from second and third class magistrates; by the Subdivisional Officers and by stipendiary and honorary magistrates vested with powers of various classes. In the sadr subdivision one of the Deputy Magistrates is Subdivisional Officer, and he tries all cases from certain specified thanas, the rest of the sadr subdivision being distributed between two other magistrates with first class powers. There is one honorary magistrate with first class powers, and a stipendiary magistrate with third class powers who assist in case a file is overcrowded. In Giridih there is a Deputy Magistrate with first class powers, and a Sub-Deputy Magistrate with second class powers, and an honorary magistrate with the same powers. In Chatra there is a Sub-Deputy Magistrate with second class powers. Two honorary magistrates with second class powers are being appointed for the Bokāro and Kargāli collieries, as they are at present very inaccessible from Giridih and Hazāribāgh. They will take cognizance of certain classes of cases both on complaint and on police report.

Statistics of Criminal Justice.

In 1915 the number of persons convicted or bound over was as follows :—

Offences against public tranquillity...	42
Murder	4
Culpable homicide	2
Rape	*Nil*
Grievous hurt	9
Hurt, criminal, by force and assault	119
Dacoity	26
Robbery	5
Theft with aggravating circumstances	6
Other thefts	336
Other offences under the Indian Penal Code	404
Bad-livelihood	51
Keeping the peace	8
Salt law	*Nil*
Excise law	41
Forest law	25
Stamp law	1
Municipal law	33
Other offences	371

The dacoits were Ghātwārs of Kharagdiha, who had been driven by poverty to revert to their old habits. Cattle thefts reported in 1915 numbered 128.

Crime.

Mr. O'Malley, in his Gazetteer of Gayā, quotes as follows from a "Description of Hindustan, by Walter Hamilton,

1820," regarding crime in Rāmgarh. The destruction of many old forts had to be "recommended by the Magistrate at an early period of the British domination, as they afforded protection to the refractory zamindars, and hordes of irregular banditti. Theft is common throughout Rāmgarh, but murder is more prevalent among a particular class, which are the slaves possessed by persons inhabiting the mountainous and inccessible interior, and of savage and ferocious habits. When petty disputes occur, these slaves are compelled by their masters to perpetrate any enormity, and are more especially employed for the purposes of assassination. Any hesitation or repugnance on the part of the slave is attended with immediate death, which is equally his fate should he fail in the attempt. On the other hand, if he succeed he is sought out by the officers of Government and executed as a murderer. The usual police have hitherto been unable to seize the cowardly instigator, and if recourse be had to a military force he retires into the jungle. On the occurrence of such an event the whole country is thrown into confusion and rebellion, during which many unoffending persons lose their lives; and the troops, after many ineffectual attempts to execute the Magistrate's orders, return to their stations worn out with fatigue, and their numbers thinned by the pestilential atmosphere of the jungles." In 1872 Colonel Dalton wrote "Hazāribāgh was always notorious for its dacoities. Formerly, in the Mughal days, the Kharagdiha jurisdiction was the worst part of the district for this crime; afterwards the Grand Trunk Road attracted attention, but a strong road police was established, and great efforts made, not always with success, to render it safe for travellers. Yet I have before me police reports which show that in 1832 eighty-seven dacoities and in 1833 fifty-eight were reported in Hazāribāgh district."

The glory of the Grand Trunk Road has departed, and travellers pass through the district by train. The annual crop of pilgrims on which first the Kharagdiha robbers and later the dacoits of Bagodar and Dumri depended for their support has now completely and permanently failed, but the 'Chakāi' Dusādhs still pilfer the carts that pass between Giridih and Mirzāganj. Even they, however, have fallen on evil times, for they are now being registered as a criminal tribe. The Ghātwārs of the old Kharagdiha pargana still occasionally kill a Bābhan or Mahuri *mahājan*, who squeezes them beyond endurance, and in times of scarcity they plunder the liquor shops. Witchcraft yields its annual crop of offences, ranging from murder to criminal house-trespass. But crime is now moderate in quantity and usually hum-drum in character. Occasionally an irruption down the railway of Karwāls, or poisoners from the west, reduces a little the balance of past injuries.

POLICE.

Liability of Zamindars.

When the revenue settlement was made the duty of repressing crime and maintaining order was imposed explicitly and unambiguously on the parties who received settlement, as will appear from the following passages quoted in the Settlement Report.

(*a*) At the time of the decennial settlement the Board of Revenue wrote to the Collector of Rāmgarh as follows :—

"We shall hold the Raja of Rāmgarh responsible for keeping up the establishment of *ghātwārs* and *cutwāls* for the protection of the country and for defraying their allowances, amounting to Benares Rs. 2,620-5-5."

In the *kabuliyats* which were taken from the *ghātwāls* of Kharagdiha, from the Chief of Kunda and from the proprietor of Rāmgarh the obligation was expressed quite clearly as follows :—

"I will guard and watch over the highways within my boundaries so carefully as to enable travellers to journey over them peacefully and safely. I will not harbour thieves within my jurisdiction. If peradventure, which God forbid, any body's property be robbed, I will conformably with criminal regulations search for and produce the robber with the property."

Original thānās.

When the proprietor of Kodarma obtained the decree declaring him independent of Rāmgarh he was charged with the duty of maintaining the police establishment of Kodarma, and likewise eight *digwārs* to guard the passes on his estate and eight *barkandāzes* for escort duty between Kodarma and the Sadr station. It was only the Kendi zamindar who was not required to undertake any responsibilities of this character. Apparently the *ghātwāl tikāit* of Gāwān kept up a thana at Gāwān, and the Rāmgarh proprietor maintained six, of which those at Rāmgarh, Pagār (in thana Barkāgāon), Hunterganj and Itkhori probably were never moved. There was another at Chatro, on the military road from Calcutta to Benares made in 1782 and abandoned in 1838, about twenty-five miles eas by south of Hāzaribāgh, and perhaps one at Ichāk. The Hazāribāgh thānā establishment was paid for half by him and half by Government, who appointed and controlled the staff. There was no thānā at all in the south-east of the district. Probably the thānā at Chatra was always kept up by Government. In the north-east besides Gāwān there were thānās at Kharagdiha and Sirāmpur, which also were probably maintained by Government. The insurrection in Rānchi in 1831, which was partly due to the abuse of police powers by landholders in that district, led, among many other administrative changes, to the partial introduction of Government control; and in 1837 it is stated that the district was divided into twelve thānās, in four of which the police were appointed and paid by Government; in seven the landholders appointed and paid them; and in Hazāribāgh the cost was divided as explained above. Possibly the four Government thānās in 1837 were Chatra, Kanha Chatti (opened in 1835), Sirāmpur and Kharagdiha, and the remainder consisted of Gāwān, Kodarma, Hazāribāgh, Rāmgarh, Pagār, Hunterganj, Itkhori, and Chatro. In 1838 the new Grand Trunk Road was opened, and the old Benares Road was closed down. The Chatro thānā was moved south-east to Gumia, and Kanha Chatti was closed, new thānās being opened at Barhi and Bagodar on the new road. In 1861 the police powers of the landholders were abolished, and by 1864 the established thānās were at Hazāribāgh, Itkhori, Pagār, Rāmgarh, Kasmār, Gumia, Hunterganj, Barhi, Bagodar, Sirāmpur, Kharagdiha, Gāwān and Kodarma.

Alterations in 1834.

Changes in 1838 on opening of Grand Trunk Road.

Abolition of Zamindari police.

Thānā jurisdiction. The distribution of the police thānās since 1872 has been as follows, the areas being approximate only. The information is derived from the census reports :—

1872.		1891.		1901.	
1		2		3	
Sadr Subdivision.					
1. Hazāribāgh	594 sq. miles	1. Hazāribāgh	457 sq. miles.	1. Hazāribāgh	456 sq. miles.
2. Gumia	624 „	2. Jageswar	599 „	2. Gumia	258 „
				3. Māndu	344 „
3. Kasmār	149 „	3. Kasmār	321 „	4. Kasmār	320 „
4. Rāmgarh	708 „	4. Rāmgarh	364 „	5. Rāmgarh	369 „
5. Tandwa	468 „	5. Tandwa	489 „	6. Barkāgāon	486 „
6. Barhi	458 „	6. Barhi	353 „	7. Barhi	358 „
7. Bagodar	450 „	7. Bagodar	442 „	8. Bagodar	426 „
8. Kodarma	371 „	8. Chatra	337 „	9. Kodarma	443 „
9. Chatra	712 „	9. Simaria	377 „	10. Chatra	347 „
10. Hunterganj	603 „	10. Hunterganj	480 „	11. Simaria	381 „
	5,197	11. Chaupāran	356 „	12. Hunterganj	477 „
			4,575	13. Chaupāran	354 „
					5,019
Pachamba Subdivision.		Giridih Subdivision.		Giridih Subdivision.	
11. Pachamba	562 sq. miles.	12. Giridih	450 sq. ms.	14. Giridih	461 sq. miles.
12. Kharagdiha	918 „	13. Kharagdiha	613 „	15. Kharagdiha	340 „
13. Gāwān	344 „	14. Dumri	509 „	16. Dhanwār	249 „
	1,824	15. Gāwān	432 „	17. Dumri	514 „
		16. Kodarma	442 „	18. Gāwan	438 „
			2,446		2,002

The changes between 1872 an 1891 were considerable. Between 1891 and 1901 they were unimportant. Jageswar was split up into Gumia and Māndu, and Kharagdiha into Dhanwār and Kharagdiha. Barkāgāon was adopted as the name of the thānā known originally as Pagār and later as Tandwa, but always co-extensive with Karanpura.

The present distribution of the police force of the district is in thirty-two police-stations, of which the names and areas are as follows :— Present distribution.

Name of thānā.	Name of police station.	Area.
1	2	3
1. Sadr Subdivision—		
1. Hazāribāgh ...	1. Hazāribagh ...	300·2
	2. Ichāk	151·7
2. Gumia	3. Gumia	261·3
3. Māndu	4. Māndu	334·4
4. Petarbār	5. Petarbār	252·8
	6. Jaridih	64·3
5. Rāmgarh	7. Rāmgarh	232·9
	8. Gola	129·7
6. Barkāgāon ...	9. Barkāgāon ...	322·6
	10. Tandwa	166·7
7. Barhi	11. Barhi	190·0
	12. Barahkatha ...	166·1
8. Bagodar	13 Bagodar	422·6
9. Kodarma	14. Kodarma	344·0
	15. Jainagar	95·6
	Total area, Sadr ...	3,435·4

N.B.—The area of Kodarma has been calculated as follows :—

Area in Kodarma Settlement	...	108	square miles.
Area in District Settlement	...	236	„ „
Total	...	344	„ „

Name of thānā.	Name of police station.	Area.
1	2	3
2. Chatra Subdivision—		
10. Chaupāran ...	16. Chaupāran ...	258.1
	17. Itkhori	97·4
11. Chatra	18. Chatra	246·5
	19. Gidhaur	107·8
12. Simaria	20. Simaria	377·6
13. Hunterganj ...	21. Hunterganj ...	285·5
	22. Partabpur... ...	171·7
	Total area, Chatra ...	1,544·6
3. Giridih Sub-division.—		
14. Giridih	23. Giridih	375·8
	24. Bengābād... ...	79·5
15. Gāwān	25. Gāwān	295·8
	26. Sātgāwān... ...	117·3
16. Kharagdiha ...	27. Kharagdiha ...	354·5
17. Dhanwār... ...	28. Dhanwār	136·2
	29. Birni	123·4
18. Dumri	30. Dumri	167·3
	31. Pirtānr	151·7
	32. Nawādih	204·1
	Total area, Giridih ...	2,005·6
	District Total ...	6,985·6

The area has been obtained from the acreage shown in column 88, Appendix G, of the Hazāribāgh Settlement Report.

Proposals have been sanctioned for the redistribution of thānā Kodarma between the police-stations of Kodarma and Jainagar, of thānā Gāwān between Gāwān and Satgāwān, of thānā Giridih between three police-stations and of thānā Kharagdiha between two police-stations. The principle has been laid down that all changes of police jurisdiction must be made within the external boundaries (as surveyed in the recent settlement) of the eighteen thanas specified above.

The sanctioned strength of the police in 1915 was one Superintendent, one Assistant Superintendent, two Deputy Superintendents, seven Inspectors, sixty-three Sub-Inspectors, one sergeant, seventy-six head constables and 499 constables. The total cost of the force in 1915 was Rs. 1,90,537. The annual payments made by the zamindars of the district in liquidation of their thānā obligations are, by Rāmgarh Rs. 2,592-12-0, and by Kunda Rs. 600.

Digwārs.

In addition to the thānā establishments the settlement-holders had to guard the roads and passes against invaders and dacoits, and for this purpose they maintained patrols known as *digwārs*, who were usually remunerated by grants of service lands, and less frequently by wages inadequate in amount, and paid at irregular intervals. There were somewhat frequent changes in the main lines of communication, and these were embarrassing to the service-holders, who were liable to be called on to guard new lines remote from their grants. Finally in 1878 the liability of the settlement holders was commuted into a cash payment of Rs. 25,760 a year, part of which was imposed on certain considerable *jāgirdars* of the Rāmgarh estate. From this income, which is collected by the Deputy Commissioner, a local fund is maintained from which the *digwārs* and *sirdar digwārs* are paid monthly cash wages of rupees four and five respectively. They are appointed and dismissed by the Superintendent of Police; and are stationed in units of three or four men at *digwāri* posts which are from time to time altered according to the varying needs of the roads. When road robberies begin to be numerous the *digwārs* escort the carts from their own *phānri* to the next; but in normal times they pass a lazy if ill-paid existence.

Village Chaukidārs.

In 1916 the village chaukidārs were 2,320 in number, of whom 251 were 'Regulation' chaukidārs, appointed by the landlord and paid by him or by the villagers, in cash or by *chākrān* lands. The remainder were appointed by the Superintendent of Police under the Chota Nāgpur Rural Police Act, and paid from the Chaukidāri Fund. A general re-assessment is being made in which the unit area is no longer the village but the entire police station, whereby the incidence of the tax is equalized. All sources of income, including agriculture, are reduced to the common denominator of an acre of first class rice-land, and the requirements of the police station, divided by this denominator, have so far been satisfied by a rate of from 2 to 2¾ annas. The minimum tax is six annas a year, and the maximum twelve rupees. Simultaneously the 'Regulation' chaukidārs are being brought under the Act, as the conditions of their appointment and pay were against their efficiency. The rate stated above is sufficient to permit of a wage of Rs. 4 (four) a month for each chaukidār with the exception of the towns of Giridih, Pachamba and Kodarma, where higher rates are necessary. There are no dafadars. The current demand of chaukidāri cess in 1916 was Rs. 1,02,541.

JAILS.

The jail at Hazāribāgh is what is known as a Central Jail, and receives long-term prisoners from other districts. It has accommodation for 1,156 male and 33 female prisoners. Attached to it is a plantation of aloes from which fibre is extracted by the prisoners, and an extensive garden contributes largely to the diet. The water-supply is obtained from the lowest of three lakes, and for some time it was suspected of being the cause of an outbreak of dysentery: but large sums have been spent in reducing the danger of contamination from surface drainage, and the health of the prisoners is now satisfactory. The sub-jails at Giridih and Chatra are new, and were used for the first time in 1916. The Giridih building is specially capacious. Prisoners convicted at Giridih are usually sent not to the Sadr jail but to Gayā, as it is accessible by rail. These sub-jails have accommodation for forty and eighteen male, and five and two female prisoners, respectively.

CHAPTER XIII.

LOCAL SELF-GOVERNMENT.

THE District Board was established in 1900, when the provisions of the Local Self-Government Act III (B. C.) of 1885 were extended to the district. It now consists of seventeen members, of whom six are officials and members by virtue of their office. Eight are non-officials appointed by Government, and three are elected by the members of the Giridih Local Board out of their own number. The Deputy Commissioner is *ex officio* Chairman, and the Vice-Chairman is one of the members, elected by his colleagues. The Board is appointed for a period of three years. DISTRICT BOARD.

The duties of the Board consist mainly in the repair of public roads and the construction of new roads, with subsidiary bridges, rest houses and other buildings, the promotion and supervision of elementary education, the supply of medical relief to human beings and cattle, the improvement of the water-supply and the custody of stray cattle. It is in respect of the first of these duties connected with communications that the Board enjoys the greatest freedom and shoulders the greatest responsibilities. Duties of the Board.

The main source of income is derived from the cess on land, and the profits of mines and forests. In a normal year these aggregate Rs. 1,30,000, but in years of scarcity delay occurs in the payment of cesses by the landlords. Government contributions amount to about Rs. 40,000 and income from cattle pounds to about Rs. 5,000. In addition to this aggregate of Rs. 1,75,000 special grants may be received from Government for specific objects, such as bridges or schools. Income.

The income from coal mines, which is so important an addition to the resources of the neighbouring district of Mânbhum, is almost negligible here, amounting in 1915-16 to Rs. 4,167 only. So much of the Giridih field as belongs to private owners is being rapidly exhausted; and the profits of the small area in the south-east corner of Dumri thānā, sometimes known as the Bokāro-Jherria field appear to be very small. The large and important mines at Giridih which belong to the East Indian Railway Company do not pay cess; for it has been held that for this purpose the company is *de facto* a state railway. Similarly no cess is paid for the colliery at Bokāro, which is managed by the East Indian Railway for itself and the Bengal-Nagpur Railway jointly. These collieries will shortly be producing annually about a million tons of first class coal. So far, however, they have not necessitated any special expenditure from the funds of the District Board for roads or medical and sanitary services. On the other hand, the Board receives a large though indirect subvention from provincial funds in the shape of the many miles of provincial roads which are maintained without expense to the district.

Expenditure. In framing its budget estimate the Board has to begin with those items on which expenditure is beyond its powers of control. These are firstly education, for which the minimum expenditure stipulated in 1915-16 was Rs. 55,026 and secondly medical and sanitary charges and water-supply for which at least Rs. 25,000 must be provided. This ordinarily leaves about Rs. 95,000 for all other charges. In 1915-16 the actual expenses were as follows :—

	Rs.
Veterinary charges	4,012
Administration	8,787
Allowances and Contributions ...	840
Stationery and Printing	1,830
Arboriculture	1,874
Establishment for public works ...	17,529
Maintenance of existing public works ...	51,751
New works	19,615

Education, as a matter of fact, received Rs. 61,334 and Medical, etc., Rs. 25,796. When the Board is in funds the last two items of communications—maintenance and new works—do not fare badly; but if the collection of cess has been poor rigid economy is unavoidable. The practical effect is that new works are possible only in case of a windfall in the shape of a grant from Government.

The Board maintains three middle vernacular schools—at Gola, Expenditure. Jori and Kharagdiha—one upper primary school, and three lower primary schools. Aid is given to three middle English schools, six industrial schools, six other schools, thirty-one upper primary and 503 lower primary schools. The inspecting staff is paid by Government, except ten pandits, who are gradually being replaced by Sub-Inspectors. Primary schools required Rs. 41,517 besides scholarships Rs. 1,005 and wages of pandits amounting to Rs. 3,055. Middle English schools cost the Board Rs. 1,933 and middle vernacular Rs. 3,176 besides Rs. 10,452 on new buildings. Further expenditure is contemplated in providing hostels for the middle vernacular schools, in which in recent times the number of pupils has decreased.

Medical and allied expenditure.

The Board maintained one dispensary (at Tandwa) at a cost of Rs. 1,729 and contributed Rs. 13,503 to other medical institutions, out of which the Sadr Hospital received Rs. 6,845, Chatra Rs. 2,119 and the Giridih Hospital Rs. 325. A Sanitary Inspector is maintained mainly at the expense of the Board to advise the villagers in matters of sanitation and assist upon the outbreak of epidemics. New wells are made and old ones are kept in order at a considerable annual expense.

Veterinary.

Two Veterinary Assistants are employed at the joint expense of the Board and Government, one at Giridih and the other at Hazāribāgh, who tour freely in the interior. Large sums are spent annually on serum for inoculation against rinderpest.

Giridih Local Board.

The Local Board at Giridih was created in 1906. The Subdivisional Officer is *ex officio* Chairman, and in addition there are eight nominated non-official members. The Board prepares a budget for the repair and original works of communication in the Giridih Subdivision, the Veterinary Assistant, pounds, ferry and wells; and this is usually adopted by the District Board so far as funds permit. In addition it exercises a local control over the execution of all works included in the budget.

Municipalities. Hazāribāgh.

The Municipality of Hazāribāgh was established on the 1st of April 1869. By 1911 it had a population of 17,009, and the rate-payers numbered 2,540 or 15 per cent. The area included in municipal limits is 7·13 square miles. The Commissioners consist of the Deputy Commissioner who is *ex officio* Chairman and fifteen members, of whom two are nominated, ten elected and three are *ex officio*. The hitherto system of taxation consisted of a personal tax of one per cent on the circumstances and property of the assesses within the municipality, practically an income-tax, and a latrine tax at 6¼ per cent. on the annual value of holdings. In the case of buildings the property of Government, the occupier pays 7½ per cent. on the annual value. A proposal has, however, been adopted to substitute a holding rate for the personal tax. Taxes are also levied on animals and vehicles and certain trades. Other important sources of income are obtained from the markets and pounds, and also from some landed property belonging to the municipality. The real income and expenditure are obscured by the responsibility which the municipality undertakes for the maintenance of the local hospital, which is, however, largely supported from extra-municipal funds. In 1915-16 the income from municipal sources was Rs. 26,798 and Rs. 3,921 were received in grants from Government, making a total income of Rs. 30,719 for all purposes other than the hospital. Receipts for the hospital amounted to Rs. 11,810. Expenditure aggregated Rs. 27,951 (including Rs. 1,642 on repayment of loan) and Rs. 15,442 on the hospital. The net cost of the hospital to the municipality in the year was Rs. 3,639. The municipality still owed Rs. 17,876 out of a loan of Rs. 20,000 taken from Government for making a new system of surface drains.

Chatra. The town of Chatra was for fifty-four years the headquarters of British administration in the province of Chota Nāgpur, but it has for the last thirty years been declining in prosperity and in 1911 the population had decreased to 9,222, the tax-payers numbering about 15 per cent. The area of the municipality is 3·78 square miles. The system of taxation is a personal tax on "circumstances and property within the municipality" at 1¼ per cent. No latrine tax is levied. Like Hazāribāgh Chatra takes the responsibility for the local hospital; and in the year 1915-16 Rs. 2,383 were received from outside sources for its support. Excluding this sum from both receipts and expenditure they aggregated Rs. 8,958 and Rs. 6,502 respectively. The Commissioners are saving as much as possible to meet the cost of the new hospital which they are about to build. The constitution of the Council is an *ex officio* Chairman, who is the Subdivisional Officer, two *ex officio* members, two nominated members and eight elected members.

Giridih. The municipality of Giridih was created in 1902. In 1911 the population had grown to 10,668 and the tax-payers formed

1·48 per cent. of that number. The area at present is 1·35 square miles, but proposals have been made for an important extension to include Pachamba. The income in 1915-16, which included Rs. 10,987 from rates and taxes, Rs. 1,067 from other municipal sources and Rs. 1,675 from outside sources, aggregated Rs. 14,428 and the expenditure Rs. 15,804. The system of taxation now in force is a holding rate of 6 per cent. on the annual value, and a latrine tax at Rs. 3-6 per cent. The council consists of the Subdivisional Officer as *ex officio* chairman, four nominated and eight elected commissioners.

Additional information about these municipalities is given in the chapter on Public Health and in the Gazetteer.

Union Committees.

There are no Union Committees in the district.

CHAPTER XIV.

EDUCATION.

An interesting account of the state of education in the district shortly after its creation is given in the following letter from Captain Louis Bird, the officer in charge of Hazāribāgh, to Captain Wilkinson, the Governor General's Agent. It is dated the 12th August 1837:—

Education in 1837.

"I have the honour to acknowledge the receipt of your letter No. 782, dated the 7th instant, forwarding for my information and guidance the Sadr Board of Revenue's Circular No. 65, dated the 1st idem and requesting me to state where I would recommend a school should be established within my Division, and instructing me to avail myself of every proper opportunity to carry into effect the wishes of the Board as expressed in the 6th paragraph. A Government Seminary is a desideratum, and should the funds at the disposal of Government be sufficient, I would recommend that one be established at the Sadr Station of my Division as it would then be under my immediate eye and superintendence. As an experiment it might be introduced on a small scale, as I do not anticipate the admission of many pupils here. This, you are aware, is an isolated situation, and the residents are confined to the camp followers and others attached to the European Regiment here, and the Amlah of my court and their dependants, with the addition of a few Mahajans. The respectable part of the Native community do not look upon this station as their home, having their families at Gayā and Patna, and if inclined to send their children to a Seminary avail themselves of the one established at the latter station. I have a small school in which the instruction is confined to the vernacular language, and which is attended by about eighteen or twenty boys. These would perhaps attend at the Seminary, and perhaps we might expect an addition of eight or ten more. The hope expressed by the Board in their letter that the opulent natives in the mufassil would employ their wealth and their influence in the promotion of the contemplated object, I see no prospect of being realized; for this district can boast of little wealth as the several zamindars, with one or two exceptions, are involved in pecuniary difficulties, and some of the Tikāits and Thākurs can hardly command a meal for the morrow. The little wealth in the district is in the hands of mahajans and they are too much interested in keeping the several *ilakadars* in that state of ignorance of which they have already taken advantage to enrich themselves, consequently no aid can be expected from them to further the object in view.

"The observation of the Government on the question brought before the Board on the 12th August 1830 as to the zamindars in the interior being remarkable for their general want of instruction, their ignorance and their prejudices, is still applicable to this district, and any plan for supplying them with useful knowledge, liberalizing their feelings and enlarging their minds appears to me to be hopeless and visionary. During my approaching annual tour I shall avail myself of every proper opportunity to carry into effect the wishes of the Board as expressed in the 6th paragraph, although I am prepared to find every suggestion on this score met universally with pleas of poverty, embarrassment and ruin. To enter into any lengthened detail would be useless, as it would contain nothing new to you, aware as you are of the general poverty and distress which pervades this district."

Education in 1872.

From the 'Statistical Account' it appears that there was no government school of any kind until 1865; and five years later government support was confined to one district school, which taught English, four vernacular schools, and three aided English schools. Altogether these schools had 403 pupils. There was a number of pāthsālas or indigenous village schools, but these were ordinarily reserved for boys of the Brahman and Kāyasth classes. About 1871 Sir George Campbell's scheme for improving primary education was drawing attention to the subject, and three old pāthsālas and forty-three new ones received aid. In 1872 when the scheme was introduced, the number increased to seventy-six, and a training school for *gurus* was opened. There was, however, in the public a general indifference about education, ascribed to innate conservatism and the absence of any immediate and tangible return in the shape of employment.

Education in 1915-16.

In 1915-16 there were in all 765 institutions recognized by the Education Department, in which the number of pupils was 21,323; and there were twenty-five schools which did not conform with the departmental standard. About twenty per cent. of the boys of school-going age were receiving instruction, the proportion for Muhammadans being eighteen. The change in the minimum qualification for literacy which was made in the Census of 1911 had the effect of vitiating comparison with 1901, and the decrease in the ten years is more apparent than real. Excluding Christians there were in 1911 2,484 people literate in English, and the total number of all classes literate in any language was 29,097 or less than twenty-three per thousand of the total population. Males were forty-three and females three per thousand.

Reasons for the slowness of growth.

There is no room for doubt that the progress of primary education has been very slow, and in 1911 the proportion of literates in Hazāribāgh was the lowest in the province with the exception of Palāmau. For this result there are several causes. In the first place the population contains a large aboriginal element, which has to a great extent been absorbed into Hinduism, with the loss of its distinctive language and religion. As such it makes no direct appeal to the proselytizing agencies which have done so much for education in Rānchi and the Santāl Parganas. Secondly, the immigrant Hindus from Bihar who made their permanent homes in the district gradually became isolated from their kindred. Living in a remote and unknown land they were suspected of all kinds of ceremonial neglect, and the natural affection of parents combined with religious scruples resulted in their refusing to give their daughters in marriage to residents in Hazāribāgh. Thrown on their own resources these latter failed to maintain the same standard of culture as their relatives in Gayā or Patna; and of this failure their lukewarm attitude to education is one of many symptoms. Thirdly, the social leaders of the district, the Tikāits and Thākurs to whom Captain Bird refers, are for the most part still uneducated and poor, and naturally do little to promote the education of others. Added to all these predisposing causes is the general state of poverty arising out of indolence which makes the contributions to the family income of even small children a matter of importance, and the complete absence of ambition in all but a few castes. Mahuris and Banias are anxious to have their children taught to cypher and write, for the purposes of their trade, and the Kāyasth who cannot use a pen is without a means of livelihood. All parents who make their living by their literacy are anxious to educate their children, and as English is the key to the most profitable employment, they make extraordinary sacrifices to obtain for them a knowledge of that language.

Inspecting staff.

The supervision of the primary and middle schools rested in 1915 with a Deputy Inspector of Schools, assisted by six Sub-Inspectors, one Assistant Sub-Inspector and ten Inspecting Pandits, the whole of this staff being subordinate to the Inspector of Schools, Chota Nāgpur Division.

College of St. Columba.

The College of St. Columba at Hazāribāgh, which belongs to the Dublin University Mission, had 164 students in the year 1915-16, a large proportion of whom live in the College. A notable feature of this institution, which makes a special appeal to many parents, is the assimilation as far as possible of the conditions of residence to those which are found in colleges of the United Kingdom.

High English Schools.

In the town of Hazāribāgh, the Zila School and St. Columba's Collegiate School teach up to the Entrance Examination of the Calcutta University, but their united accommodation is unequal to the demand for such teaching. There is another high school at Giridih, and a fourth was opened in 1915-16. The number of pupils at these four institutions was 883.

Middle English Schools.

There were seven schools with 595 pupils teaching up to the middle scholarship examination, in which English forms part of the recognized course of studies. Two are aided by Government and three by the District Board.

Middle Vernacular Schools.

There were four schools which read up to the middle scholarship, wherein the vernacular is the only recognized course of studies. Of these three were maintained by the District Board and one by Government, and in order to add to their usefulness it is proposed to build hostels for the residence of pupils from a distance. These schools are not popular with parents; but there appears to be a need for them for the education of boys who intend to adopt teaching in the primary schools as their career. The three schools had 262 pupils.

Primary Education.

There were forty-seven upper primary and 623 lower primary schools, with 2,531 and 14,710 pupils respectively. Of the former five were maintained by Government and the remainder aided by the District Board. Of the latter three are managed by the District Board and 481 receive aid. The remainder of 139 are unassisted. The tendency in recent years has been to improve the quality of primary education at some sacrifice of numbers. The largest total of pupils in lower primary schools was 15,032, as long ago as 1902, when there were only 1,408 pupils in the upper primary schools. The *gurus* are trained for their duties in special schools of which there are now four, at Mirzāganj, Bagodar, Chitarpur and Simaria; and when a sufficient supply of more or less trained teachers is forthcoming the multiplication of primary schools can be resumed. The District Board has recently spent large sums placed at its disposal by Government in building and equipping school houses; but many of the schools continue to be held in verandas and sheds which are badly lighted and ventilated, and fail to keep out the rain. The *guru's* fees are paid very irregularly by the parents of the pupils, and many of the more amateur teachers look to other sources for additions to their income, such as keeping accounts, writing letters, etc.; and they are inclined to neglect their schools in the quest of such windfalls. Less than twenty per cent. of the *gurus* have received professional training, but the number is increasing steadily.

Guru Training schools.

Technical schools.

Four blacksmiths, one carpenter and one potter receive subsidies for teaching their trades to a limited number of boys, and the Baniādih Industrial School, with a Government grant of Rs. 50 a month, had thirty-seven apprentices.

Female education.

There were seven upper primary schools for girls with 304 pupils, twenty-nine aided and twenty-one unaided lower primary schools, with a total of 898 pupils, and seven maktabs with 147 pupils. The total expenditure from public funds was Rs. 5,678.

Giridih Girls' High School.

There is a high school for girls at Giridih with seventy-two pupils, of whom thirty-five were in the advanced stage.

The year's expenditure was Rs. 7,607, of which Government paid Rs. 4,950. This institution, however, is scarcely a district institution as its pupils are obtained not merely from the whole province but also from Bengal. The reformatory school, which also serves the two provinces, had 461 convict-pupils, and the expenditure in the year was Rs. 1,22,918. It occupies the old jail for European troops at the town of Hazāribāgh, which has now been remodelled and equipped with every sanitary precaution for the welfare of the pupils and staff.

Hazāribāgh Reformatory School.

There were thirteen *tols* with 302 pupils, but none has won any marked position in Sanskrit education.

Sanskrit tols.

The education of the Santāls is largely looked after by the Pachamba and Tisri Missions, of which an account has been given in Chapter IV.

Santāl education.

The East Indian Railway owns extensive collieries at Giridih and provides for the education of the children of the settled mining population. There are thirty-one primary schools with 2,225 pupils; education is free, and the Company as employer is able to compel the attendance of the children.

East Indian Railway schools.

The total expenditure on education in the district, after excluding the Giridih Girls' high school and the reformatory school, was Rs. 2,23,845, of which Government contributed Rs. 64,582, the District Board Rs. 60,582, Municipalities Rs. 4,455, fees Rs. 53,478, subscriptions and other sources Rs. 40,748.

Expenditure on education.

There are no public libraries nor are any newspapers published in the district.

Libraries and newspapers.

CHAPTER XV.

GAZETTEER.

Badam is situated towards the eastern end of the Karanpura valley in thāna Barkāgāon. It was for a long time the residence of the family which now owns the greater part of the district; and in A. D. 1642 a fine fort was constructed for Hemat Singh by a builder from Patna of which extensive ruins still remain. The place was, however, abandoned about 1670, and the family removed to Rāmgarh probably in order to free itself from the undue proximity of the Muhammadans.

Māhudi hill caves.

About five miles to the south-west is Māhudi Hill, where there are caves, carved in the sandstone rocks, the earliest dating from about 1660, with an inscription in which reference is made to the Rājās of Bādam.

Bādam military road.

After the British occupation a military road was made from Hazāribāgh to Rānchi which passed through Bādam. It went to Khapriāon south of Hazāribāgh, and down Motra Ghāt into the Karanpura valley, of which it crossed the eastern corner by Bādam and Doka Tānr. Instead of seeking the valley of the Haharo it climbed over the Aswa range to Jarjara, and crossing the Dāmodar to Jainagar Patratu, it made its way up the Rānchi plateau to Pithauria. It is now completely abandoned for the route by Rāmgarh bridge.

Chatra is the headquarters of the western of the three subdivisions, and is about thirty-eight miles north-west of the sadr station at a height of 1,400 feet. It is connected with the railway at Kodarma Road Station by a metalled road of which the stages are as follows:—

1. Chatra to Itkhori, twenty miles, with the wide and unbridged Mohani river at the 19th mile from Chatra. There is an inspection bungalow at Pitij, about fifteen miles from Chatra furnished, but with no arrangements for food.

2. Itkhori to Chaupāran, ten miles. Chaupāran is on the Grand Trunk Road and has an inspection bungalow but no arrangements for food.

3. Chaupāran to Barākar Bridge, nine miles. The road to Kodarma is on the north side, just west of the bridge.

4. Barākar Bridge to Kodarma Road Station, fourteen miles. There is no bungalow nor arrangements for food at the station.

There is a choice of routes from Hazāribāgh to Chatra. In the rains it is best to go to Barhi on the Grand Trunk Road, and the Barākar Bridge, and then reverse a portion of the journey described above. The only trouble is given by the Mohani river at Itkhori, which is unbridged. At other seasons the best way is via Lepo and Simaria ; there are several small unbridged streams, but they do not give trouble to a motor car. There are streams with heavy sand on the Damol Ichāk and Katkamsānri routes. Formerly Chatra was connected with the outside world by a road which led down Jori Ghāt to Hunterganj and Sherghāti ; but the ghāt is too steep for wheeled carriages, and cannot be realigned, and the sandy bed of the Lilājān has to be crossed. Southward there were roads to Bālumath in Palāmau and thence to Doisanagar in Rānchi and the Tributary Mahals, and by Tandwa to Lohārdaga ; but these are now of no importance.

There is an inspection bungalow at Chatra, but there is no arrangement for the supply of food.

When the district of Rāmgarh was created in 1780 Sherghāti and Chatra were alternate headquarters, and this arrangement continued till 1834. With the constitution of the present district in that year the headquarters were fixed at Hazāribāgh ; but Chatra, where a munsifi was created, remained for many years the trading capital of the province. It lies on a comparatively level tract between the upper plateau of Hazāribāgh and the tangled mass of rock and ravine which form the western limits of the district, and was the open highway from Gayā and the Ganges valley to the south and west of Chota Nāgpur. As such it was the natural recipient of the country produce of Palāmau, and the Tributary Mahals, and the centre from which the luxuries of the north were distributed in payment therefor. The construction of railways diverted this trade, and Chatra has now been left with a comparatively limited field for its commerce, which has dwindled with its population till the latter numbered only 9,222 in 1911. There is, however, a considerable trade still left. At the *Dasahara* festival a large business is done in cattle.

In November 1914 a subdivision was opened with an area of 1,545 square miles, made up of thānās Simaria, Chatra, Hunterganj and Chauparan, of which the population is 223,403. The Subdivisional Officer is also the Munsif, and he is ordinarily assisted by a Sub-Deputy Magistrate. There is a sub-registration office; and arrangements are being made for a new hospital, in the charge of the Assistant Surgeon who looks after the jail. Particulars of the municipal administration are given in Chapter XIII; the area in municipal limits is 3·78 square miles.

In the course of the Mutiny Chatra was the scene of a small but locally important engagement between the rebels and the British troops. The Rāmgarh Battalion had mutinied at Hazāribāgh and Rānchi; and though the sepoys received very little local support they were strong enough to compel the retirement of the government officials, and for two months they were masters of the situation. They then decided to leave the province by way of Chatra, and join Kuar Singh at Bhojpur. At Chatra they were attacked by a mixed force consisting of a portion of the 53rd Regiment of British troops, and a detachment of Rattray's Sikhs, numbering in all 320 men. Apparently they were to some extent surprised; but they took up a strong position on the brow of a hill, and resisted stubbornly; for in the orders conferring on them the Victoria Cross Lieutenant J. C. C. Daunt of the 70th Bengal Native Infantry and Sergeant Dynon of the 53rd Foot are stated to have acted with "conspicuous gallantry in capturing two guns by pistolling the gunners, who were mowing down the detachment with grape." The rebels lost 150 men killed, and all their guns and ammunition; and those who scattered and escaped ceased to be a military force. There is a graveyard in Chatra where are buried the Europeans who were killed in this fight.

Dharwar is a large village, about thirty-five miles north-west of Giridih, and nineteen miles north-east of Hazāribāgh

Road Station with which it is connected by a road metalled but intersected by three unbridged rivers. It is the residence of the proprietor of the Dhanwār estate, of whose family an account has been given above in Chapter III. It is the centre of a small trade and has a few brass and bell-metal shops. The proprietor maintains a small but useful dispensary.

Giridih is the headquarters since 1881 of the north-eastern subdivision which has an area of 2,006 square miles, and had in 1911 a population of 452,656. The town owes its existence to the neighbouring Karharbāri coal-field ; for in 1871 a branch line of railway was made, simultaneously with the construction of the line from Barākar to Luckeesarai, from the station of Madhupur to the neighbourhood of the coalfield. The rail-head was about three miles from and very welcome to the busy commercial town of Pachamba on the old road from Nawāda to Sirāmpur and Tundi ; but the upstart village which slowly grew up there has gradually superseded its older rival. In 1881 Pachamba ceased to be the subdivisional headquarters, and in 1902 it saw its rival attain to the dignity of a municipality ; and now finally Giridih is proposing to inflict on its former patron the indignity of inclusion within its boundaries.

Unfortunately the town was allowed to grow up with insufficient regard to future needs, and the area east and south of the railway bridge is at present rather congested. The roads in this quarter require careful attention to prevent excessive scouring of the drains ; and as a result of unchecked encroachments in the past they are inadequate to the present comfort of traffic. The new quarter to the north of the public offices is occupied by bungalows, many of which are owned by Bengalis who find the dry climate very beneficial after the humidity of the lower province. Further to the north the extension of the town is restricted by the Usri river, which is ordinarily so dry that carts and foot passengers find no difficulty in passing through its bed, and yet occasionally stays in flood sufficiently long to interrupt seriously communications between the two banks. The construction of a bridge for carts would make the land on the northern bank very valuable for building purposes ; but as it is not the property of the municipality the tax-payers on the southern bank can scarcely be expected to bear the expense of an improvement of which they would not reap the profit. Meantime the extension of the town is proceeding north-westwards towards Pachamba. The town had a population of 10,668 in 1911, and covers an area of 1·38 square miles, which will be largely increased if the proposed inclusion of Pachamba is sanctioned.

In spite of the coal dust, which is never entirely absent, the town is extraordinarily healthy, and the death-rate is ordinarily far below that of Hazāribāgh and Chatra. There is a good high school for boys, and in the last few years a high school for girls has been opened, which is frequented by pupils from Bengal and Bihar. There are a number of private medical practitioners, but the Rattray Charitable Hospital, which depends mainly on charitable subscriptions, is inadequately supported, and in consequence is not maintained as efficiently as the importance of the town requires.

Giridih is seventy-two miles distant from Hazāribāgh, with which it is connected by provincial roads, in which the only interruption is at the crossing of the Barākar river, eight miles from Giridih. After rain the water is often so high that carts cannot pass through its bed ; and though a boat is kept there the current is so strong that it is hazardous to take a motor-car across. By rail a very circuitous route from Hazāribāgh Road leads to Sitārāmpur and Madhupur. There is a dâk bungalow with rooms and food at Giridih, but it is inconveniently situated in the middle of the town.

Gola is situated in the south of the district about fifteen miles east of Rāmgarh on the road which leads to Jhālda, a station on the Purulia-Rānchi line in Mānbhum. It serves as a centre for the receipt of country produce from the Dāmodar valley, and the distribution of goods imported by rail. It possesses a sub-registration office, and a middle vernacular school. In 1854 a road was made from Gobindpur on the Grand Trunk Road in Mānbhum to Rānchi by Mahoar (four miles north-west of Chās) and Gola, but it is no longer of any commercial importance. It passes close to Hundrughāg Falls on the Subarnarekha river, which are just outside the district. For a short time there was a Subordinate Judge stationed at Gola, with jurisdiction over Hazāribāgh and Rānchi, but this arrangement was satisfactory to neither district and was soon terminated.

The Grand Trunk Road was completed in the district of Hazāribāgh about the year 1838, replacing as the military route to the north-west the road made about 1780 from the neighbourhood of Chās in Mānbhum through Gumia, Chatro, Hazāribāgh and Kanha Chatti to the Dhangāin Pass and thence to Sherghāti. It was not, however, till ten years later that much progress was made with the bridging of the new road; for when Doctor Hooker visited the Suruj Kūnd hot springs he found in progress the building of the bridge over the Bārahkatha river near by. The road enters the district at the 193rd mile from Calcutta, near Munia Ghat and enters Gayā at Guāri bridge at the 268th mile. Till 1858 the rail-head from Calcutta was at Rāniganj; and the Grand Trunk Road had been the most important means of military communication between the lower provinces and the north of India during the preceding twenty years. Since 1858 it has dwindled in importance with the construction in succession of the Loop Line, the Chord Line and the Grand Chord Line. The latter runs roughly parallel to the road; and since its opening in February 1907 the road possess merely a local importance.

The opening of the road led to a great change in the distribution of the police; and in a short time thānās were opened at Dumri, Bagodar and Barhi, and the intervening portions of the roads were protected by posts of *digwārs* and patrolled by mounted police. Colonel Dalton, writing in 1872, stated that "Hazāribāgh was always notorious for its *dakāitis*. Formerly in the Moghal days, the Kharagdiha jurisdiction was the worst part of the district for this crime; afterwards the Grand Trunk Road attracted attention, but a strong road police was established, and great efforts made, not always with success, to render it safe for travellers. The transfer of traffic to the railway reduced the attraction, and though the police were also reduced, the road is still fairly patrolled, and the few sawars allowed are of great value." In the great days of the road it must have presented a scene of extraordinary interest, with the regiments pressing to the Afghan War, and the pilgrims crowding to Jagannāth: and the *chattis* or permanent bazars which were attached to the camping grounds of the troops doubtless drove a busy trade. Now only those shops remain whose owners have lacked the enterprise or means to move to new centres of trade, and for customers they have penniless emigrants to the coalfields, and a few mendicant fakirs. The regiments still use the road occasionally in the cold weather, but the *chattis* no longer suffice for their needs; and the proprietors of the Rāmgarh Estate, by whom the matter is regarded as closely touching their *izzat*, make due provision for the comfort of the King's troops. The usual stages are at Dumri, Bagodar, Barhkatha, Barhi and Chauparan, where there are extensive reserved camping grounds, each with a well which is carefully disinfected before the marching season begins in December. Throughout the district the road is metalled, with a good surface, and ordinarily so straight and open that there is a long clear view ahead. The villages are few, and the prudent driver of a motor car can enjoy long stretches when a rapid pace can be maintained with safety; but in the *chattis* a moderate speed is necessary.

The road enters the district six miles west of Topchānchi and is overhung for miles by the great and imposing mass of Pārasnāth Hill. After Nimia Ghāt (198) the Grand Chord line is crossed at mile 200 and at Isri (202), the railway station for the pilgrims is passed on the north side. At **Dumri** (203) the dâk bungalow is reached where rooms and food can be obtained, and Pārasnāth Hill or **Madhuban visited.** The metalled road running north by the bungalow goes to Giridih, 26 miles away, of which the first 18 down to the banks of the Barākar, pass through the beautifully-wooded lower spurs of Pārasnāth. The river is unbridged, and after heavy rain is often unfordable for several days, and the ferry boat is too small for the safe carriage of a motor car. The scenery north of the river to Giridih is devoid of interest. There is a military camping ground at Dumri.

Bagodar (216) is reached after thirteen rather uninteresting miles; and a road branches off to Hazāribāgh Road Station on the north (eight miles). There is a convenient dâk bungalow with food. The next stage is to Atkadih (222), where there is an inspection bungalow (without food), from which place to Bārahkatha (231) the road approaches the north-east corner of the higher plateau, which descends by steep and well-wooded cliffs. At mile 229 **Suruj Kund** is reached, where there are hot springs impregnated with sulphur, which lie about half a mile south of the road. These springs were examined by Dr.

Hooker (Himalayan Journals, Vol. i., Ch. ii) in 1848. There are four hot springs, with temperatures of from 169 to 190 degrees, and between two of them a cold spring arises two paces away. A *mela* is held each year in January which is much frequented, but for the rest of the twelve months the place is almost deserted. The inspection bungalow makes no provision of food. Between Barahkatha and Barsot there are a number of striking well-wooded hills on the south, but from Barsot to Barhi (248) the road is rather dull.

At **Barhi** there is an inspection bungalow, but food is not obtainable. The bungalows belong to the period when opium was widely grown along the Grand Trunk Road ; but since the closing of the agency in 1911, the place has lost much of its importance. There are also the ruins of a jail, a relic of the subdivision which was closed in 1872. There are a camping ground, police-station, sub-registration office and dispensary ; and opposite the last is a small walled cemetery by the side of the road, in which the most interesting grave is that of Colonel Knyvett, the officer in charge of the Grand Trunk Road at the beginning of the Mutiny in 1857, a post which must have been full of anxiety in those eventful days. He died at Barhi before the crisis of the mutiny had been reached. From Barhi a provincial road leads to Hazāribāgh (22 miles), and with the similar road from Bagodar completes a triangle, with sides of thirty-two, thirty-two, and twenty-two miles, which makes an excellent tour for a motor car. Two miles beyond Barhi the Barākar river is crossed by an iron bridge which has been built near the site of a stone bridge, a hundred yards to the north. In June 1913, the rains burst with unusual strength, and at the headquarters station twenty inches of rain were measured in nineteen days. Then came a great fall of ten inches in twenty-four hours, and the news came in that the old Barhi bridge had collapsed. Just beyond, a metalled road leads north-east to Kodarma station, fourteen miles away through uninteresting country. The next stage on the Grand Trunk Road is reached at **Chauparan** (259), where there is an inspection bungalow, but food is not obtainable. A metalled road leads to Chatra (30 miles) on the south-east, passing through Itkhori and Pitij. The road is quite good, and after the crossing of the broad and sandy Mohani river, which is unbridged, the scenery is pleasant right on Chatra; but that small town has little of interest and no food can be obtained. Chaupāran has the usual police-station and military camping ground, and immediately to the west begins the descent to the Gaya plans, by the Danua Ghāt. In seven-and-a-half miles the drop is 737 feet; the hills are well covered with woods and the scenery is beautiful. The hill which overlooks the pass from the north is Lohābar, 1,788 feet high. Not far beyond the foot of the pass the road leaves the district at Guāri bridge, 268 miles from Calcutta.

Hazaribagh town is situated in 23° 59[1] east longitude near the centre of the higher plateau at a general elevation of two thousand feet. In the immediate neighbourhood a few rocky hills break the landscape, of which Chendwār or Seotāgarha Hill is 2,815 feet high. The population in 1911 was 17,009, residing in a municipal area of 7·13 square miles. The town is the meeting-place of three first-class roads, of which one connects it with Rānchi, fifty-eight miles away, and the others with Bagodar (thirty-two miles) and Barhi (twenty-three miles), respectively, on the Grand Trunk Road; as a centre for motoring it is unsurpassed in the two provinces. The nearest railway station is at Hazāribāgh Road on the Grand Chord Line, which is reached by means of a public service of motor cars in about three hours, and the journey to Calcutta occupies about seven hours more. The accommodation provided for travellers consists of a dāk bungalow at the railway station for Indians, and another at Bagodar, eight miles on the road to Hazāribāgh, where rooms and food can be obtained by Europeans. At Hazāribāgh itself there is a staging bungalow near the church which also provides rooms and food: while for officials travelling on duty there are the Circuit House and a Public Works inspection bungalow. The comparative coolness of the climate and the pleasing scenery of the surroundings make the town popular with visitors both European and Indian, especially in the rains and autumn. From time to time the subject of railway connection has been mooted, and plans and estimates have been prepared for a narrow-gauge line to Hazāribāgh Road; but so far nothing has been done.

The town owes its existence to the raising of the Rāmgarh Battalion about 1780, and the decision to station it permanently near the villages of Okni and Hazāri, on the read from Chatra to Ichāk, which had become an important place after the zamindar of Rāmgarh had made it his residence in 1772. Rennell's map published in 1779 shows the road, and the present town appears therein as Ocunhazāri. In 1834 it was made the headquarters of one of the new districts which were then carved out of the old ' conquered provinces ' of Rāmgarh. For a long time it was intensely unpopular with the Bihāris whose official employment compelled them to live there; and they were reluctant to bring their families with them. The distance from Gayā and Patna was very great, and the roads were so poor that *sagars* were the only form of wheeled carriage; moreover, the district was then, and for many years later, notorious for its dacoities. Those who brought their families to the district quickly found that it was difficult to keep in good caste standing with their kinsmen in Magadha; and doubtless in many cases this led to the abandonment of rules which are of prime importance in Hinduism. As a glaring example of this backsliding may be mentioned the case of certain Brahman families near Tandwa who now permit widow-remarriage. Gradually, however, better roads were made, and more securely guarded, and the drawbacks to residence in Hazāribāgh disappeared, until at the present day it is a favourite station, especially with Bengali officials.

The history of the military cantonment has been given in Chapter XI in connection with the Sarkāri Hāta government estate. Abolished in 1842 it was restored in 1859, and again abolished on the 15th May 1884. In 1857 a detachment of two companies of the 8th regiment of the Rāmgarh Battalion was sent to Hazāribāgh, but it mutinied in August, and the officials had to leave the station. They returned to Bagodar, but after receiving a small force of Rattray's Sikhs reoccupied Hazāribāgh, and early in October the 53rd Regiment and the Sikhs destroyed the rebels at Chatra. The most valuable legacy of the military occupation is the manner in which the town is laid out. After the cantonment was re-established it was decided to improve the sanitation; a large additional area was acquired from the proprietor of the Rāmgarh estate, the old bazars were uprooted. A spacious block known as the Boddam Bazar was laid out with wide roads intersecting at right angles; and on this the Indian quarters has been built, at a distance from the barracks where the troops were placed. As a result of these measures the town is orderly, spacious, well-drained, and practically free from those areas of congestion which disfigure so many Indian towns.

In addition to the offices usually found at the headquarters of a district there are a number of institutions of more than local importance. St. Columba's College is built on a very fine site beyond the eastern boundary of the extensive military camping ground, which the students are permitted to use for their games. St. Columba's Zanana Hospital is a large and well-equipped building, at the south of the town. On the north side are the Reformatory School for the two provinces of Bengal and Bihar with about 500 inmates, originally used for the reception of European military prisoners, and the Central Jail whose extensive grounds are planted with aloes. Between these two buildings and the town are three large artificial sheets of water, skirted by well-made roads which make a pleasant promenade for the townspeople. The Police Training College of the province is also now stationed at Hazāribāgh, where it occupies a large building formerly used as a Roman Catholic convent school. The Anglican station church is well situated in the midst of the open spaces which were formerly used for military purposes. The cemetery has been laid out with taste, and is kept in admirable order under the care of the Chaplain, and its heavy massive tombs recall the early days of the last century.

About four miles away on the west of Seotāgarha Hill the Jains of the province have built an extensive range of sheds and stalls for the reception of old and worn-out cattle, of which a very large number, mainly from the neighbourhood of Calcutta, are to be found in the adjoining pastures. It is a matter of great regret that this solicitude of the public for adult cattle does not serve to stop the cruel practice which is followed by many local Goālas of causing the death of female calves by intentional starvation. From the town roads lead to the edges of the plateau; and northward over Katkamsānri and southward from Marāngi extensive views are obtained over forest-clad valleys, which are specially beautiful at the end of the rains. The Sadr Subdivision now covers about 3,435 square miles, with a population of 612,544 in 1911.

Hazāribāgh Road Station is on the Grand Chord Railway, 215 miles from Howrah. It was opened in February 1907 and is connected by a metalled road with the sadr station forty-two miles away. A number of traders have established, themselves near the station, but so far the place is in its infancy.

Ichāk lies about eight miles to the north of Hazāribāgh, two miles to the east of the Barhi road. Tej Singh took up his residence there, after the capture of Rāmgarh by the British in 1772, and his successors built a *garh* of brick three storeys high which fell into decay after the succession of the Padma branch in 1867. The town has declined rapidly in population and now contains only about 5,000 people. There are two large *maths* or religious foundations, presided over each by a *mahanth* , and well endowed by the Rāmgarh family ; but they contribute little to the spiritual or material improvement of the dirty and congested little town.

Itkhori is about ten miles south of Chauparan which is at the head of the Danua pass from Gaya, on the Grand Trunk Road. From Chaupāran a *pucca* road leads through Itkhori to Chatra ; so that it is readily accessible. Prior to 1770 it was the seat of a petty chief—one of the so-called *rajas* of Chhai—and ruins of his residence are in the village, near a large *bandh* on which is an old temple with stone images. About a mile to the west of the village on an upland now overgrown with jungle, and close to the bank of the Mohani river among the débris of old buildings, are two temples which still survive in a half ruined fashion, with a number of a black stone images. The ruins have not been examined by an expert ; and it is very desirable that this omission should be repaired, as their character and probable date may possibly throw some light on the question of the date of the Hindu migration into the district.

Kharagdiha lies twenty-seven miles north of Giridih, on the road which leads to Gāwān and Nawāda. Formerly it was the centre of the old pargana of Kharagdiha, the land of the Bhuiya Ghātwāls ; and roads radiated to Sirāmpur, Doranda, Nawāda and Chakai. From 1834 it was the site of a munsifi and later on a great centre for poppy cultivation. Now it is derelict, and trade has gone to Mirzāganj, two miles to the south, where are found a number of branch firms from Pachamba, and a repetition of the insanitary conditions of that very dirty town.

Kodarma is about four miles north-east of the station of the same name on the Grand Chord Railway and is about forty-three miles distant from the district headquarters, with which it is connected by a series of metalled and bridged roads. It is a large village in the centre of the government estates, of which the northern portion consists of the Kodarma Reserved Forest, famous for its mica mines. The latter have been described at length in Chapter II, and the history of the estate will be found in Chapter XI. The village has a small Anglican Church, and a cemetery; and a local committee maintains a hospital and dispensary very efficiently. For travellers there is a District Board bungalow, but no arrangements are made for food. About half a mile away, inside the protected forest area, there is a bungalow of the Forest Department from which there is a pleasant view of Banda hill and the jungle to the west.

Kuluha Hill lies about six miles south-west of Hunterganj. Though its height is only 1,575 feet it is very striking when seen from the north, as it overhangs abruptly the low Lilājān valley. It contains some ruined temples and other buildings, and as it is now a place of pilgrimage for Hindus, these were for some time thought to be of Hindu origin. Dr. M. A. Stein, however, visited the hill in 1900, and was satisfied that they were built by the Jains, who venerated it as the birth-place of the tenth Tirthankara, Sitala Swāmin, and frequented it till about one hundred and fifty years ago. It is curious that it is now entirely unknown to the ordinary Jains, and is associated by the local Hindus with the Pandava brothers.

Pachamba. See Giridih.

Padma is two miles west of the Barhi road, about fourteen miles north of Hazāribāgh. Upon the break in the succession of the Rāmgarh family in 1866 there was litigation between various claimants which ended in favour of the Padma branch, descended from Tej Singh *faujdar* by a second wife. Following a common Hindu practice the new owner abandoned the residence of his predecessor, and stayed on at Padma, which is built on rather low ground near the bank of a small tributary of the Barākar river. There a new *garh* has been commenced but is still incomplete. The village has no features of interest of any kind.

Pārasnāth. South of the Himalayas the highest mountain for many hundred miles is Pārasnāth Hill. It is situated in

Hazāribāgh district, not far from the boundary of Mānbhum, and is 4,481 feet high, the effect of this elevation being accentuated by its comparative isolation and the beauty of its form. It rises immediately north of the Grand Trunk Road at about the 200th mile, and has been easily accessible ever since the construction of that road in 1838. Formerly, however, the route from the north and west led from Patna and Nawāda through Kharagdiha to Pālganj; whilst travellers from the south and east came by the road which led from Jaipur in Mānbhum through Nawāgarh to Pālganj. As both these roads led through wild Ghātwāl tracts, which were not reduced to any semblance of order before the arrival of the British about 1770 a pilgrimage to Pārasnāth must have been costly and dangerous. It is much to be regretted that there is no account of such a journey: and it is significant that the oldest of the temples appears to date only from A. D. 1765. In 1780 the new military road to Benares was made, and brought travellers within sight of Pārasnāth "from Bānkura to Katkamsānri"; and an interesting account of a visit paid in 1827 is reproduced in the "Statistical Account". In 1871 the railway to Giridih was opened, and there was left a gap of nineteen miles only to be covered by road across the Barākar river to Madhuban at the northern base of the hill. Finally the Grand Chord Railway brought pilgrims to the very foot of the sacred mountain, and in the season from December to March a motor service connects Isri station with the temples at Madhuban. European visitors can halt at Dumri bungalow, a mile from Isri, where food and lodging are obtainable. They can make arrangements there for climbing the hill up its steep southern face; or they can proceed ten miles down the provincial road towards Giridih, whence another three miles of good road (branching off at mile 16) brings them to Madhuban, and the hill can be climbed on its easier northern side. A good path suitable for a pony or a dandy leads to a dâk bungalow on the summit, where there is ample accommodation and furniture, but no food, water or servants, for which visitors must make their own provision. The nearest spring is at a considerable distance from the top, and a bath is a luxury. The local residents believe the place to be haunted, and will not voluntarily stay alone at night; and it is impossible to retain a Hindu or Muhammadan caretaker. The hill commands magnificent views, and is

Roads to the hill.

comparatively cool: but the absence of any level ground at the top is a great drawback, and it is difficult to obtain supplies cheaply. The bungalow is in the charge of the Subdivisional Officer of Giridih, and it is necessary to obtain his permission in advance of occupation.

Dr. Hooker, who ascended the hill in February 1848, writes thus of the view of Pārasnāth from near Taldanga in Mānbhum:—

Hooker's description of the hill.

"As the sun rose Pārasnāth appeared against the clear grey in the form of a beautiful broad cone, with a rugged peak of a deeper grey than the sky. It is a remarkably handsome mountain, sufficiently lofty to be imposing, rising out of an elevated country, the slope of which upward to the base of the mountain, though imperceptible, is really considerable; and it is surrounded by lesser hills of just sufficient elevation to set it off. The atmosphere, too, of these regions, is peculiarly favourable for views; it is very dry at this season; but still the hills are clearly defined, without the harsh outlines so characteristic of a moist air. The skies are bright, the sun powerful; and there is an almost imperceptible haze that seems to soften the landscape, and keeps every object in true perspective."

The view from the hill itself he describes as follows:—

"The view from the saddle of the crest was beautiful, but the atmosphere too hazy. To the north were ranges of low wooded hills, and the course of the Barākar and Ajay rivers; to the south lay a flatter country with lower ranges, and the Dāmodar river, its all but waterless bed snowy white from the exposed granite blocks with which its course is strewn. East and west the several sharp rides of the mountain itself are seen; the western considerably the highest. Immediately below, the mountain flanks appear clothed with impenetrable forest, here and there interrupted by rocky eminences, while to the south the Grand Trunk Road shoots across the plains, like a white thread as straight as an arrow, spanning here and there the beds of the mountain torrents."

Sanitarium for troops.

Portions of the hill have been variously used since the British occupation of the district as a sanitarium for British troops (1862-68), for which the confined space and absence of water made it unsuitable; for a tea-garden, of which a few scores still survive and grow a poor tea which is sold to pilgrims; and for a fruit garden.

Santāl religious hunt.

Pārasnāth is the "Marang Buru" or hill deity of the Santāls of Hazāribāgh, Mānbhum, Bānkura and the Santāl Parganas; and each year they assemble at the period of the full moon in Baisakh from these districts, and celebrate a religious hunt for three days; after which a great tribal session is held for the trial of charges against *mānjhis* and *parganāits*, and of other grave matters which affect the outcasting of individuals. The entry of this custom in the record-of-rights which was prepared in 1911, and of the similar right of the Ghātwārs was followed by the institution of a suit by the Swetambara Jains to have it declared that no such custom exists. That suit was dismissed by the Judicial Commissioner, and an appeal, preferred against his order, has been rejected by the High Court.

The Jains.

The special sanctity of Pārasnāth for the Jains arises from the tradition that the twenty-third of the Tirthankaras (the religious saints who are the objects of their worship), Pārsva or Pārsvanāth, like nine of his predecessors, attained *nirvāna* on the hill. It is said that he was born at Benares, and died at the age of one hundred years when fasting, along with thirty companions. He is usually depicted with a blue complexion, and his cognizance is a hooded snake.

The twenty-third Tirthankara Pārsvanāth.

The last Tirthankara Mahābir.

The foundation of Jainism is attributed by European scholars to the 24th and last Tirthankāra, Vārdhamāna Māhāvira, a contemporary of Buddha in the reign of King Bimbisara (about 519 B. C), whose kingdom of Magadha then coincided with the limits of the modern districts of Patna and Gaya. Mahābir was related to the royal family, and spent many years of his ministry in that kingdom, where he gathered a large following of monks who afterwards spread his teaching over the greater part of India. At the present time the majority of the Jains belong to western India; and a large proportion of the Mārwāri traders who are to be found in every centre of trade belong to one or other of the Jain sects.

Jain sects.

The two most prominent of these sects are the Swetambaras and Digambaras. The word Digambara means 'sky-clad', a euphemism for *nude*; and apparently their habit of taking their food naked, and refusing to decorate the images in their temples with any kind of ornament, are survivals of a wider

(1) Digambaras.

(ii) Swetambaras. practice, to which they owe their name. The Swetambaras or 'white-clad' on the other hand take their meals clothed, and adorn the images of the Tirthankaras with a profusion of golden ornaments. They admit that women can obtain *nirvāna*; and they hold that an ascetic should use a face cloth to guard the mouth and a brush for sweeping away insects, differing in all these matters from the Digambaras. At present they control the ceremonial at the temples and shrines on the hill; and once the pilgrim has crossed the boundary just above Madhuban he must place himself in their hands, even though he be a Digambara. This has excited great bitterness between the sects, each of which is making strenuous attempts to obtain a more assured position on the hill. So far, the Swetambaras have had the greater success, for they have for some years enjoyed a lease by which they are entitled to build their shrines wherever they choose on the hill; but unfortunately for them the High Court has recently declared this lease to be void. The hill is included in the old geographical division of Kharagdiha, and is shown in the map prepared by Rennell in 1779 as lying entirely within Pālganj *gādi*. Recently, however, the owner of the Nawagarh *gādi* in Mānbhum obtained a decree in a Civil Court that he was entitled to the southern face of the hill, and the question is now on appeal before the High Court. A further complication in the present tangle has arisen out of a proposal made a few years ago to build houses for Europeans on the Hill. The Jains disliked this; and offered to buy the hill from the Encumbered Estates Department, which was at the time in charge of the estate of the *tikāit* of Pālganj: and the Digambaras claim that in the subsequent negotiations they were given a definite and enforceable promise of sale, and this claim they are prosecuting by a civil suit. To add completeness to this maze of litigation which is financed by the subscriptions of the faithful throughout India the two sects have a suit pending between themselves regarding the manner of worship to be observed at the shrines on the hill.

Quarrel about Pārasnāth.

Buildings. It has been stated above that the oldest date borne by any building is A.D. 1765, and it is believed that none of the edifices whether on or below the hill are of much earlier age. The officers of the Archæological Department who have examined them have found nothing of special interest. The main building on the hill is a temple on the south-east side of the summit, which was described in 1827 as follows :— The Temple on Pārasnāth.

"About three-quarters of a mile on the southern descent from first *math* at which I arrived, and snugly sheltered from the northern and western storms, stands the principal and the most beautiful of all the temples in this neighbourhood. The same observation that I have made regarding the mixture of Musalman and Hindu architecture in the temples of Madhuban will apply to this *mandir*, which, as I descended through the thick jungle upon it, looked more like a Muhammadan *dargāh* than a building belonging to the original people of Hindustan. The pediment and body of the temple were ornamented with arched entrances between single pillars, such as are common in the larger houses of the Hindus; but above this all was in Muhammadan fashion. Five handsome fluted domes, one large one in the centre, surrounded with four small ones each forming the roof of a corresponding apartment, seemed too heavy a crown for the edifice from which they rose. These domes were well ornamented, and were pointed with those spires composed of golden or brazen balls, and ending in arrow heads, which are generally to be seen shooting out from the tops of minarets. The four sides of the building are alike, but to mark the principal approach, a large *chabutra* lies in front of the eastern archways.

On entering the centre and holy chamber of this temple, it is impossible to avoid being impressed with the simple beauty of the place. The pavement is composed of fine slabs of blue veined marble; and on a white marble pediment opposite to the entrance five very beautiful idols of the Jain Tirthankaras sit in dignity waiting for the prayers of their disciples, which are rendered more deep-toned by the echoing influence of the dome that forms the ceiling of the sanctuary. The centre figure, which represents Pārasnāth as a naked figure sitting cross-legged in an attitude of abstract meditation, is cut out of a beautiful piece of black marble. It measures between three and four feet high, as sitting, and is a remarkable graceful idol, in full preservation. The other four are each about two feet and a half high, all of them of white marble, and one of them wearing the same hood which adorns the head of the central image, as the peculiar ornament of Pārsvanāth. On the pedestal of each idol the same inscription appears that Shugal Chand Jagat Seth erected it in

A.D. 1765. The chamber which constitutes this sanctuary is about twenty feet square and between thirty and forty high to the centre of the dome. There are no ornaments beyond those I have described, but the marble pavement, pedestal, and idols are the handsomer for being unadorned. Of the four smaller apartments at the corner two remain empty, and the other two contain each seventeen idols of all sizes (but all of the Jain form and posture) ranged along a ledge in the wall. These appear to have been left at will by pilgrims who may have been anxious to consecrate their household gods at the shrine of Pārasnāth."

The shrines on Pārasnāth.

"It is held to be necessary that every *gumti* or *tuk* should be visited and receive an offering at the hands of each pilgrim; and as many of the peaks are several *kos* distant from the *math* of Kuntnāth to which the ascending path arrives, and as some of them can only be mounted by climbing, this is indeed a penance of extreme labour and fatigue. The length and tediousness of this duty is increased by their strict forbearance from committing any kind of impurity whatever within the holy precincts; and as it is their custom to eat by daylight only to avoid incurring the destruction of the smallest insect, several excursions to the summit are necessary for the accomplishment of the pilgrimage. Each *gumti* is a solid pile of brickwork, varying in height and size according to the facility its station afforded to the builders. The largest does not exceed eight feet in height, and the same in length and breadth, while some appeared not to be larger than one-fourth of these dimensions. In each of these buildings is a small recess, on the flat of which is marked the print of a foot revered as the *charan* (or last footmark upon earth) of the Tirthankara whose name is engraved beneath.......... The visits and salutations to several *charans* on the peaks are concluded by a more deliberate adoration at the temple of Pārsvanāth. After concluding the duties on the mountain, those who desire to leave no claim to a sanctified character unadvanced perform a circuit round the base, starting from Madhuban, to which they again return after traversing a circle of at least thirty miles. From this place the greater part of the pilgrims depart for the other temples at Pawapuri in Bihār, and Champapuri near Bhāgalpur."

The highest peak of Pārasnāth is covered by a ofty pointed temple, which has replaced shrines, of which at least two had been successively destroyed by lightning. This temple is a conspicuous landmark for many miles.

The administrative headquarters of the two sects are at Madhuban on the north side of the hill near the beginning of actual ascent. It is connected by a good road about three miles long, with one unbridged stream, with the provincial road which runs from Giridih to Dumri on the Grand Trunk Road. The temple and rest-houses of the two sects are congregated in the closest proximity ; and though none of the buildings appears to be of any antiquity, yet the collection of white-washed edifices, gay with flags and the golden balls of their cupolas, rising out of a green bed of thick foliage, is very beautiful when seen from the various stages of the ascent. Madhuban.

Ramgarh is about thirty miles south of Hazāribāgh on the road to Rānchi at the crossing of the Dāmodar river, which since 1914 has been spanned by a cart-bridge. The place was the residence of the Chiefs of Rāmgarh for a hundred years, after Bādam had been abandoned in 1670 ; and the ruins of their fort remain, but they are in complete decay. Rāmgarh was attacked and captured by the Muhammadans under Hidayat Ali Khan in 1740, but the complete subjugation of the district was cut short by the necessity of moving away to meet a Marātha invasion of Bihār. It was again captured in 1772 by a British expedition under the command of Lieutenant Goddard, who replaced Makund Singh by Tej Singh as Chief of Rāmgarh. Makund Singh fled, and shortly after died, as did his infant son. Tej Singh established himself at Ichāk, and the former capital quickly fell into decay. There is a telegraph office which is useful on occasion, and a comfortable staging bungalow near the south bank of the Dāmodar, where food and shelter are obtainable. The view up and down the river is interesting from the top of the bridge, which was made of greater height than the original plan as a consequence of the unprecedented floods of 1913. A black band on one of the piers marks the greatest height which the waters then reached.

Tandwa lies on the west bank of Garhi river twenty-eight miles west by south of Hazāribāgh, at the western end of the

Karanpura valley, and six miles from the borders of Palāmau. It collects whatever trade there is in the neighbourhood, and forwards it to Chatra, and it now possesses a hospital and dispensary. There are deposits of coal in the neighbourhood, which may give the place an increased importance in the future.

INDEX.

T

B. . O. G. P. (P. A . E.) No. 231—450—22-2-1918.